FED UP.

GEMMA HARTLEY

FED

UP.

EMOTIONAL LABOR, WOMEN, AND THE WAY FORWARD

HarperOne
An Imprint of HarperCollinsPublishers

HarperOne

HarperCollins books may be purchased for educational, business, or sales promotional use. For information, please email the Special Markets Department at SPsales@ harpercollins.com.

FIRST EDITION

Designed by Yvonne Chan

Library of Congress Cataloging-in-Publication Data

Names: Hartley, Gemma, author.
Title: Fed up : emotional labor, women, and the way forward / Gemma Hartley.
Description: First edition. | New York, NY : HarperOne, 2018 | Includes
  bibliographical references.
Identifiers: LCCN 2018033285 (print) | LCCN 2018036096 (ebook) | ISBN
  9780062856487 (e-book) | ISBN 9780062855985 (hardcover) | ISBN
  9780062856463 (pbk.) | ISBN 9780062884947 (audio)
Subjects: LCSH: Sex role—Psychological aspects. | Sexual division of Labor—
  Psychological aspects. | Emotions. | Sex differences (Psychology)
Classification: LCC BF692.2 (ebook) | LCC BF692.2 .H374 2018 (print) | DDC
  155.3/33—dc23
LC record available at https://lccn.loc.gov/2018033285

ISBN 978-0-06-285598-5
ISBN 978-0-06-290649-6 (Intl)

18 19 20 21 22 LSC 10 9 8 7 6 5 4 3 2 1

For Lucas, Avery, and Thomas

CONTENTS

CONTENTS

AN INVISIBLE JOB IS NEVER DONE

> We are brought back to the question of what the social
> carpet actually consists of and what it requires of those
> who are supposed to keep it beautiful.
>
> —ARLIE RUSSELL HOCHSCHILD

For Mother's Day I asked for one thing: a housecleaning service. Bathrooms and floors specifically, windows if the extra expense was reasonable. The gift, for me, was not so much the cleaning itself but the fact that for once I would not be in charge of the household office work. I would not have to make calls, get multiple quotes, research and vet each service, arrange payment, and schedule the appointment. The real gift I wanted was to be relieved of the emotional labor of a single task that had been nagging at the back of my mind. The clean house would simply be a bonus.

My husband waited for me to change my mind to an "easier" gift than housecleaning, something he could one-click order on Amazon. Disappointed by my unwavering desire, the day before Mother's Day he called a single service, decided it was too expensive, and vowed to clean the bathrooms himself. He still gave me the choice, of course. He told me the high dollar amount for completing the cleaning services I requested (since I control the budget) and asked incredulously if I still wanted him to book it.

What I wanted was for him to ask friends on Facebook for a recommendation, call four or five more services, do the emotional labor I would have done if the job had fallen to me. I had wanted to hire out deep cleaning for a while, especially since my freelance work had picked up considerably. The reason I hadn't done it yet was part guilt over not doing my own housework, and an even larger part of not wanting to deal with the work of hiring a service. I knew exactly how exhausting it was going to be. That's why I asked my husband to do it as a gift.

Instead, I was gifted a necklace for Mother's Day while my husband stole away to deep-clean the bathrooms, leaving me to care for our children as the rest of the house fell into total disarray.

In his mind, he was doing what I had most wanted—giving me sparkling bathrooms without me having to do it myself. Which is why he was frustrated when I ungratefully passed by, not looking at his handiwork as I put away his shoes, shirt, and socks that had been left on the floor. I stumbled over the large Rubbermaid storage tub sitting in the middle of our closet. My husband had taken it down from a high shelf days before, because it contained the gift bags and tissue paper necessary to wrap his mother's gift and mine. He had taken out what he needed, wrapped the gifts, and left the tub on the floor: an eyesore, an obstacle, and (at least for me) a source of endless ire. It impeded me every time I needed to toss clothes in the hamper or pick out something to wear. It was shoved, kicked, and rolled onto its side, but it wasn't put away. To put it back, I had to drag a kitchen chair into our closet so I could reach the shelf where it belonged.

"All you have to do is ask me to put it back," he said, watching me struggle.

It was obvious that the box was in the way and needed to be put back. It would have been easy for him to just reach up and put it away, but instead he had stepped around it, willfully ignoring it for two days. It was up to me to tell him that he should put away something he had taken out in the first place.

"That's the point," I said, now in tears. "I don't want to have to ask."

And therein lay the problem. It was a simple and obvious task that required minimal effort for him. So why hadn't he done it? *Why did I always have to ask?*

It was a question that led to a tear-filled fight as I tried to get my husband to grasp why it is exhausting to be the household manager who notices problems, delegates solutions, and has to ask in a singsong voice to get anyone to comply, how I find myself carrying all the domestic upkeep that relieves others of the mental load. I am the one who notices when things need to be done, and my options are limited. I either complete these tasks myself or delegate them out to others. If we are running low on milk, I put it on my grocery list or ask my husband to pick it up at the store, even if he was the one to use the last drop. I'm the one who notices when the bathroom or kitchen or bedroom needs to be cleaned, and my attention to *all* the details often makes one task turn into twenty. I start taking socks to the laundry, then notice a toy that needs to be put away, which leads to tidying the playroom, and then a stray bowl needs to be put in the sink, so I do the dishes, and the cycle continues ad nauseam.

Housework isn't the only thing that becomes a drag. I am also the schedule keeper who makes appointments and knows what is on the calendar at all times. I am the person who has all the answers to where my husband left his keys, what time that wedding is and what type of dress code is necessary, do we have any orange juice left, where is that green sweater, when is so-and-so's birthday, and what are we having for dinner? I carry in my mind exhaustive lists of all types, not because I want to, but because I know no one else will. No one else will read the school handbook. No one else will plan what to bring to our friends' potluck. No one else will lift a finger unless asked, because that is the way it has always been.

Yet asking, and asking in the right way, is an additional layer of labor. Delegating, in many situations, requires repeating requests, which is often perceived as nagging. Sometimes it's simply not worth the effort of asking again and again, and continually asking in the right tone (and still risking being called a nag). So I do the task myself. Many mornings I bring my daughter her shoes and put them on her feet, not because she is incapable but because I do not want to ask her to put them on ten or more times before yelling that it is time to leave and no one has their shoes on. When I want my husband to clean up the yard, but I also want to keep the peace, I have to monitor my tone so it doesn't betray the resentment I feel, because he never notices tasks that need to be done without my reminders. I find myself curbing my own emotions to cater to those around me, simply to keep our life running smoothly and fight-free. Otherwise, I do all the work myself. My kids certainly don't have to make this choice, and neither does my husband. It's my job. It always has been.

And it seems no matter how much I do, there is always something more on the horizon. It is a kind of work that is far more time consuming than the tasks in which it culminates, but which goes largely unnoticed by those around me. It's a feeling that is all too familiar to many women. While reading Tiffany Dufu's *Drop the Ball*, I bristled with recognition as she recounted her postbaby resentment toward her husband. "Both of us worked full-time outside the home, but inside the home, I worked harder," Dufu writes. "And, maddeningly, he seemed unaware of half the things I did to keep our household running smoothly. In other words, not only did he do less, he didn't appreciate that I did more."[1] Yet in his mind, he probably thought he was doing more than enough. Most men think that, because they *are* doing more than previous generations. The amount of time spent on housework more than doubled for fathers between 1965 and 2015, and the amount of time spent on childcare nearly tripled, but these leaps and bounds haven't brought us to full equality. The gender gap at home persists in a big way. Women are still spending double the time men do on both domestic labor and caring for children.[2] Yet even in more equitable relationships where we are evenly distributing the physical labor of domestic work and childcare, it still *feels* like women are doing more . . . because they are. Even when there is a fifty-fifty split in domestic labor and childcare, we aren't quantifying the emotional labor that goes into these tasks. Often it's easy to miss the "more" that we do, because much of that "more" is invisible. At the heart of so much emotional labor is the mental load that goes into ensuring everything gets done. For every task that produces a physically visible result, there are many mental steps behind it that remain unseen. Those steps are largely noticed, tracked, and executed by women.

That Mother's Day, it wasn't simply the storage tub on the floor, which I had noticed time and again—or my husband's failure to give me the gift I truly wanted, because it required too much emotional labor—that pushed me to tears. It was the compilation of years and years of slowly taking on the role of the only person in our household who cared, until the labor that went into caring about everything and everyone became utterly invisible.

I reached my boiling point when I realized I couldn't explain to my husband why I was frustrated, because I could no longer trace the source. When had the gap become so wide? Hadn't emotional labor always been my forte? Hadn't I opted to care for our home, our children, our life, our friends and family? Wasn't I better at this than he was? Was it asking too much to recalibrate this balance?

I wasn't merely self-questioning for my own benefit. If I didn't own emotional labor as my domain, what would happen to everyone around me? I cared about the outcome: where the pieces would fall and who would pick them up. If I let the domestic upkeep and home management slide, who would suffer? If I became less concerned with how my tone and demeanor affected my husband, what darker depths would our fights reach? I had been conditioned my whole life to think one step ahead, to anticipate the needs of those around me and care about them deeply. Emotional labor was a skill set I had been trained in since childhood. My husband, on the other hand, hadn't received that same education. He is a caring person, but he is not a skilled carer.

Yet assuming that I was not only the better but the best person for the job meant I took over everything. I was better at soothing the kids' tantrums, so I was the one to do it. I was better at keeping the house clean, so I was the one who took on the bulk of organization and delegation. I was the one who cared about the details, so it felt natural that I should be the one in control. But as Sheryl Sandberg points out in *Lean In*, being the only person who cares about these things can lead to a damaging and harmful imbalance. "Each partner needs to be in charge of specific activities or it becomes too easy for one to feel like he's doing a favor instead of doing his part."[3] For my husband, the work that fell under the larger umbrella of emotional labor had become a favor he performed for me. His efforts in emotional labor weren't linked to carefully curating a life or having a deep sense of responsibility. When he did a task without my asking and absorbed any small piece of the mental load, it was a "treat" for me. It was an act that required praise and gratitude that I could not expect in return for the same work. For me, on the other hand, emotional labor became an arena in which my worth was interwoven with each task.

I was angry and completely spent. I didn't want to walk that fine line of protecting his feelings while still getting my point across. Managing your partner's emotions—anticipating needs, preempting displeasure, and keeping the peace—is something women are taught to accept as their duty from an early age. Built into this premise is that it is "natural" and acceptable for men to be defensive, annoyed, or even angered in response to being asked to pull their weight in resolving emotional disputes. "In general, we gender emotions in our society by continuing to reinforce the false idea that women are always, naturally and biologically able to feel, express, and manage our emotions better than men," says Dr. Lisa Huebner, a sociologist of gender who both publishes and teaches on the subject of emotional labor at West Chester University of Pennsylvania. "This is not to say that some individuals do not manage emotion better than others as part of their own individual personality, but I would argue that we still have no firm evidence that this ability is biologically determined by sex. At the same time (and I would argue because it is not a natural difference) we find all kinds of ways in society to ensure that girls and women are responsible for emotions and, then, men get a pass."[4]

Even having a conversation about the imbalance of emotional labor involves emotional labor. My husband, despite his good nature and admirable intentions, still responds to criticism in a very patriarchal way. Forcing him to see emotional labor for the work it is feels like a personal attack on his character. It gets to a point where I have to weigh the benefits of getting my husband to understand my frustration against the compounded emotional labor of doing so in a way that won't end in us fighting. Usually I let it slide, reminding myself that I'm lucky to have a partner who willingly complies in any task I decide to assign to him. I know compared to many women, including female family members and friends, I have it easy. My husband does a lot. He does dishes every night habitually. He often makes dinner. He handles bedtime for the kids when I am working. If I ask him to take on extra chores, he will, without complaint. It feels greedy, at times, to want more from him. After all, my husband is a good man and a good feminist ally. I could tell, as I walked him through it, that he was trying to grasp what I was getting at. But he didn't. He said he'd try to do more cleaning around the house to help me out. He restated that all I ever needed to do was ask him for help, but therein lies the problem. I don't want to micromanage housework. I want a partner with equal initiative.

In a popular Babble article on the lack of help she gets around the house, Chaunie Brusie recalls thinking to herself, "Wouldn't it be faster, if we all pitched in to clean this mess after meals, so we could all relax together? Wouldn't it be better, if my children learned that mothers alone aren't meant to be the only ones who clean? Wouldn't it make more sense, to treat the space we share as a shared responsibility?"[5] Wouldn't it be nice, basically, if all the emotional labor didn't fall to her? If perhaps her husband, maybe someday her children, would take the initiative to notice what needs to be done and then do it? Brusie works full-time from home, earning a six-figure salary as a freelance writer; a little "help" is more than warranted. In fact, her whole point is that the sole responsibility of taking care of their shared home should never have fallen to her in the first place. And yet it has. She writes in her article that she makes the choice to delegate out some of the after-dinner chores. She not only keeps her tone upbeat but even throws in the added lure of playing a game together afterward when she is ignored upon her first request. If she wants "help," she has to ask nicely, even if that "help" involves cleaning up their own damn mess. "We treat doing chores around the house as 'helping Mom out' instead of just doing what needs to be done," Brusie writes. "I want kids who realize that taking care of our home is important work, and because it's important work, we should all do it." Yet that's a hard sell when you have a partner who isn't taking the same initiative to notice what needs to be done—who isn't equally sharing in both the mental and physical labor of keeping a home. Taking out the trash is great, but taking the responsibility to notice when it needs to be emptied is where it's really at.

When I tried explaining this to my husband, though, he struggled to see the difference. As long as the task gets done, why does it matter who asks? What was the big deal? On the spot, I couldn't put it into words, so eventually I wrote it down—all the struggles and frustrations that had led to that mess of a moment—and published it as a feature article in *Harper's Bazaar*.[6] I knew there would be women out there who intrinsically understood what I was talking about. We do this type of invisible work—greasing the wheels that keep the whole operation running—every day. We face the frustrations of constantly shouldering more than our fair share of emotional labor. Still, I was surprised when my *Harper's Bazaar* essay "Women Aren't Nags—We're Just Fed Up" went viral in spectacular fashion (as of this writing, it's been shared more than 962,000 times). Thousands of readers responded with comments and replies. People were sharing their own "Mother's Day moments" where they were caught in the crosshairs of it all being too much to bear and too much to explain to a partner on the defense. Millions of women from all walks of life were nodding their heads and saying, "Yes. Me too." It was a satisfying, but also disheartening, moment of solidarity. And it made me wonder, *Why now?*

After all, I was far from the first person to explore the concept of emotional labor. Sociologists originally coined the term to describe how flight attendants, maids, and other service employees must project happiness and cheerfully engage with strangers as part of their job descriptions. This definition of emotional labor came into the spotlight in Arlie Russell Hochschild's 1983 book *The Managed Heart*. Hochschild used the term *emotional labor* to designate the management of feeling to create a publicly observable facial and bodily display that has exchange value and is sold as a commodity, while she used the terms *emotion work* and *emotion management* to refer to emotional labor done in a private setting.[7] Her study focused on the deep acting and surface acting required of flight attendants to not simply appear warm and friendly on the job but *become* warm and friendly in order to better manage the emotions and expectations of customers in flight. She explains that for the flight attendant the smile is part of her work, which requires a marriage of self and feeling so that the work of being pleasant seems effortless and masks any fatigue or irritation that might cause the customer to become uncomfortable. Flight attendants were taught how to best regulate their own emotions and bury their righteous anger by thinking of drunk or unruly passengers as being "like a child" in need of attention. They were asked to conjure empathy from stories they made up about the customer in their own heads. It was all about connecting with the customer's emotions while disassociating from their own. It was customer service to the extreme.

Other sociologists expanded on the topic of emotion work in academic journals, exploring the ways women are expected to perform emotional labor in the home. In 2005, Rebecca Erickson linked the emotion work women perform to the unfair division of household labor. Her study revealed that emotion work was a critical component in understanding the gendered divide in domestic labor—women are doing more, delegating more, and trying to keep everyone happy while doing it.[8] The divide in who does what when it comes to housework persists because of our gendered expectation for women to perform emotional labor. We are the ones who decide whether to do a task ourselves or to delegate it to someone else, and doing the physical labor is often the easier road. Our cultural gender norms tell us who is supposed to be "in charge" of the home, thus creating and maintaining the deep imbalance many couples face.

Yet it wasn't until much more recently that the topic started gaining more widespread interest outside the academic world. In 2015, Jess Zimmerman opened the public conversation about emotional labor as she homed in on the way women perform emotion work in the personal sphere—in fact, how we perform it *all the time*. We lend an ear. We offer advice. We soothe egos and acknowledge the feelings of others while muting our own. We nod. We smile. We care. Perhaps most importantly, we do so without expecting any reciprocation, because emotional labor is women's work. We all know it. "We are told frequently that women are more intuitive, more empathetic, more innately willing and able to offer succor and advice," Zimmerman writes. "How convenient that this cultural construct gives men an excuse to be emotionally lazy. How convenient that it casts feelings-based work as 'an internal need, an aspiration, supposedly coming from the depths of our female character.'"[9]

Zimmerman's article sparked a lively, internet-famous Meta-Filter thread wherein thousands of women rallied around the term and shared their own experiences with emotional labor in story-rich comments.[10] Across the board, readers seemed to see emotional labor as a special kind of invested effort encompassing the anticipation of needs, the weighing and balancing of competing priorities, and the empathy of putting oneself in someone else's shoes, among other factors. MetaFilter users saw emotional labor in everything from the shame and guilt they felt over chores undone, to the effort they put into considering their partners' feelings over their own, to the charm and conversation that sex workers offer their customers.

Rose Hackman expanded the definition even further in her viral article for *The Guardian*, which proposed that emotional labor might be the next frontier of feminism.[11] She talked about not only the emotion work that Zimmerman explored but also the emotional labor that takes place in the details—the planning and thoughtfulness and care that women bring to the table. Hackman covered many of the small yet insidious ways emotional labor is woven into our lives, from being asked where household belongings are (where do "we" keep the kitchen towels), to creating a pleasant work environment by remembering birthdays and organizing happy hours, to faking orgasms to pad a partner's ego.

The topic of emotional labor continued to gain steam and attention throughout the next couple of years. Countless articles were written on emotional labor and its many iterations. Indeed, my *Harper's Bazaar* article wasn't even the first time I had written on the topic. A mere month before it appeared, I had written for Romper on the emotional labor of stay-at-home motherhood.[12] Emotional labor was everywhere. So why, then, did my article in *Harper's* touch such a nerve when it came out?

Quite frankly, I think it was because women were fed up. When my piece appeared in late September 2017, we were a year shy of Hillary Clinton's presidential loss, Trump's election victory, and the Women's March following his inauguration—which has been cited as "likely the largest single-day demonstration in recorded U.S. history."[13] It would be barely a week before Tarana Burke's #metoo movement resurfaced in the face of the Harvey Weinstein accusations. Women were angry, awake, ready to force change. We were done managing male emotions and expectations at our own deep expense.

This was the perfect moment for women to own that emotional labor isn't just a wellspring of frustrating domestic gripes, but rather a primary source of systemic issues that touch every arena of our lives, in damaging ways that make clear the pervasive sexism in our culture. The deep social expectation that women will shoulder the exhausting mental and emotional work at home—a type of labor that goes largely unnoticed by those it benefits most—has made it all too easy for such insidious expectations to follow us into the world, as we step gingerly through a culture that has left us little choice in the matter. We alter our speech, our appearance, our mannerisms, our own internal expectations to constantly keep the peace. We have been feeling the toll this work takes, in ways that are too often invisible. When my article came out, we were ready to see how our dynamics in the home are writ large in the world, and we were ready for a change.

As many journalists before me had, I expanded the definition of *emotional labor* just a little bit further, hoping to give readers a new lens through which they might see their own relationship dynamics more clearly. *Emotional labor*, as I define it, is emotion management and life management combined. It is the unpaid, invisible work we do to keep those around us comfortable and happy. It envelops many other terms associated with the type of care-based labor I described in my article: *emotion work*, *the mental load*, *mental burden*, *domestic management*, *clerical labor*, *invisible labor*. These terms, when separated, don't acknowledge the very specific way these types of emotional labor intersect, compound, and, ultimately, frustrate. It is work that is mentally absorbing and exhausting, and emotional labor has repercussions that follow us into the world. Judith Shulevitz outlines the high cost of such work in her *New York Times* article on the emotional labor experienced by mothers. "Whether a woman loves or hates worry work, it can scatter her focus on what she does for pay and knock her partway or clean off a career path," Shulevitz writes. "This distracting grind of apprehension and organization may be one of the least movable obstacles to women's equality in the workplace."[14]

It takes time and effort to be the "designated worrier," as Shulevitz calls it. Taking a strictly homebound example, maybe you orchestrate a system of organization to help everyone's morning run smoothly—such as having a key hook on the wall. It takes "nagging" to get the key hook installed. It takes multiple tempered reminders to pick up the supplies from the hardware store, or else you add it to your to-do list and get it all yourself. It takes multiple tempered reminders that maybe this quick job could be done tonight, or tomorrow—all suggestions drawing on your knowledge of what other competing priorities are on the schedule. Then no matter how many times you reiterate the convenience of hanging up the car keys, the keys are left elsewhere. Then you are the one who is asked, "Where are my keys?" You weigh whether to dole out the information or bring up the key hook. If you decide to do the latter, it becomes a fight in which you must always think one step ahead. You have to be careful with your words, careful with the way you voice your frustration. You have to regulate your emotions and manage your partner's emotions at the same time. It's exhausting, so often you choose to simply tell your partner where they left their keys. It saves you both time and grief.

Except it doesn't, because this compounded emotional labor becomes the norm across so many seemingly minor issues. Your life becomes, in time, an intricately woven web that only you can navigate. You must guide everyone else along the careful system of silken strands, so they don't get stuck or fall. It's noticing when you're running low on toothpaste or changing the roll of toilet paper when you use up the last bit. It's being expected to plan the after-work happy hour for your coworkers. It's keeping mental lists and knowing what needs to be done. It's noticing and acknowledging other people's emotions while restraining your own. It's keeping things running and doing so with great care. It takes a great deal of time and energy to perform this type of labor—and it is never fully shut off in our brains. And it costs us dearly, using up untold reservoirs of mental capacity that we could be using in ways that serve us, our careers, our lives and happiness. It made sense to group these formerly disparate terms under one umbrella, because they are deeply connected. Emotional labor means caring not only about the outcome but about the people affected by our emotions, words, and actions—even when doing so comes at our own personal expense.

Women are, in many unpaid ways, expected to keep those around us comfortable at all costs—including the cost of self. We create an altruistic persona, allowing ourselves to be subsumed by the needs of others. We become the listening ear, the sage advice giver, the trip planner, the schedule manager, the housecleaner, the reminder, the invisible cushion that everyone can comfortably land on—with little regard for how it depletes us. When we perform emotional labor, we put the needs of those around us ahead of our own needs. The way we exist in the world becomes, in many ways, invisible. We bury or morph our emotions to cater to those around us—to keep the peace with our husband, to stop our kids from throwing tantrums, to avoid a fight with our mother, to stop street harassment from turning into assault.

Managing other people's emotions and expectations means jumping through hoops to be heard, using up precious time you could be harnessing in more productive ways. You have to make sure your responses are carefully thought out with the other person's emotions in mind. You have to ask in the right tone when you need to delegate work. You have to use restraint and be agreeable in uncomfortable situations. Putting yourself in the most advantageous position means thinking of how the other person is going to react. Don't deliver your work along with a side of charm and meekness? You may be labeled negatively, hurting your chances for career advancement. Don't smile and keep your mouth shut while a man yells lewd comments at you on the sidewalk? You may be followed, attacked, or worse.

There is a high price to pay for not playing to the established power dynamic through both our words and our actions. As Sandberg describes in her book, women often hedge their statements in the professional setting for fear of labeling. "Fear of not being con-

sidered a team player. Fear of seeming negative or nagging. Fear
that constructive criticism will come across as plain old criticism.
Fear that by speaking up, we will call attention to ourselves, which
might open us up to attack (a fear brought to us by that same voice
in the back of our heads that urges us not to sit at the table)."[15] We
do the same sort of hedging at home to get the "help" we so desperately need without a fight. It's constant and exhausting work that
is largely invisible.

Hochschild talked about how flight attendants were tasked
with creating a warm atmosphere of home during flights, and what
that manufactured feeling cost them when they clocked out. They
were emotionally depleted and found it hard to transition between
their work personae and their true selves. They struggled to find
authenticity within themselves, perhaps because their emotional
labor wasn't strictly confined to the service sector. As women, we
are tasked with creating that same warmth in all areas of our lives.
We do it not only at work but also at home and out in the world,
with our friends and family, with coworkers and strangers. Women
are fed up because we've realized we can't clock out. Emotional labor is expected from us no matter where we turn. We are fed up
with the ongoing demand to be the primary providers of emotional
labor in all arenas of life because it is taxing, it is time consuming,
and it is holding us back.

We fill our mental space with the minutiae of household details
and use our time disproportionately for the benefit of others. We
perform emotional labor to advance our careers in a way men are
simply not required to do, from self-policing our tone to being a
sounding board for the ideas of others. We must carefully weigh the
risks of how we interact with strange men in public to ensure our
safety. All these types of required emotional labor are symptoms of
a larger, systemic inequality that actively harms women, especially
women with less privilege. As Hochschild puts it, the way men and
women interact in terms of emotion work is "a common mask for

inequality in what is presumed to be owing between people, both in display and in the deep acts that sustain it."[16] Women always owe emotional labor in society, endlessly indebted to whomever needs us. And we will continue on in deficit until both men and women rewire their expectations about who should do this work and what it is truly worth.

This is where we must all shift our perception of emotional labor to reclaim the value of the skill set behind it. Emotional labor can be our kryptonite, yes, but it can be our superpower as well. We need to see that this work has worth and bring it into the light. This type of caring and emotional intelligence is a valuable skill—an intensive exercise in problem solving with the added benefit of empathy. According to Dr. Michele Ramsey, associate professor of communication arts and sciences at Penn State Berks, emotional labor is often synonymous with problem solving. "The gendered assumption is that 'men are the problem solvers because women are too emotional,'" she explains. "But who is really solving the bulk of the world's problems at home and in the office?"[17] As the household manager for my husband and three kids, I'm fairly certain I know the answer. For all the frustration emotional labor may cause us, inherent within this care-based labor is a valuable skill set. We expertly envision the big picture, we think about the consequences on a broad scale, we adapt easily to the unexpected, and we put heart into the work we produce, the relationships we nurture, the interactions we stumble upon. These skills are assets that ensure our mental and emotional work is done with care, in both attention to detail and attention to other people. The way emotional labor presents in our lives creates an elaborate tapestry woven from the very threads of civility that hold our society together. We cannot live without emotional labor, and we should not want to.

Instead we need to reclaim emotional labor as a valuable skill that everyone should have and understand, because it makes us more attuned to our lives. It brings us more fully into the human experience. It allows us to be the truest and most fulfilled versions of ourselves—as both men and women. There is benefit both in lessening the overwhelming load we have placed on women and in bringing men into a new and fulfilling realm of their lives. We should want not simply to divide the weight of emotional labor but to understand what comes along with carrying the weight. Even with the imbalance we are currently saddled with, we live longer and healthier lives because of emotional labor.[18] We put planning and foresight into our lives, concern ourselves with creating and maintaining strong relationships, and work tirelessly to make others comfortable. Our partners, unsurprisingly, also benefit from this. A study from Harvard has shown that married men tend to live longer, healthier lives than unmarried men.[19] They experienced less stress and fewer instances of depression, and were in better physical health than their unmarried counterparts—in large part because their wives are managing their lives in a way that keeps them healthy. Multiple studies have found that widowed and divorced men don't fare as well as their widowed and divorced female counterparts, because without the partners who put time and care into managing their lives, their health, comfort, and social bonds suffered.[20] When a wife is the only one who responds to party invitations, the only one who gathers together the family for events, the only one who keeps social bonds strong and healthy, then losing her means losing everyone. It also means those bonds don't belong to men in the first place.

Women are holding together their bonds with friends and family. They are making sure their partners eat healthily and exercise. They are unburdening them of the tasks that would otherwise fall to them—acting as their second brain to remember the "small stuff" that isn't important enough for them to remember. Yet when men never learn emotional labor, they miss out on a large and important part of their lives. It is a comfortable life in many ways, certainly. But when someone else is taking care of all the details, your life is never fully your own. The current imbalance of emotional labor continues the expectation that men are not meant to forge their own social bonds, to care deeply about the details of their lives, to find meaning in creating lives and homes that they are truly invested in. It creates an environment where toxic masculinity thrives—where women are still expected to take care of men in a myriad of ways so they never learn to take care of themselves, not only physically but emotionally and spiritually as well. We tell men as a society that they cannot handle emotional labor, that they *need* every last detail delegated or handled for them, that they cannot rise to the occasion and learn these skills, which could deeply change their lives. We leave them with buried frustration at the half-life they are given, even with all their power and privilege. We are feeding a cycle that hurts us all. Changing this dynamic will not hurt men while helping women; it will help set everyone free. Setting an expectation for a more equal distribution of emotional labor is not the transferal of a burden but an invitation for all of us to change our lives for the better.

Balancing emotional labor gives all of us the chance to live fuller and more authentic lives. Women whose loads are lessened can reclaim their mental space and time, make decisions in their careers with clarity, and feel more connected to their partners from a place of true equality. Men can lean into their humanity in new ways. They can step into roles that break from toxic masculinity, live in a place of deep connection, and feel truly unafraid as they help us fight for a more equal world.

Hochschild said that the very ways we acknowledge the rules for emotion work in our lives reflect where we stand in the social landscape. I believe we are ready to break with the old rules and move to new ground. To do that, we must recognize the points where we get snagged on emotional labor, so we can move beyond frustration and decide how to best use our skills of caring deeply. Emotional labor doesn't need to be a detriment to our well-being.

In fact, it's the very glue that holds the world together. Once we become aware of it, acknowledging the many ways it affects our lives for better or worse, we can own emotional labor. We can transform the way we use these skills. We can reclaim them as our own.

We can learn how to better model equality for our children, so they do not repeat our patterns. We can give men the opportunity to step into roles where they can experience emotional labor and come more fully into the human experience as fathers, partners, and men. We can draw clear boundaries instead of meeting expectations for emotional labor every which way we turn. We can use this as a skill rather than a handicap. In the words of Maxine Waters,[21] we can reclaim our time, using emotional labor only where it truly makes sense to do so, in ways that will make the world a better place for everyone, including ourselves. By doing this, we will improve not only our lives but our partners' lives and the lives of generations to come. By working together to address the inequality of emotional labor, we can change the course of our children's future. Our sons can still learn to carry their own weight. Our daughters can learn to not carry others'.

PART I

EMOTIONAL LABOR AT HOME

CHAPTER 1

HOW DID WE GET HERE?

The two-year-old screamed at the top of his lungs as we pulled out of the driveway. He had been screaming from the moment he woke up, about half an hour earlier. The four-year-old started screaming at him to stop screaming before we reached the end of our road. The six-year-old told them both to stop it, which led to them all pointing and yelling, "Stop it!" at one another, round-robin style. I would say it was a difficult way to start the day, but my day had started hours earlier. I had already dealt with email, budgeting, making breakfast, packing school lunches, cleaning the counters, and washing the dishes—all while listening to a podcast on time management. Even as I managed the toddler meltdown, I had done homework with the six-year-old, checked backpacks, filled water bottles, got everyone dressed, combed and braided my daughter's hair, and herded the kids into the car. As I drove, I tried to organize my thoughts about everything that needed to be done that day, which was difficult given the noise level around me. I needed to remind my husband to text his mom and ask about dog-sitting over Christmas. I needed to remember we were out of hand soap and low on diapers. I needed to read the school email that was still open on my laptop. I needed to do a lot of things that I knew I was forgetting, because I had to drive while attempting to smooth over the escalating fight taking place in the backseat. That's when I saw my husband's car approaching in the opposite direction.

Rob had left for work two hours before, so I knew it wasn't likely that he had left his keycard or laptop. I had Siri text him to ask why he was home. When I arrived at my daughter's preschool, I saw his reply: "Let's talk when you get back."

I didn't need him to tell me. From the sinking feeling in my gut I already knew. There had been rounds of layoffs at his company, and it was that time of year again. I breathed deeply before heading for the second school drop-off, immediately going into planning mode. I could figure this out. I knew exactly where our budget stood. We could withstand quite a bit of time on one income. He could take a whole six months off if we were careful about our spending. In fact, perhaps he *should* take a whole six months off.

That was exactly how long I had until my book manuscript was due. My career was taking off, and my income was secure. He could take his time finding the job that felt right for him, while taking over the home front and caring for our two-year-old (who, by the way, was still screaming in the backseat). The timing seemed downright serendipitous. I had always been able to rise to the occasion as my freelance career demanded more and more from me, but recently I felt like I was nearing my limit. There was still so much emotional labor that remained invisible to Rob, and I had so much more on my plate than ever before. I imagined that having him home would change things. He would be confronted with the day-to-day running of our household, the emotional demands of full-time at-home parenthood, and everything would come into focus for him. What would have been a moment of panic at any other point in our lives seemed instead like a door of opportunity opening wide.

We had been talking about the imbalance of emotional labor constantly since my *Harper's Bazaar* article came out a couple months earlier, but it still hadn't quite clicked into place. He could see the physical manifestation of it; I was the one doing the bulk of the cleaning and lunch packing and list making and calendar keeping. But he didn't understand how to take over, even when I desperately needed him to. My job was no longer part-time, yet my load at home hadn't changed to reflect our new situation. While Rob had started occasionally doing laundry and other chores as it suited him, the planning and any delegation of domestic or family work still fell squarely on my shoulders. The mental load was heavy; the emotional labor that went into explaining it to him was even worse. I felt guilty for immediately thinking about how his unemployment would benefit me, but I couldn't help but believe that this big shake-up was exactly what we needed. *This will be the turning point*, I thought. *This is when the shift will finally happen.* I was now the sole breadwinner. He would naturally have to take on the management of the household while he was at home. The role would finally make sense to him. How else could this scenario possibly shake out?

When I arrived home and he broke the news to me, I kept my plans to myself. I knew what he needed from me in that moment was empathy. I told him I was sorry and that we would be okay and mirrored him when he stated how much it sucked.

"It does suck," I said.

Rob was obviously in shock. Today would be a wash on the emotional labor front. Probably most of the week would be. He could start taking over next week, once we'd discussed our expectations and plans. I wanted to give him time to absorb the pain and frustration of the layoff, to talk it out, to feel confident in how he was going to move forward during this period. I wanted him to see this time as an opportunity for himself as well, to find space to enjoy himself while he had all this unbound freedom. If I had been doing all the emotional labor up until this point, surely we could find a new balance with him at home that could make us both happy. We could tackle large-scale delegation together, and then I could lean back at home and lean into my work without the endless to-do list pinging through my mind in the background. I imagined what it might feel like to walk into my home office, knowing that everything at home would be taken care of while I was "away." It was a dreamlike prospect, but I felt confident we would find our groove effortlessly. We were off into this new chapter of our lives.

That afternoon, we took our (still whining) two-year-old to the park. We walked along the creek that ran beside the park trail. The air was crisp, the ground covered in bright yellow leaves from the cottonwoods. The path wove its way through tall Sierra pines. The changing landscape, our changing lives—it all felt steeped in meaning. The more I thought about it, the more confident I felt that the change, unexpected and unsettling as it might be, was exactly what we needed in our lives. It would be a fresh start, not only for his career but for our relationship dynamic as well. I mentioned to him, gingerly, that the layoff was perhaps a positive event. Look where we were—literally, figuratively. I had my book to focus on. He had severance pay for three months. This could be a good thing.

"I'm allowed to be mad about this," he said.

I could tell he was annoyed with my optimism and scaled back. When we returned home and he went to the computer to job-search, I went back into planning mode. I consulted close friends who had been through spousal job loss to gauge the emotional arc we would be facing. I needed to know how to tread lightly here, how to keep moving forward while protecting my husband's feelings. My friends told me stories of husbands who became listless or suffered massive identity crises when unemployment stretched longer than expected. On the car ride home Rob had mentioned he expected the job search to take two weeks. It was wishful thinking on steroids. I had to figure out how to best dole out that reality, while assuring him of my confidence in his abilities. I would have to maintain a careful level of optimism while empathizing with the plight of the job search and understanding the difficulty of adjusting to his shifting identity. I was exhausted just thinking about it, and I didn't dare check in on my own emotions. The fine line I had to walk in our relationship to keep the peace was about to become razor thin.

Rob took the reins of the morning routine as my schedule became increasingly hectic. It was a rare morning when I wasn't sucked straight into emails, interviews, podcasts, or research. I referred him to our calendar constantly to keep track of what was on the schedule each day. I was still taking our daughter to preschool every morning. We were a whole month into Rob's unemployment and my full-time book writing.

"Today I have a podcast recording for an hour and a half, then I need to work until around one to get the updated outline finished and sent in to my editor," I told him. The timing was ideal. I would wrap up work right around the time the two-year-old would need to go down for a nap just after his lunch. I could put him down, eat lunch myself, and get right into the reading I wanted to do. Maybe I'd even read for pleasure. Meanwhile, Rob could go mountain biking.

To my surprise, however, when I emerged from my home office, the two-year-old hadn't eaten lunch yet. I scrambled to make him ramen noodles and quickly put him down for a nap while Rob changed into his riding gear. He left as I tried to console the two-year-old, who was now blindsided by the fact that naptime and Dad leaving were happening in tandem. He took over an hour to settle down and fall asleep. When the battle was finally over, I staggered into the kitchen to finally eat my own lunch. When I saw the dining room table, I almost screamed.

Abandoned coloring books, crayons, markers, printer paper that I had told my six-year-old time and again *not to steal from my workspace*, pencil shavings, and a library book I feared to look inside blanketed its surface. There was kinetic sand in two colors, both of which were scattered in small lumps well outside their designated trays and all over the floor. There were dishes from breakfast, half-eaten food taken off the plates, and milk hardening on the finished wood top of the table. There were small beads from a craft project everywhere—in the sand, in the food, on the floor.

The urge to scream grew harder to suppress when I started clearing the plates and food from the table and realized that none of the dishes from the previous night had been put away. None of the breakfast dishes had been done. None had even been rinsed. The counters were covered with cereal boxes left open, and oatmeal had hardened in the pot on the stove. I went to put the library book back on its designated shelf in the living room and found a half-finished popcorn bowl and a floor covered with half-eaten kernels. Shoes and sweaters were strewn across the couch. Toys had been taken out and never put away. As I moved from one small job to the next I found more things left undone. The laundry was overflowing. The trash needed to be taken out. I could feel the resentment bubbling up inside of me. *What the hell has he been doing all day?*

I had spent the last five hours working intently, trusting him to take care of the rest. The house wasn't just a little messy. It was a disaster. You might be able to walk through without stepping on anything if you were particularly nimble, but how on earth could you not *see* it? His laptop was perched on the end of the horror show that was our dining room table. He had no doubt been sitting at that table half the morning, planning out a route for his bike ride or watching biking videos. Then he had gotten up, looked right past it all, and left.

It was the punch line to a bad joke I'd heard before: that men have a film of dust over their eyes which stops them from seeing the mess. The things they don't want to see they render invisible. Every woman I knew had a story of the things her partner never sees. One leaves the kitchen cabinets wide open. Another leaves the cooler out for weeks after they host a party. The socks and shoes are in every room but the closet. The clothes land right outside the hamper. The towel is always scrunched up behind the bathroom door. I feel these frustrating blind spots on a spiritual level. My husband leaves cups of coffee all over our *property*. I find them in the garage, on the barbeque, outside the front door, in the closet, on the side table next to the bed. I'm lucky if I find the coffee the same day it was made. I've found mugs I had to throw straight in the trash because they harbored their own ecosystems. These are the kinds of jokes that are funny when you're a couple glasses of wine in, and out of the house. They're not much comfort when you're staring down the consequence of your partner's selective sight skills and seeing red.

When Rob returned home, he waxed poetic about his amazing ride as he peeled off his mountain biking gear and threw it onto the floor next to the hamper in our closet. I picked up the sweat-drenched clothing and started the load of laundry I had sorted in anticipation of his arrival. I had spent the entirety of the two-year-old's nap on a fury-fueled cleaning spree. To say I was frustrated would be an understatement.

"The house looks amazing," he said when he finished showering.

"Yeah," I said tersely. "It still needs to be vacuumed, though."

"It looks really good, babe. I'm sorry I didn't do more earlier."

I stepped aside so he could access the vacuum closet, sure that he was going to complete the task I had just mentioned. Instead he turned and walked toward the kitchen to get himself a snack. I got out the vacuum, left it in the hallway, and still nothing. An hour later, I vacuumed the house myself. Then I asked him, for the fifth time, if he had remembered to call his parents to see if they could watch our dog while we traveled during the holidays. He had not.

How did we get here? I didn't understand how this was happening. We'd talked about emotional labor. He said he wanted to help. In the weeks after my *Harper's Bazaar* article appeared, he was getting the kids ready for every outing and doing full loads of laundry every few days. I thought he understood how to pick up his share of the burden. I truly and naively thought that we had changed, and that my husband's unemployment would be the opportunity of a lifetime to balance out emotional labor once and for all. So why was I back to picking up his laundry off the floor and stewing in resentment?

Every wise woman I know understands that *balance* doesn't always mean "split right down the middle." There's push and pull. Our relationships, no matter how well established, are never static. In fact, one of the key predictors of a successful relationship is being able to adapt to change.[1] This applies not only to stressful or traumatic life events but to predictable changes as well. How quickly and efficiently can we adapt together to a change in schedule, a move, a job loss? I had thought because we'd had our aha moment after Mother's Day that the changes would be permanent. The realization that we could slip backward so quickly scared me. I had heard from so many women who harbored overwhelming resentment toward their partners, who felt browbeaten into the role of emotional laborer with no way out, who felt hopeless. I could now see how easy it would be to end up in that position if we didn't figure out how to change our dynamic—and soon. That night, as I sat with the fear, I read Sarah Bregel's essay on the buildup to her divorce, "How to Say You Maybe Don't Want to Be Married Anymore." It had been making the rounds, and I knew the author from freelancing around the same subjects: parenting, life, love. I did not expect to see one iota of myself in the essay, or at least I hoped I wouldn't. Yet I saw the strain of emotional labor peeking through the cracks of the divorce essay almost immediately. "I talked about being a better parent when I'm alone, about disappointment, about resentments that have been coming and going then jolting me so hard that I know, at least in that moment, I've given up."[2] I had never felt like I'd given up, not even close, but had I been disappointed and full of resentment and thought to myself, *Why is this so much easier when he's not around?* Yeah. I had. But we were fixing things. We'd had the talk about emotional labor. We were moving forward, or at least we had been, and we would be again as soon as I figured out the magic formula. Then I got to the point in Sarah's essay where she describes her husband cooking breakfast, doing dishes, helping with the kids—all the things she's been asking him to do and more. It feels hopeful, almost, until she reveals the kicker I should have seen coming. "It always reverts," she writes. "And part of me knows it will keep reverting until it's so ingrained that all I can remember about my life is how to be someone's angry wife." I reread the essay. It's all about emotional labor, even the parts I didn't catch the first time because they are second nature to me. Of course she is the one who is holding it together for her kids. Of course she is the one to schedule the appointment with the therapist for them both. *Of course.*

When I spoke with Sarah on the phone, I wondered aloud if there was a distinct turning point when she realized the imbalance of emotional labor was getting way out of hand. I asked, somewhat desperately, if there were warning signs she could have spotted along the way, but she revealed what I most feared: the emotional labor had always been imbalanced in this way, especially since having their two kids. She could have been describing my own life as she described her well-meaning husband who just didn't get it. He was a man who had watched his own father not take on any of the emotional labor in his family. In their relationship, as a result, when it came to pitching in, there had always been an undercurrent of "this is not my job." He'd feel proud when he loaded the dishwasher, fishing for praise though Sarah did the same job three times over without the work being noticed, let alone lauded. When she would bring up emotional labor, it always turned into her being the "bad guy." Her husband would become self-deprecating, beating himself up over never doing enough. The guilt trip that came with that response sometimes made it easier to just quietly pick up the emotional labor and get back to it alone.[3] I felt more than a hint of recognition now. It was like looking in a mirror.

I thought back to the beginning of my own relationship, trying to find the differences between my relationship with Rob and Sarah's with her husband—differences that would reassure me we would be okay. I wanted to know, with unwavering doubt, that we were different. But had there ever been a time when the balance of emotional labor had been more evenly distributed between us? Rob and I first started dating in high school. When we were seventeen, we went, together, to the teenage wedding of mutual friends of ours. Choosing the wedding gift—knowing we were supposed to bring a gift, even—had fallen to me. I bought a waffle iron, wrapped it, and signed a beautiful card from both of us. The car ride to the wedding was tense. Rob was extremely uncomfortable that we were attending a wedding as a couple, though he wouldn't say so out loud. Instead I was clued in by his deliberate silence and his refusal to look directly at me or the present between us. The tension in the car was suffocating. When he stole a nervous glance at the box, I asked him if he wanted to know what was in it. He said he didn't care. I rolled my eyes and asked him if he needed me to cross his name off the stupid card. *I knew how much he hated signing cards.* The latter part was a dig at the fact that he had given me a card that was blank inside for Valentine's Day. That upset him. I smoothed it over. I wasn't as skilled at emotional labor then as I am now, clearly, but I was already practicing—whether I knew it or not.

Rob spent a large portion of the ride home railing against the institution of marriage and how he felt pretty confident that he would never want to get married.

"I want to get married someday," I said matter-of-factly, digging my heels into the tattered floor of his truck. I set my steely glare on the road ahead.

I often joke that we couldn't have known what we were getting into when we got married at twenty. Then I think back to that moment. *Or maybe we did.* He wasn't one for grand romantic overtures. I wasn't one to back down from what I wanted. These things haven't changed. Yet even if I did have an inkling of how our personalities would butt against or complement each other, I didn't have the self-awareness at seventeen or at twenty to realize the emotional labor I would be taking on, nor how it would evolve throughout our adult lives. Back then it was so innocuous it feels like child's play. In fact, I distinctly remember that buying the waffle iron was fun for me. It was playing grown-up. Back then I would have relished the idea of buying gifts from both of us for the rest of our lives, because writing our names side by side was an act steeped in romance. I had been raised to view performing emotional labor as inherently romantic and adult, two things I, as a teenager, desperately wanted to be. The joint waffle iron card was the equivalent of scrawling "Mrs. Gemma Hartley" in a schoolgirl notebook, but more thrilling because I didn't have to hide it. In fact, I could shove his uncomfortable face in it. It was a glimpse of what our future *could* be.

I didn't realize that should have scared me a hell of a lot more than it scared him. Indeed, it was a glimpse of what our future *would* be as I took over gift buying and card writing for both of our families, just as I had seen my mother and aunts and grandmothers do in their families. I watched these women in my life come together to plan holidays and family vacations. I saw them put dinners on the table and masterfully arrange family schedules and make sure that every last thing from chores to homework got done. I was able to see emotional labor as a sustaining act of love in the way my female relatives took care of everyone, and their husbands rightfully loved them for it. Respected them for it. From where I was standing, I could see that love required everything, at least for women. And as a love-obsessed teen with no grasp of the real world, giving up all of myself for love seemed totally worth it. I never would have imagined myself resenting the act of writing our names and the names of our three children on forty Christmas cards each year. At seventeen, the thought would have made me swoon.

Which is perhaps exactly how I got here. As a woman in American culture, and furthermore Christian culture, I had been conditioned since childhood to romanticize performing emotional labor. I knew that godly women "served" their husbands as a veritable path to better faith. I attended a small, unregulated Christian school where the distinct and separate roles for men and women were drilled into us from kindergarten. We learned extensively that our strength as women came from our ability to serve and give and build community and hold the faith together in a family. It was our job to lift up men so they could lead, basically clearing the path for their success both in faith and in life. Even as I later began to question and move away from many of the misguided teachings of my childhood, the messages I had absorbed didn't completely disappear. I still believed that emotional labor was more naturally my responsibility, if for no other reason than I was "naturally" better at it. It was quicker, more convenient, if I was in charge of that realm. It was one of the few things that still appeared true when I looked around at the world outside my limited experience. My Christian grandmother and my atheist aunt and our lush neighbor were all doing emotional labor for their husbands. I never even questioned that there might be another way. When I thought about my future, I imagined performing emotional labor. That was the mark of a good girlfriend and later a good wife. It was the unifying thread of all strong and lasting relationships I saw growing up. Women did the emotional labor and men stayed with them, loved them. In fact, I absorbed this ideology so fully that I was practicing it even in middle school with my first serious crush. On basketball game days, when he had to wear a tie (a team ritual at our small Christian school), I would straighten and fix it for him. I knew his schedule, though he never bothered to memorize mine. Emotional labor was my job even then.

Whether we start dating at twelve or twenty, most of us encounter the expectations for emotional labor for the first time when we begin to explore romantic relationships. Where boys are encouraged to be unattached and aloof, avoiding emotional attachment like the plague, girls are faced with an entirely different objective: how do I make this person happy? We're encouraged to put ourselves in the background and our romantic interest in the forefront, entangling our self-worth with how good we are at performing emotional labor. When we start partnering up, we already have a lot of societally reinforced ideas about what makes a good girlfriend and later a good wife and mother, in addition to the consistently reinforced gender roles we've grown into. Girls become communal, are emotionally intelligent, and know how to forge bonds—behaviors that are discouraged in adolescent boys.[4] It becomes "natural," then, when we pair up, to fill in the emotional skills our partners lack—and we furthermore glean through culture all the things we "ought" to be. Girlfriends are supposed to be nurturing and caring, but not overbearing. Thoughtful of others' needs but low maintenance with their own. Easygoing and flexible. These are, of course, in addition to a cavalcade of other patriarchal expectations that dictate acceptable appearance, sexual behavior, intelligence level, and style of humor, just to name a few. In the romantic arena, the need for women to keep men comfortable and happy is amplified to the extreme. The work that goes into presenting ourselves physically, the easygoing yet nurturing interactions we foster, the planning and forethought we put into our relationships are exhausting, yet all signs of effort must be masked. Everything must be perfectly smooth; the seams can never show. Indeed, there are few insults greater than being deemed "high maintenance," a term almost explicitly reserved for women who ask for emotional labor from their partners. Emotional labor, when seen for the work that it is, is incredibly unsexy. Men want emotional labor from women, certainly, but they prefer to see it as a natural extension of our personalities—something effortless and joyful—rather than difficult work that will eventually run us into the ground.

Men don't face the same expectations for emotional labor unless they are attempting to woo as a means to an end. They are then supposed to *perform* emotional labor, switching roles for a brief romantic moment to "get" the girl. I was a chick-flick junkie in my early teens. A whole tree was sacrificed for the amount of tissues I used watching and rewatching *The Notebook* (and reading and rereading it as well). Ditto on *A Walk to Remember*. I have only recently relinquished my large collection of Nicholas Sparks novels to my grandmother. These novels and films were my "hopeless romantic" staples. The premise of my favorite rom-coms was always the same—a man would step out of the traditional masculine stereotype to prove his love for a woman. In *A Walk to Remember*, Landon Carter risks the disapproval of the cool kids and takes on fulfilling the bucket list of his dying girlfriend as his own personal mission—finding creative and well-thought-out solutions to her life's desires. In *The Notebook*, Noah Calhoun builds Allie the house of her dreams without her ever having to ask or nag, without even knowing if his efforts would ever be recognized. In *10 Things I Hate About You*, Patrick Verona enlists the school band to publicly woo Kat Stratford. Harry sprints after Sally on New Year's Eve to relay all the reasons he loves her in the now classic *When Harry Met Sally*.

It's no wonder that Nicholas Sparks novels have garnered so many movie deals and a multimillion-dollar empire—and not just because I was an obsessed fan in my teen years. He takes emotional labor to the extreme, and then hands the load over to men. That's what young heterosexual women call romance. These acts are steeped in emotional labor that is scarcely found in real life. Few men take the initiative to think deeply about the needs of their partners and put planning and foresight into grand gestures. Though the cultural script may say men ought to perform some emotional labor in the dating and boyfriend stage, in general our culture is more lenient with men who don't fit that mold. When I talk to my friends who are still in the dating game, there are few, if any, who are still caught up in the fantasy of finding the man they were promised in chick flicks. They've found far more horror stories out there than romantic comedies. Men who won't stop talking about their exes and expect a sympathetic shoulder to cry on. Men who expect you to be cool with waiting around while they play video games. Men who take you out to a meal at their favorite restaurant (Hooters!) and after downing 80 percent of the meal, show their "progressive" nature by wanting to split the check. Not quite the makings of "prince charming."

Yet even men who do perform emotional labor in the early stages of a relationship do so as a means to an end. For men, performing emotional labor isn't a reward in and of itself (as it is supposed to be for women). It's how you get the girl or win her back. It's the ticket to your "prize." The times when men have to think about our desires and needs and emotional responses are culturally viewed as exceptional acts. It's above and beyond, and it's not meant to last forever. There's an expiration date on the demand for men's emotional labor in a relationship. Women, on the other hand, must offer it in perpetuity.

There's a scene in *When Harry Met Sally* that illustrates the letdown women experience when the emotional labor disappears from a relationship. As the character Harry Burns explains, "You take someone to the airport, it's clearly the beginning of the relationship. That's why I have never taken anyone to the airport at the beginning of a relationship." When Sally asks why, he responds, "Because eventually things move on and you don't take someone to the airport, and I never wanted anyone to say to me, 'How come you never take me to the airport anymore?'"

The exchange is funny, because we don't typically consider a ride to the airport a grand romantic gesture. The common trope is that a man stops taking a woman dancing or out to a particular restaurant or any number of experiences that would signify an act of thoughtful, caring emotional labor during the early stages of a relationship. In pop culture, this transgression signals a relationship that is in great peril, and more emotional labor must be done to "win back" the girl. In reality, it is a commonplace experience that women learn not only to live with but to expect. Reasonable acts of caring left unfulfilled become the norm. Perhaps this is why the airport is such a poignant example after all—it's a gesture of caring and foresight and planning that we *want* to be able to expect. It's the sort of thing we do for others all the time.

Harry's approach of keeping expectations for emotional labor low by never taking a woman to the airport is perhaps fairer than the alternative, which is to put in a great deal of emotional labor at the start of a relationship and drop it bit by bit as the relationship progresses. Dating someone who goes above and beyond to show caring and attentive behavior in the beginning as a means to a comfortable end is a far more disappointing prospect than knowing what you're getting into from the start.

When Caitlin Garrett was twenty-five years old, she thought she had found a man who fit the fairy-tale romance we swoon over. He went above and beyond in his thoughtfulness at the beginning of their relationship, never missing a chance to showcase his ability to be caring and thoughtful. She has a photograph of massive logs spelling out *Love U Babe* from the days when he worked in his uncle's log yard, his rural Oregonian version of skywriting— more personal, even, given the brawn and sweat that went into it. On another job site, he spent his break picking blackberries for her and brought them by after work, during a time when she was rarely able to pull away from her job as an escrow assistant to enjoy the outdoors. "He knew I was bummed about being too swamped to pick," she says. "He was so sweet and attentive." The random acts of romance should have, in her mind, led to a relationship that would be equally attentive to her needs, but as time went on things shifted.

When they moved in together after six months of dating, he expected her to pay exactly half of all their living expenses, though he decided on the budget without her. "I was making $15 for every $50 he made," she said. "I was so embarrassed about how poor I felt I'd just overdraw my account frequently to cover 'my share.'" She was barely able to make it work and found it hard to do while keeping up with his other expectations. "I was supposed to be home cooking breakfast, lunch, and dinner, doing all the housework, and pampering him like I'm the Mother Teresa of foot rubs." She was allowed to expect the grand gestures for only a brief moment in the scope of their relationship, but the acts of emotional labor that would truly sustain their life together fell entirely on her shoulders. She was there to give. He was there to take. The sad thing is how normal the imbalance felt across the nearly four years they were together. "It didn't feel right, but it didn't seem shockingly wrong either. I just kept thinking things would get better and made up excuses when they didn't." Now, a couple of years after a messy breakup, she looks back on it all as a learning experience, but one that came with a high cost of emotional labor and a whole lot of heartache.[5]

Which is perhaps why many women value the pragmatism of not getting swept up in the fairy-tale romance. We lower our expectations for the great falling-in-love story to decrease the chance of crippling disappointment when our "prince" turns out to be the guy who eventually stops taking us to the airport. Irina Gonzalez, a thirty-two-year-old freelance writer and editor from Fort Myers, Florida, definitely gave up on grand gestures by the time she began dating her husband. What she wanted instead was someone who wouldn't keep taking and taking without giving anything back. "The men I casually dated, as well as my two serious relationships before meeting my husband, often leaned on me for advice but rarely provided the same," she says. "They also didn't really understand the concept of being in an equitable relationship." When she met her husband, she could tell by the end of the first date that she had found something different, more valuable, than the fairy tale most girls are taught to look for. Their four-hour coffee date didn't feel like the therapy sessions she was conducting for most guys. There was give-and-take, genuine interest, and true equality, which set the tone for the rest of their relationship. Speaking of her newlywed life, she says, "We do our hardest to split things in our house as much as possible, and we try to do so based on each other's strengths—our likes and dislikes."[6] It's nice to know she doesn't have to ask him to vacuum or wash the dishes or take out the trash, because he knows these things are his responsibility. This isn't to say that she doesn't take on the mental load of emotional labor in other ways—she is still the person to take care of finances, trip planning, and scheduling, which she admits could become a point of contention if they decide to have children—but for now, the divide in domestic labor is working for them. She has her happy ending. There's less movie-worthy gravitas in being the person who always vacuums the house, but it's worth more in the long run.

When I look back at my own relationship, I know this is true. The daily acts of emotional labor matter far more than grand gestures. A burst of big romance here and there is nice, certainly, but it isn't the type of behavior that keeps a relationship humming along day after day, year after year. We prime ourselves for disappointment when we pine after the big romantic story, not only because this behavior is rare but because we're taught to expect the wrong kind of emotional labor from men. Wooing, if you get it, involves big bursts of thoughtfulness, but it is not the everyday emotional labor that sustains a relationship. It's not taking you to the airport or remembering your mother's birthday or noticing the dishes in the sink. That part of the equation we are still leaving to women. We're chasing the wrong sort of fantasy from the beginning, and it often takes us far too long to figure it out.

I remember feeling a flood of relief when one of my friends revealed that she and her husband had simply decided to get married rather than having a swoon-worthy engagement story. By this point, I had spent years lying about an engagement story that never happened. It involved a ring that wasn't there and romantic words that were never spoken. I tried not to veer too far from reality, but as friends and coworkers pressed for details upon the news of our engagement, the story grew until it was sufficiently romantic and life affirming. In the embellished version we were lying in bed, and he was going on about all that he loved about me. (At this part, I would laugh and joke that I thought he wanted to have sex, so I rolled away from him because I was tired.) Then he scooted up to me, leaning over to place a ring box in front of me *just* as I was about to fall asleep, and whispered in my ear, "Will you marry me?" In reality, we were just lying in bed talking about getting married, as we had many times before, and then we concluded that we were going to get married. He still asked the question. I still said yes. We picked out a ring later. But it wasn't something I could weave into a magnificent story without sufficient imagination and outright lying.

The fact that I felt it was necessary to lie was something that bothered me for years. I cringed every time someone asked me to tell the story of how we got engaged. I didn't want to admit that my fiancé hadn't taken on the emotional labor that society expects for this momentous occasion, even if it didn't matter to me personally. I confided in my friend who also had an unremarkable engagement that our decision-making process had always made me feel affirmed that we were making a decision based on both love and reason, away from an audience that might sway me. Why should one of the biggest decisions of our lives be made into a public spectacle? Yet I can't ignore the fact that the teenage chick-flick junkie inside me still longed for the big romantic gesture I never received in that proposal. Now I know why. In the real world, the proposal is supposed to be the last big gesture of emotional labor before the slow and steady shift of power takes place.

The movies focus on the sweeping proposals and fairy-tale weddings, but what they don't show is what "happily ever after" actually looks like. We are presented with the beginning of a relationship, or else an act of emotional labor serves as a second chance, a promise for the future. The movies show us that the beginning of love requires an investment of emotional labor on the man's behalf. Sometimes we get that in real life, albeit on a smaller scale. Sometimes we don't.

From what I've seen, however, we all end up in a similar place. As the romance fades into a more comfortable and stable relationship, the expectations for emotional labor begin to shift as well. Men who may have taken on a larger role in caring for the home and emotional state of their partnership in the beginning slowly let go. Emotional labor is handed off because women are "just better at this stuff." By adulthood women are already far more skilled at emotional labor, and that disparity in experience makes it seem logical for men to hand over the reins. Whether consciously or not, men tend to perform emotional labor as a means to an end, whereas women perform emotional labor as a way of being. That's how we get from a happy and equitable relationship at the onset to the simmering resentment that appears years later.

In my marriage, taking on all the emotional labor for the relationship wasn't something I did overnight or even consciously. It was a long and gradual process, especially since Rob and I started dating so early in life. When we first met, there was another woman folding his laundry and preparing his meals and writing his name on holiday cards: his mother. Yet even men who have had time out on their own, once in a relationship, tend to give up many aspects of their independence in order to be relieved of the mental load. Either slowly or all at once with a sudden life change, such as moving in together, men hand off their emotional labor responsibilities to their partner. The ties with families and friends, including social engagements, suddenly become the domain of "the couple" instead of the individual, which is problematic enough. But as women are trained to be more responsive to responsibilities related to emotion, kin, and domestic work, they become the member of the couple responsible for maintaining those ties.[7] That's how I became the one looking at the calendar and reminding my husband of his family members' birthdays, the one writing all the cards he didn't care to sign.

Not only do they allow their familial social bonds to lapse, but men's participation in the running of an efficient and well-cared-for household also tends to slide over time. Men often have a slower timeline or lower standard when it comes to domestic work, so women take it on themselves, choosing to delegate work only when it's most desperately needed. This may be in part because women tend to associate a clean home with their personal success, whereas men's success is tied strictly to their work outside the home.[8] Our worth is tied up in this work, whether we realize it or not. There's also still a societal expectation that women are the ones who need to keep the home in order. If someone comes to the house and it's an utter mess, I'm the one who feels guilty, not Rob. I'm the one people expect to care. So I always have.

It's not always in-your-face overwhelming, but the overwhelm is always brewing beneath the surface. And it almost always leads to a boiling point where we're facing the frustration of being the only one doing this work and wondering how the hell we got here without ever noticing. Taking control of all emotional labor is a gradual process that coincides naturally with the progression of a relationship. It's a cultural norm that is so ingrained in both partners that it happens without discussion, but women are the ones who pay for that lack of communication. We give up our time, our emotional energy, our mental space to solving the issues of emotional labor or taking on the full workload ourselves. The onus is on women to find the solution, to make men's responsibilities clear to them—which reinforces the notion that this is "naturally" our job. Unless we communicate our needs and desires for emotional labor, we can't expect men to take on that role. By the time we become frustrated with how much emotional labor we are performing, it's "our fault" for taking control in a way that produces a learned helplessness on our partner's behalf, and it's "our job" to fix it or deal with it, because no one else will.

The cultural pressure to be the good wife and good mother, along with my long history of thinking about and performing emotional labor, is what made the transition so easy. I don't think Rob ever meant to put all the housework, the mental load, the kin work, and the domestic organization entirely in my court any more than I did. It seemed natural. For a long time, I didn't even notice, as many women don't. The cumulative effect of the handoff often goes unrealized, because we're not doing everything at once. At least not at first. We pick up the pieces one by one.

You are the first one to RSVP to a party for both of you, and an expectation is born. You buy presents for his family when he says he doesn't know what to get for them: another expectation is born. He does a sloppy job cleaning the floors once, maybe twice, and you decide to take over. The dishes are left in the sink, and you don't want to leave them until the situation is unbearable, so that becomes your domain as well. He leaves his laundry next to the hamper, then by the time he returns home the clothes are picked up, washed, and put away. In the waiting game of "who is going to notice this thing first," women beat men to the punch nearly every time. While you don't do the physical tasks every time, you still end up delegating, because noticing the socks on the floor, thinking about the birthday coming up, caring about whether all the grandparents get Christmas cards—that whole sprawling mental load is your job now because you touched it last.

The answer to how we got here is usually: one step at a time. We spend our childhood watching the world around us, picking up on the subtle and not-so-subtle messages that tell us emotional labor is women's work. That it is our birthright, our natural forte, our romantic destiny. There is no shortage of practice for us as we wade through the world of dating, hoping to find "the one." Then, if we're lucky, we get to a point where we find a good guy, a progressive guy, a guy who will help when we ask him to help. This is how the fairy tale really pans out. We get our happy ending and begin a new journey of slowly picking up each piece of emotional labor. A little worry work here, a little reminder there. Nothing huge. Nothing noticeable. Certainly nothing to complain about. We take these small steps toward deeper inequality, so small we hardly notice them at all, until maybe one day we see some tiny blue lines on a pregnancy test and take a sudden plunge.

CHAPTER 2

THE MOTHER LOAD

The moment I looked at that positive pregnancy test, my world was forever changed. Not only because of the depth of love I experienced through motherhood but because of the depth of emotional labor I dove into the moment I knew I was pregnant. I shrieked and cried tears of joy and stared at the test in wonder, then within the hour I had set up a pregnancy appointment, ordered *What to Expect When You're Expecting*, found a gestational calculator to give me all the facts I needed to know at this stage, and begun scouring the internet for nursery inspiration. It was go time: Emotional Labor 2.0.

As the birth of my first child approached, I overprepared and overresearched in every possible way. I wanted to be fully armed for whatever was ahead, because I knew the stakes were high. Every decision I now made affected another person. The pressure to "get it right" was unlike anything I had ever experienced before, and it was especially intense because, even though it took two of us to make this baby, it was *my* responsibility to know what to do.

I felt the weight of this new mental load acutely as Rob and I made our way through Target, scanning items for our baby registry. I stared at the extensive list of suggested items in my hand. I also had in my mind all the suggestions friends and family had given me on things I did and did not need. Much of that advice was conflicting. We stopped in the baby food section. Did I need a microwavable bottle sterilizer, or would we boil our bottles in a pot? I put it on the list, just in case. Then we came to a specialized bottle-drying rack. It looked like a patch of rubber wheatgrass. For some reason, this item stumped me. I didn't know what to do. I had reached the edge of my mental capacity. I asked Rob to make the decision, and he flat-out wouldn't. "I don't know. You're the one who knows these things. You know what we need more than I do." Except that I didn't, and what I did know had much more to do with my personal research than some magical mom knowledge I was endowed with upon conception. Moms don't innately know what the next steps look like, from what to put on a baby registry to how to diagnose common infant illnesses to what questions we should ask our doctors. But we learn. We put in the hard work, the time, the research, even when we don't find these things necessarily compelling or interesting. Because if we don't do it, who will?

Pregnancy was physically exhausting but perhaps even more mentally and emotionally draining. Rob was there for support when I asked him to be, but the details—anticipating the needs of a child not yet born—were mine to worry about. I was the one tasked with carrying around this encyclopedia of new information in my head, hoping that pregnancy brain wouldn't make me forget any of it. Rob could have read the baby books. He could have looked up the articles on what to get for the baby or how to prep and freeze homemade purees or how to make DIY padsicles for my recovery period. But it never even crossed his mind. He didn't need to educate himself on these things. I had educated myself for the both of us. And although I was stressed and bone tired, I wasn't upset with

Rob. It was a division of labor that was already so embedded in our psyches neither of us ever considered another way. I never even asked him to read the baby books—partly because I knew I would regurgitate the most pertinent information to him and partly because I knew he wouldn't read them.

Fathers-to-be don't take on the same emotional labor responsibilities very often, and we accept this as normal. We allow this line to be drawn between us: helper on one side, responsible party on the other, even before the baby is born. We're responsible for the knowledge, the worry work, *and* the untransferable growing of a tiny human. And we're told to enjoy it. We're subject to the cultural myth that all the emotional labor we do in preparation for a baby is natural, and therefore not real work. The registry, the research, the room decor—it was all supposed to be fun. Certainly, some of it was, but much of it was plain and simple work. There is so much to prepare for, so many balls already in the air by the time we set foot in the delivery room. Though I heard many people tell me that birth is when the real work begins, as I look back over my pregnancy, so much of my emotional labor had already started.

Still, I kept hoping that our egalitarian ideal would be met after the baby arrived. I felt confident that once our son was brought into the world, surely my husband and I would coparent like champions, but I was swiftly and unceremoniously corrected.

My son's birth was a traumatic event that spanned twenty-two hours and involved multiple unwanted interventions. The beautiful, drug-free birth I had spent months preparing for had been completely turned on its head. I was bruised, shaking, and bleeding profusely when they transferred me to my recovery room. In some small corner of my mind, I wondered if I was going to die. The pain was still intense. My mind didn't feel fully present. The entire time I was in the hospital, I needed help hobbling to the bathroom a mere ten steps away. I was constantly watching the clock for the next dose of Percocet, though it didn't help much. It would be weeks before I could stand alone in the shower without my husband to steady me and wash my back. I couldn't imagine going home and having to care for another human being. It seemed unbearably cruel, this whole childbearing and child-caring arrangement.

This was, of course, compounded by the fact that my husband didn't have any paternity leave. He had less than a week of vacation time at his retail job and was also still in school. In fact, he had to leave me in the recovery room twice to go take finals. (This would happen again when our daughter was born. Our children have impeccable timing.) Since I had worked retail up until the night I went into labor, I would simply not return to work. There was no conceivable way we could get our job schedules to sync up in a way that would allow us to access daycare. Even if we could, we wouldn't make enough to cover the cost of even the most questionable childcare. I would have to eventually figure out how to use my newly acquired English degree; in the meantime, I would work on pinching pennies and keeping this new little human alive.

While the prospect of quickly becoming the sole caregiver for our child was harrowing, it wasn't unexpected. The fact that we would not be able to afford childcare and would cut out my job because it paid slightly less was a factor we had discussed and agreed upon before we even conceived. I was prepared for that. What I wasn't prepared for was the sudden shift in our roles as we went from partners to parents. Before we'd even left the hospital, the expectations for each of us were set out clearly. It was a foreboding peek at how motherhood would exacerbate the inequality of emotional labor between us.

By the time we were settled into our postpartum recovery room, I had been awake for the better part of two days. To be honest, I was grateful for the exhaustion if only because it was intense enough to make sleep more important than my pain. Yet as soon as I began to drift off, my baby tucked into his bassinet beside me, there was a knock at the door. A stack of paperwork was placed on my hospital tray. The nurse pointed to the one on top and explained to me that I was responsible for keeping track of each bowel movement, feeding, and duration of feeding on this paper. When was the last time he breastfed? How was the latch? Was I producing colostrum or milk? Had the meconium been expelled yet? Was it normal? *How on earth was I supposed to know?* I currently had a big whiteboard on the wall in front of me that told me when I could get my next dose of Percocet and ibuprofen, respectively. I had to hit a call button whenever I needed to use the bathroom so someone could assist me. I was a hazy mess, still coming off the drugs and in so much pain I was afraid to sit up to look at the mountain of information in front of me. I had just given birth. Why was this my responsibility? My husband was sitting next to me, physically and mentally intact. It would have been so easy for him to jot down feedings and diaper changes as they happened, to read through the paperwork, to fill out the forms. Considering the state I was in, it was really the only solution that made sense. Yet for the duration of our hospital stay, the nurses spoke exclusively to me. I was the one tasked with remembering the onslaught of information all on my own. I desperately needed Rob to be my representative as I recovered and came out of the haze, but to the doctors and nurses filing into our room at all hours, he seemed entirely invisible.

I was the only one they seemed to speak directly to. And yet, during the three days we were hospitalized, none of the nurses learned my name. They simply called me "Mom." There was a deep desire within me to tell them I had a name, that I didn't want my personhood erased by this new role, but that would have disrupted their comfort. So I let it go. They kept calling me "Mom." Every interaction seemed imbued with the same meaning: you're a mom now; this is your job.

There isn't much I remember about those first few sleep-deprived days of motherhood, but I do remember my husband asking, often, "What can I do?" It was a question meant to help me.

He didn't know what to do because he hadn't been inundated with hospital pamphlets, he hadn't read the baby books and blogs, he hadn't prepared in the same way I had. Instead, he looked to me for direction. It was my job, after all. Yet all I could think was, *I don't know either!* Reading the baby books and bringing home an actual living, breathing baby were two entirely different experiences. I crossed the threshold of our home with our infant and immediately realized I had no idea what I was doing. The hospital had clearly made a terrible mistake in letting us leave. I was very unqualified for this job, and yet here we were. Rob was asking me what to do, asking for delegation because I was *supposed* to know what to do. Despite not knowing the answer, it was clear that I would need to figure it out and fast. I needed to know for both of us, and so a much deeper divide in our domestic dynamic began. I became the person who knew what needed to be done. Rob became the person I informed. This isn't to say he didn't do his part in parenting. He did. He changed diapers when I told him to. He learned the ropes when I showed him. He did far more than my friends' husbands, who required endless coercion and praise for simply watching their own kids. In time, I could walk out the door and not expect a panicked call or a text asking for the most basic of parenting information. Now, I don't even hesitate before leaving for a yoga class or dinner with my friends. I can trust that he'll step into the role of primary parent without missing a beat or expecting a pat on the back for "babysitting." I know plenty of women who don't have that luxury.

I realized this recently when I brought dinner to a friend with a newborn while her husband was out of town for work. I came alone, not wanting to add my three older children to what was already a stressful time for her. She seemed surprised when she opened the door, my arms full of lasagna rather than a toddler.

"Where are the kids?" she asked, looking around me to see if they were hiding.

"They're at home with Rob."

"That's so nice of him."

She says this, as many of my friends do, with no hint of sarcasm. Many women I know think that by letting me leave the house he is doing me a great favor—one that must presumably be repaid. In their experience, full-fledged fatherhood comes with a catch. Taking care of their own kids is never simply their job. It's a favor to be traded. A show of unusual good faith. As I left my friend's house that evening, she asked me to thank Rob for her, and I felt like shaking her.

"He doesn't need to be thanked for watching his own kids," I said.

"Thank him anyway."

It's an exchange I can't imagine her husband, or even my own, has ever encountered. No one asks where the kids are when a father is out in public. Friends would never marvel at how nice it is for me to allow my husband to leave me with all three of our children while he spends time out on his own. For mothers, being the primary parent is generally a given. For men, it's extra credit.

This is amply clear in the high standards we impose on single mothers compared to the compassion and sympathy we give to single fathers. In Stephanie Land's essay "The Mental Load of Being a Poor Mom," she describes the heavy burden not only of caring alone but of doing so with very little money. "Nobody offered to help. . . . My extended family, limited in their own resources, spent little time with my daughter. They never asked if they could take her for an overnight or even out to dinner. Her dad paid minimal child support. Asking him for help, for instance to take his kid for an extra day so I could work, meant giving him the power to drop out at the last minute, leaving me with the responsibility to suddenly find child care or possibly lose my job."[1] Her mental load did not consist only, or even primarily, of simple chores left undone, like those she saw in Emma Lit's popular "You Should've Asked" cartoon, which depicts the unequal load in what appears to be a middle-class heterosexual couple.[2] The decisions Stephanie weighed in caring about every last detail included whether she could put food on the table. Not only was the emotional labor she undertook heavier, but it was judged more harshly. It is evident every time she writes about the intersection of poorness and motherhood. By doing it all and still coming up short, she is accused by strangers on the internet of moral failing.

The bar is impossibly high, and resources to help single mothers find reprieve from emotional labor are simply nowhere to be found. Our culture lauds motherhood, holds it up as "the most important job a woman can have," then does little to nothing to support us (just look at the outlandish cost of childcare) and admonishes us when we fail to do the job as expected—even when we're going it alone. This is truer than ever when we look at black mothers and women of color, who face layers of judgment and castigation across their intersecting identities. They become responsible not only for the emotional labor of their households but for the emotional labor of the entire black community. "If I had a dollar for every time a single mother got blamed for the problems in the African American community, I'd be rich. If I had two dollars for every time someone said a single mother's problems would be solved with the addition of a man to the household, I would be even richer," Rasheena Fountain writes in her *Huffington Post* op-ed titled "Black Single Mothers Are More Than Scapegoats."[3] She explains her frustration with conversations that so often blame black mothers for the ills that haunt the black community—ills that are far more rooted in a culture of white supremacy than the product of black single mothers on welfare, a stereotype that is both harmful and incorrect. She notes the decline in unwed motherhood across black and Hispanic communities, the rise in single mothers pursuing higher education, and the many prominent examples of valuable citizens raised by single black mothers. No matter how high a hurdle single mothers clear, it's never enough.

Single fathers simply do not face those same standards. A quick Google search of communities rallying around single fathers produces results such as a father being inundated with kindness from strangers when he publicly wrote about his struggle to pay for his three sons' insulin.[4] There are "heartwarming" internet stories about men who learn to do their daughter's hair or play dress up because Mom isn't there to do it. These actions are lauded in a way a mother doing the same thing never would be. The bar set for fathers is incredibly low, even when they simply want to be seen as equals.

Recently, when I had a busy workday, Rob took it upon himself to get the kids out of the house for a while so I could have some quiet space to concentrate. He took them all to Costco (the easiest shopping trip thanks to the large carts to hold them all) and then out for ice cream. It's a big trip to be sure but one I've done many times. It's not uncommon for me to get the comment "You have your hands full," but that's about the extent of stranger interaction when I'm out with all three. My husband, on the other hand, is inundated with praise and admiration for his brave efforts. Multiple people stopped him on his shopping trip to comment on what an outstanding parent he was. He spent the entirety of the ice cream trip being commended by an older gentleman for taking on this "dad day" to give me a break. Nearly everyone he encounters thinks that simply being out in the world with all his kids is an extraordinary and novel accomplishment.

Fortunately for me, he doesn't feel the same way. To be honest, he was offended when he came home from the ice cream shop. The "dad day" comment got under his skin, because it undercut how much he does. He doesn't have dad days. He is a dad.

My husband knows nearly all the same details about our children that I do. He takes them to the grocery store as often as I do. He puts them to bed as often as I do. He cooks for them as often as I do (probably much more, actually). The few things he misses—the naptime rituals, the morning routines, the occasional idiosyncrasy here and there—are merely because I am the at-home parent. I have more time around them. He puts in the effort to be a father in the same capacity as I do as a mother, which makes the low bar of fatherhood frustrating for him. He craves a higher expectation, because he regularly goes above and beyond.

Moments like these remind me why it's so hard for men like my husband to helm the ship of emotional labor in a family. It's not the norm. It's not the expectation. The societal pressures he grew up with were the polar opposite of mine in terms of emotional labor. Caring was not an expectation for him; in fact, it was tacitly frowned upon as not masculine. The men in his life did not take the time to write letters to their grandmothers, or prepare meals for the family, or take charge as equal parents and partners. Men's main societal pressure is to be breadwinners. They are expected to put this priority above family, above caring, above emotional labor— always. There is no open space for him to learn, no support system that will help him achieve the full equality he may desire at home. As Tiffany Dufu writes in *Drop the Ball*, "Until the contributions that women make at work are seen as just as valuable as the contributions women make at home, the contributions that men make at home will never be considered as valuable as the contributions men make at work. Just as women need affirmation on both fronts, so do men."[5] Yet so often, that affirmation never comes. Their efforts, though praised, are undercut by the overplayed manner in which we give that praise. The pat on the back men get for parenting is akin to the exaltation we give children for messily making their bed or dressing themselves with two different socks and sparkly sandals. We praise the effort and turn a blind eye to the incompetence. Yet unlike children, men often do not learn to do these things better in time. Instead, without the equal support necessary to take on emotional labor, they hand it back over without giving it their best effort. Unlike us, they have the ability to believe it's not their job.

It is a mother's job to care about every last detail, and when it comes to caring for children, those details add up quickly. In her *Huffington Post* article "The Mental Workload of a Mother," author Jami Ingledue writes out just a few of the things she must constantly keep track of: the stuff in the house (toys, clothes, literally everything), gift buying, kin work, all things school related, the calendar, the meal planning, and the emotional needs of her family. These don't even begin to scrape the surface. "The list is endless and could fill a whole book," she writes. "Which I do not have the brain space to write."[6]

Every mother has "the list" in her head, and it grows and shifts with each passing day. The field-trip form is now done, the check written and sent: this task gets removed. My daughter's closet door has come off the tracks, and my husband needs to be told to fix it. I've updated the bath schedule in my mind: the oldest needs one tonight, the youngest and middle should take one tomorrow. My daughter has decided lettuce is now acceptable. My son has decided that grapes are not. These are mere drops in the well of information I always carry. My husband's list, while quite extensive, never nears my level. It doesn't have to. If something is truly important for both parents to know, it's up to Mom to pass on the crucial information.

When you're the only one keeping track, becoming the delegator is all you can do to help yourself. It becomes increasingly hard to lighten your load without asking for help, because dropping the ball is not an option. You have to make a pass, and you must do it skillfully.

In motherhood, the role of household manager becomes a full-fledged beast, because emotional labor is no longer simply expected—it is required. Living with a partner before kids may not be easy, but it is easy in comparison. If you take an "each man for himself" approach in a relationship, you'll have tension but no one will die. Once you have a baby, that's no longer the case. Kids require intense physical and emotional labor, none of it optional.

Someone is going to pick up a crying baby, and the person who does it over and over again naturally becomes the primary caregiver. That is usually the person home with the baby, and given the sad state of paternity leave in this country, that person is typically the mother, whether either partner wants that or not. You become the one who knows and cares about the child's needs. You become the first responder. And caring for another human who can do literally nothing for themselves is overwhelming. Women simply learn to live with the overwhelm. It's expected that we do. And it doesn't seem to matter if we are stay-at-home mothers or working demanding full-time jobs.

Brigid Schulte, author of *Overwhelmed: Work, Love, and Play When No One Has the Time*, writes, "These days, even as mothers put in extreme hours on the job, the New Domesticity movement urges the ideal mother to raise chickens, grow organic gardens, knit, can vegetables, and even home school her children."[7] The time we spend mothering is intense. We take on the impossible task of "doing it all" at the expense of our health and sanity. We shoulder more emotional labor than we can possibly survive, and we don't get much help in balancing it with our partners. Kids need immense portions of emotion work and mental labor, and the bulk of that labor consistently falls to us. We take on the drudge work, the worry work, the extracurriculars of parenthood, while men, on the other hand, take on a less demanding load, if they're taking one on at all.

While fathers are certainly spending more time with their kids than ever before, how they spend that time is very different. In 2006, Australian sociologist Lyn Craig analyzed time-use diaries to see if women were still spending more time as the primary caregiver (they were) and if the quality of care provided by moms versus dads differed (it did). Mothers are still the "default" parent, the ones who do the mental and physical labor of childcare. Fathers, on the other hand, were more likely to be the "fun" parent. Their time spent with kids involved talking, playing, and recreational activities more than any other type of care. "Even in relative terms, the time women spend caring may be more demanding than the time men spend caring," Craig writes. "Therefore, even if fathers do spend more time with their children than in the past, they may not relieve mothers of some aspects of the work that is part of caring. . . . If the tasks that men and women undertake with their children, or the time constraints or level of management responsibility for care are different, increased father time with children may still leave mothers inadequately assisted in the challenge of balancing work and family commitments."[8]

Yet men often don't see the split in emotional labor as unfair. Even when the data show otherwise, they believe domestic labor and childcare is split equitably between themselves and their partners—or at least it is close enough to being equal. Based solely on information from the American Time Use Survey (ATUS), they aren't too far off the mark. In dual-income heterosexual households where both Mom and Dad work full-time, mothers average 10 hours on childcare versus men's 6.7, and women spend nearly 12 hours on housework compared to men's 8.4 hours per week.[9] In both instances, this is about a half-hour difference per day in childcare and housework, respectively, between men and women. What this information doesn't account for, however, is who is in charge of ensuring that the work is done. In addition to the extra hour a day women put into this type of labor, they also tend to take on all the mental and managerial work to make sure it actually happens.

Because our societal expectations for fathers are lower, they often get a pass when it comes to knowing all the idiosyncrasies involved in caring for their own children. They expect their partners to remember everything for them, because they always have. They aren't accounting for the extra work that this emotional labor adds to our plates. They don't even see it. They see their "help" as enough, because fatherhood isn't considered their job in the way motherhood is considered ours.

Part of this is because as mothers, we approach parenting with the preconceived notion that parenthood is our domain, and fathers are often relegated to the role of helper, whether they want to be or not. While many of us no longer subscribe to the outdated stereotype of the bumbling father, we still don't trust them to be in charge. We've usually seen, by the time we have children, a level of ineptitude when it comes to emotional labor. We've spent our pregnancies doing the research they don't even think to do, and postbaby the stakes are higher. The mistrust, to some extent, is warranted. Then our lack of faith is cemented by a cultural lack of paternal responsibility. We don't, as a society, value men's work as fathers or hold them to the same rigid standards as mothers. This not only sets up women for an overwhelming dive into the deep waters of emotional labor but also inhibits men from growing and stepping fully into the role of parent. They are instructed by their partners in what they need to know and what tasks they need to perform. It may be less effort, but the gender imbalance in emotional labor also mitigates men's emotional payoff in parenthood.

We need to allow and encourage men to share in emotional labor, not only to give mothers relief but to give fathers a chance at a more full and rewarding experience of parenthood. Michael Kimmel, author of *Angry White Men* and *The Guy's Guide to Feminism*, highlights that gender equality, especially in regard to the emotional labor that takes place in the home, helps men live the kind of lives they desire. "The more egalitarian our relationships, the happier both partners are," Kimmel says in his TED talk "Why Gender Equality Is Good for Everyone—Men Included." "When men share housework and childcare their children are happier and healthier, their wives are happier and healthier, *the men* are happier and healthier."[10] He notes that *sharing* is the key word here. "We often have two phrases that we use to describe what we [men] do: we pitch in and we help out," Kimmel says. These terms don't reflect equal responsibility. They don't reflect true balance. It's not enough. We have to *share* this load. Though our current imbalance may look, on the surface, like a sweeter deal for Dad, in truth both partners are hurt by the unequal distribution of emotional labor. Neither men nor women can live their best, their fullest lives until we fundamentally change our expectations not only for motherhood but for fatherhood as well.

CHAPTER 3

WHO CARES?

"Just let me do it," I told Rob as I watched him struggle to fold our daughter's fitted sheet shortly after he took over laundry duty. It's a phrase I'm sure he's heard from me countless times, and even when I'm not saying it out loud, I've often implied it with a single you're-doing-it-wrong stare. I cannot pretend that I have not played a part in creating such a deep divide in the emotional labor expectations in my home. I want things done a certain way, and any deviation from my way can easily result in me taking over. If the dishwasher is loaded wrong, I take it back on instead of trying to show my husband how to load it. If the laundry isn't folded correctly, I'll decide to simply do it myself. On occasion I have found myself venting with friends that it is almost as if our male partners are purposefully doing things wrong so they won't have to take on more work at home.

While I don't think this has been the case in my own home, for some women this is a reality. A 2011 survey in the UK found that 30 percent of men deliberately did a poor job on domestic duties so that they wouldn't be asked to do the job again in the future.[1] They assumed that their frustrated partners would find it easier to do the job themselves than deal with the poor results of their half-hearted handiwork. And they were right. A full 25 percent of the men surveyed said they were no longer asked to help around the house, and 64 percent were only asked to pitch in occasionally (i.e., as a last resort).

Even if men aren't consciously doing a poor job to get out of housework, their lackluster "help" still frustrates. A similar survey conducted by Sainsbury's in the UK found that women spent a whole three hours per week, on average, redoing chores they had delegated to their partners.[2] The list where men fell short left little ground uncovered: doing the dishes, making the bed, doing the laundry, vacuuming the floors, arranging couch cushions, and wiping down counters were all areas of complaint. Two-thirds of the women polled felt convinced that this was their partner's best effort, so perhaps it's not surprising that more than half didn't bother "nagging" them to do better. They simply followed their partners around and cleaned up after them.

The ways in which women cling to maintaining rigid standards is what sociologists call "maternal gatekeeping," and what we refer to, prebaby, as simply "perfectionism."[3] We actively discourage men from becoming full partners at home, because we truly believe we can do everything better, faster, more efficiently than everyone else. Because we are the ones who control all the aspects of home and life organization for our families and especially our children, we become convinced that our way is the only way. We are hesitant to adjust our personal expectations, especially because we have put so much work into caring about our household systems. We've carefully considered how to best keep everyone comfortable and happy, so it seems natural that everyone should conform to the best-thought-out plan available: ours.

This thinking is consistently reinforced by a culture that tells us that we *should* hold ourselves to this higher standard. That if we don't strive toward perfectionism, we are failing as women. We feel as if we are letting our families down, we are letting womankind down, we are letting ourselves down when we don't perform emotional labor in the most intense possible way. Yet this level of perfectionism can be exhausting, and it dissuades those men who would help from even trying. Instead of assuming that men can hold down the fort while we are out of town, we leave a veritable handbook on how they should best care for their own children. Dufu writes in her book that she once wrote a list for her husband titled "Top Ten Tips for Traveling with Kofi," which included, among other things, a reminder to feed their child. I have left freezer meals and detailed instructions for my husband on how to feed himself when I am out of town so he doesn't wander into the grocery store and spend $200 on two days' worth of food, instead of involving him in the process of meal planning so he could take it on himself. It's not just society but also my maternal gatekeeping that contributes to the mental load I've taken on. I don't leave room for mistakes, and because of that, I don't leave room for progress. Then again, when I do, I've been let down.

We had both been warned by my oral surgeon that my wisdom tooth extraction was likely going to put me down for a few days, but instead of the intense prep I would normally do ahead of time, I assumed my husband would take over what I couldn't do. He'd been slowly but surely picking up his share of emotional labor since my *Harper's Bazaar* article had appeared three months earlier. He seemed ready to take on the type of full day I would have put in before he was laid off. The day of the surgery, I felt mostly fine immediately afterward. I took my pain pills but was moving around, had minimal swelling, and spent the evening going over the plans for the next day with Rob. I had worked with our son on his homework, but there was still one page that needed to be finished in the morning. He was allowed to bring in a Game Boy for the special "electronics day" their class had earned. Our daughter needed to go to preschool at 8:30 a.m., but her needs were simple—get her dressed, brush her hair, fill her water bottle. Our son had the option of hot lunch if the morning got out of hand, and I encouraged Rob to use it but just remember to pack him a snack. He had been around and helping with the morning routine for weeks since his layoff. I assumed he could do it alone just this once, though we both thought he wouldn't have to. After all, I was fine.

Well, I was fine until 11:45 p.m., when I woke up crying and frantically scrambling for pain pills. The left side of my face had swollen to the size of a baseball, and I spent hours awake in excruciating pain. When morning came, the situation was even worse, and I could barely function. Rob woke me at 8:30 a.m. to tell me he was taking our daughter to school along with our youngest. Our six-year-old would have to be walked to school in half an hour. I set an alarm on my phone in case I dozed off, and our son came into the room and talked with me. I asked him if he had everything ready—his lunch, his clothes, his homework. He said yes, and I lay back relieved. I was barely able to get myself out of bed to walk him to school and found myself resenting the fact that his dad hadn't thought to take all of them to drop off like I had done when he was working. My face throbbed with pain as I slipped on shoes and a jacket, then instructed our son to do the same. Then I came into the living room at the moment we had to leave and realized that my six-year-old had been wrong. His homework hadn't been done or checked. His lunch hadn't been packed. He didn't have a snack or fresh water. He didn't have an electronic device to bring to school for their special day.

Now not only was I suffering the guilt of not getting him ready, but he would have to suffer the consequences of no one helping him. He would have to stay in at recess to complete his homework. He wouldn't get the thirty minutes of electronic time his friends would have. I was able to grab an orange and throw it in his backpack for a snack, but it was too late for the rest of it. Even though my husband had been the one on duty for the morning, I was the one left with the guilt of taking my son to school ill prepared. I felt like I should have better prepared my husband to take over for me. I should have implemented my system better. If letting Rob take over was going to mean my kids' needs falling through the cracks, I wasn't here for it. I needed a better option, and that better option seemed to be doing things my way.

When I later brought up the morning mishap with Rob, he felt guilty also, but not in the way I had. He was able to acknowledge the problem, say he was sorry, and move on. He didn't beat himself up over his mistake in the way I was beating myself up for not hovering more diligently. Parenting mistakes aren't a moral failing for him like they are for me. Dads get the at-least-he's-trying pat on the back when people see them mess up. Moms get the eye rolls and judgment. Everything that happened that morning was still "my fault," because I wasn't living up to the standard I *should* set for myself as a mom: the standard of perfection.

I was still expected to be the one in charge, even when I was incapacitated, because isn't that just what moms are supposed to do? He wasn't expected to have the morning routine locked down. He was still a dad—still exempt from judgment. Despite now being the at-home parent, at least for the time being, it still wasn't his primary job or responsibility. It was mine, just as it had always been. I was trying to treat my husband as an equal partner. I was trying to let go of control, or adjust my expectations, or compromise my standards, but we kept coming up short. We kept missing that elusive balance, and more frustratingly, I was the only one who felt bad about it. I was the one who cared.

The day my *Harper's Bazaar* article on emotional labor went live, I went out for wine with my friend, and we immediately dove into the conversation. I wasn't asked to explain the concept or clarify any points. She had an intrinsic knowledge of this problem that previously had no name, as did every woman I spoke to for weeks afterward. After a day spent walking on eggshells trying to further clarify the issue of emotional labor for Rob, it felt good to let loose with someone who got it. Someone who cared in the same way I did.

My friend told me how she had set a pile of bedding and other things that needed to be taken up at the bottom of the stairs. Much like my blue Rubbermaid storage bin in the closet, the bedding was difficult for her to put away and quite easy for her husband. It was also impossible not to notice—you'd have to jump over two steps or push it all to the side to go up the stairs without it. Yet that was exactly what her husband did, ignoring the obvious task in front of him, not out of spite but out of what seemed to be sheer ignorance that this was a problem at all. If it was, she would have asked him for help, right? It wasn't up to him to notice. Realizing what needed to be done in the home was her job. She decided to go the passive-aggressive route of taking it all upstairs herself and putting it away in front of him (clearly, we are kindred spirits), getting an apology for a problem that wasn't fully understood, and coming out on a wine date with me so she could explain to someone who would get it.

I have had conversations with my friends about emotional labor more times than I can count, most of them long before I chose to write on the topic. Women talk to each other about the emotional labor we perform, because we all understand it deeply. We all care in similar ways. We all know how hard it is. Emotional labor is rooted in our relationships in a way that seems unshakable, even when we reach our final breaking point. One woman, upon becoming overwhelmed with the emotional labor she was performing, told her partner the only way they were staying together was for him to go to a therapist. He asked her to find one and make an appointment for him. "It went right over his head," she says. "He's never going to get it."

It's no wonder women come to each other with our problems instead of hashing them out with our partners. We talk about all the work we do—emotion work, kin work, domestic work, clerical work—because we know other women will not only recognize it but validate its worth, whereas men, through their actions, and the larger culture do not. There is so much behind-the-scenes work that we do day in and day out, and it often feels thankless and unseen. We share our stories with one another, talking to our girlfriends instead of our partners because that is where the understanding is. Our conversations with each other help us feel seen, make visible the invisible. It doesn't change the dynamic with our partners, but it helps us feel a little less alone when we go home.

But while feeling seen by women helps, it doesn't provide a solution to the frustration we feel when work is left unnoticed and unappreciated at home. The mental load still waits for us. The delegation of labor must be done, and a fine line must be walked to ensure our frustration doesn't show. So why not just talk about it with our partners, rather than behind their backs? The truth is, that's easier said than done. Most women have had the talk about emotional labor at some point in their relationships only to have the talk become a fight. Our words fall on deaf—or at least defensive—ears. Talking about emotional labor requires emotional labor.

When I try to explain emotional labor to my husband, it sounds to him like I'm saying, "You don't care at all." He hears that I don't appreciate the work he puts in. But his response ignores the extensive emotional labor that goes into the way I live my life. We usually don't go near the heart of the problem. It's why my conversations about emotional labor have always been so cyclical. I try to talk to Rob, and we don't see eye to eye. The emotional labor of the conversation becomes too much for me, so I instead talk to other women who will understand. We vent, we share, we bolster each other until we reach the breaking point again. Most of the time, the struggle takes place in my mind. On the outside, I look fine—maybe a little stressed but fine. Which is why the outbursts of overwhelm seem so out of nowhere when they occur.

"Men aren't privy to the conversations that we have with one another, so for them it looks like we have it all together," Dr. Froswa Booker-Drew, author of *Rules of Engagement: Making Connections Last*, tells me the first time we talk.[4] We've been talking about the wisdom of womanhood and how sharing our stories with one another helps ease the burden of emotional labor, but now for the first time, I'm wondering if *only* talking to one another has been harming us as well. Having space to tell our stories, to bring our invisible work into the light is vital, but nothing changes if men cannot also see, hear, and tell each other these stories.

As we talk about her personal life, she tells me about the disconnect between her husband's view of her as a force of nature, able to get all these things done with ease, and her frequent feeling that she needs help. What he sees is her ability to come up with all the solutions to keep things running smoothly. In his mind, if she needed the help, she would speak up about it, they would hire someone, and that would be the end of it. What appears to him as an innate ability to make sure everything is taken care of, however, is not as simple as it looks. He doesn't understand the cultural pressure she feels to "do it all." He doesn't understand the mental work, not to mention guilt, that would have to be factored into changing the system.

"He doesn't have the same lens that I do," she says. "He means well, he just doesn't get it."

That lens Dr. Booker-Drew talks about is the lived female experience. She counts herself lucky, because her husband was raised with sisters who taught him to pull his own weight, but there is no denying the difference in how they approach the home front. He cooks and cleans and helps, but as a man, this makes him exceptional. The fact that Dr. Booker-Drew does not *always* cook and clean has often made her feel as if she isn't doing enough. This strikes me as absurd, because she is squeezing in this interview from a hotel room in Las Vegas where she has spent all day presenting a workshop on community involvement while suffering from a cold and allergies. It seems like these domestic duties should be the last thing on her mind as she focuses on important community-building work, yet it is always right there beneath the surface. There is no compartmentalized Dr. Booker-Drew that can be separated from her roles as wife and mother and daughter and black woman and southern woman and good Christian churchgoer. She says when she shows up in the world, she shows up as all of it, and there is added cultural pressure for her specifically to get it perfect. She even recalls as a child being told she had to be a hundred times better than everyone else because as a black woman, she is held to a different, higher standard. "You're representing not just women, you're representing your own ethnic group," she says. "The weight is so heavy." For women, and women of color especially, we are subject to the cultural expectation that we should fill all these different roles—they are, after all, the roles that help keep those around us comfortable and happy.

One of our biggest problems seems to be that we can never simply focus on any one part. We are always juggling the whole of our lives, no matter where we are or what we are doing. Even now, as I sit here writing, I am calculating the drive time to the restaurant where we are meeting my in-laws for a birthday celebration, thinking of the housework that needs to be done, refreshing email for my freelance work, trying to convince myself the mental noise will calm when I write another massive to-do list, even though I know it will simply lead me down the rabbit hole of connecting one task to another to another to another.

If it seems men don't have this problem, that may be because it's true. Men might be better at compartmentalizing, because their brains are wired differently. In a 2013 study published by the National Academy of Sciences, scientists found significant differences in brain connectivity patterns between men and women. On average, men had greater connectivity in each individual hemisphere of the brain, while women have much greater connectivity across hemispheres.[5] Our broadly connected wires can be a great blessing or a great curse, depending on the circumstance. When we're tackling the problem of orchestrating the schedules of five family members from memory, it can really give us a leg up. When we need to disconnect from home and focus on the work at hand, the connectivity of our mental and emotional load can drag us down. It can also be a big roadblock in trying to communicate the burden of the mental load and emotional labor to our partners. We're living such different experiences through both our social conditioning and our manner of thinking that it's hard to see eye to eye. That's why we call our girlfriends. It's why women I've never met before get it, and my partner of thirteen years doesn't. It's also why the most common answer I get when talking to women who feel like they've reached a balance is this: you have to let go. The clean house, the perfect motherhood, the laundry, the mental lists, the worry—it all has to go.

Tiffany Dufu, author of *Drop the Ball*, spends her entire book detailing a journey from total control freak (she refers to herself as recovering from "home control disease") to a truly equal partnership with her husband. I immediately recognized her situation before I was halfway through the introduction as she writes about the bubbling resentment she feels upon realizing what an unfair load she has opted to take on in comparison to her husband.

"I was his solution to having it all. What would be mine?" she asked herself.[6]

So she made a change and handed off some responsibility (and mental load) to her partner. I was swept into her story but somewhat horrified when I learned what dropping the ball meant for her. Handing over the reins to her husband seemed to also mean turning a blind eye to a job done incredibly poorly. She tells about how she handed over mail duty to him, and it piled up on the table for three months before being opened. There were parking tickets that went to collections, birthday invitations that went without an RSVP, not to mention the eyesore of a mountain of mail. When he offers to take over meal prep duty after she receives a job opportunity, he makes a single stew for them to eat all month long. It's not the way she would have done it, but it's efficient, and it works. She says she feels capable of letting her preconceived standards slide because she is clear on her priorities. "It's important to disrupt what a standard even is," says Dufu. "I take issue with the narrative that a woman's standard is either the best way or the most efficient way."[7] I have to admit, it's a pill that's hard for me to swallow. She tells me they have come to a bit of a compromise on the stew (he has added a bit of variety and makes a different meal each week nowadays), but they don't have a lot of back-and-forth to perfect the way he does his part. They never have. The work she is doing in lieu of micromanaging is more important than making sure everything is done "her" way.

Clearly going completely hands-off works for her. She shifted her priorities and let the less important balls drop, along with any guilt she felt. She even tells me about a birthday party her daughter had recently missed because she does not handle the calendar (that task is squarely in her husband's court). Since most parents don't forward invitations to dads, this isn't an unusual occurrence. Her daughter was in tears. All her classmates were at the party, and she wasn't, and for a second grader, that's total devastation. Dufu knows she could have prevented this and other calendar heartbreaks. But she won't. She doesn't pick up the balls she has decided to drop, or the guilt that goes with them. Instead she takes her daughter out for a pink-sprinkle doughnut and knows another party will come. She knows her value as a mother doesn't hinge on one missed party or anything else she has decided to forgo for the sake of fulfilling her best and highest purpose. "There are so many things that I don't do, that I have decided are okay for me not to do." I feel envious of her freedom though perhaps not of the method she used to achieve it.

"I would die," I told Rob as I relayed the mail story.

"You would kill me," he corrected.

But she was onto something. I could feel it as I read through her book and listened to her speak. I was struck by the fact that she didn't sound mad that things weren't being done her way; she sounded happy, content. In relinquishing some of the mental load, she had gained something more valuable than the picture-perfect life she had been striving for. She had more mental space and more focus, and she was more available to her family in ways that truly mattered to her. She had taken a long, hard look at her life and re-assessed what she really cared about. She gave the rest of the emotional labor to her husband, and gave up not only control but the idea that the things she handed over must be done *perfectly*. She doesn't get an interesting, well-balanced dinner on the table each night, but she seems to have an interesting and well-balanced life. It doesn't take a rocket scientist to figure out which one is worth more.

I later spoke with Karen Brody, author of *Daring to Rest*, who told a similar tale of going completely hands-off with the running of her home for a couple of years.[8] She dropped all the emotional labor. She didn't send Christmas cards or buy clothes when her sons were outgrowing them or worry over anyone's schedule but her own. Her boys would go for trips to Grandma's house in the winter having packed only shorts. They ate dinner at 9:00 p.m. every night because that's when her husband put dinner on the table. She wrote her book and relieved herself of the major stress of being the "cruise director" for her family, and from her view, it was totally worth it. I could hear the passion in her voice as she told me this. Yet still, I couldn't wrap my mind around letting go of emotional labor and feeling peace with wherever the pieces fell. Dufu's and Brody's tales of shifting their focus and dedication to boldly go after what they needed were inspiring, but they unnerved me. I didn't want bills to go unpaid or have a pile of laundry that has to be pulled from the dryer and is never, ever finished. It didn't seem worth it to me. How is it balance if one person is half-assing his part? We can say we have "different methods" all we want, but isn't there a way to maintain a reasonable standard and divide the work?

Letting go works, certainly, but I couldn't stop thinking that the onus was still on these women to make the compromise, to deal with the discomfort of things left undone. Why can't we expect our partners to care more, so we can then shift some of our attention to those things we care about most? Why can't we ask our partners to rise to the occasion in a way that satisfies our needs, that gives us peace, that keeps *us* comfortable and happy?

Even after listening to the sage advice of Dufu and Brody, I was still stuck with three choices, none of them ideal: do it alone, be a nag, or let it go. The last option was supposed to be my golden ticket, but it felt more like another path to the same type of resentment. In many cases, it seemed downright unrealistic. I had a two-year-old, a four-year-old, and a six-year-old to care for. You can take an each-man-for-himself approach in certain things, but at some point, there are balls you simply can't put down.

Have you ever been accused of being a control freak?" It was one of the first questions Piya Chattopadhyay asked me during an interview for the CBC radio show *The Current* following the publication of my *Harper's Bazaar* article.

"I'm sure I have been." I laughed half-heartedly and shifted uncomfortably in my seat. It was her gotcha question, the one that would expose me for what I really was: not a journalist interested in plumbing the root causes of emotional labor imbalance but a high-maintenance woman unfairly demanding that everything be done my way.

She went on to lay out the old chestnut that, by this time, I was sick of hearing: women simply expect too much. We can't let good enough be good enough. We have control issues. There are plenty of ways to say it, but they all boil down to this: we have no one to blame but ourselves. We become nags because our standards are too high, and it's unfair to ask men to live up to our unreasonable expectations. Emotional labor wouldn't weigh on us so heavily if we'd just ease up. Could it be possible that all my emotional labor boils down to me expecting too damn much of my husband? Had I become my own worst enemy, creating a standard that no one can live up to but me?

In her book, *Overwhelmed*, Brigid Schulte describes a patronizing lunch with sociologist John Robinson where he said that if women feel imprisoned by housework—feel compelled to get cooking, cleaning, caring done in a certain manner—they have only themselves to blame. "Women are their own worst enemies," he relays to her confidently after chiding women who have kitchen floors clean enough to perform open-heart surgery on. "He has not seen my sticky kitchen floor," Schulte says in an aside to the reader. "Nor does he seem to understand that when everything else feels like it's coming apart at the seams, at least having the house tidy somehow helps you breathe."[9]

The people who argue that emotional labor is an issue of wanting or needing control are missing the point. They are playing into a sexist narrative that forever blames women for struggles that originate within the patriarchal structure we are trying to critique. It's a finger-pointing blame game that distracts us from digging for the root of the problem—which isn't an issue with control but a problem with how we value emotional labor. Women aren't fed up because we "expect too much"; we're fed up because we're told we shouldn't expect anything at all. We should just "let it go," as if it were so easy. As if our work were so easily disposable. The only reason the control argument is so sticky is because perfectionism *does* often become internalized. It's easy to blur the line between a desire for control and the pressure for perfection, because they go hand in hand. We *do* feel that cultural pressure to live up to an impossibly high standard, and maintaining control is the only way for us to keep up that chase for perfection. But when you strip away the perfectionism, the imbalance of emotional labor still exists. The control freak argument ignores the true problem: that we do not, as a society, value the work of women. We don't think emotional labor matters.

The truth is, women don't keep their houses at a certain level of cleanliness because sparkling floors are a path to womanly redemption (although cultural pressures still do apply—we'll return to that issue later). We carefully craft a household system that works for us, one that keeps everyone happy and sane, and we make sure it's executed well. For some women the way they run their household is a point of pride, while for others the system is a minimalist tool for survival, but in any case, it is an act of care—not just for ourselves but for all those around us.

Those who make the argument that we should simply lower our standards are not only saying we should care less; they are considering only how the rebalancing of emotional labor would negatively affect the partner who isn't currently carrying the burden—in other words, cause him to do more work. Why should our partners have to live up to our standards? Why should they care? The argument seems sound until you bring the emotional aspect back into it. You should care because the person you love cares. You should be willing as partners to come up with standards that will make everyone happy. Of course there is room for compromise, but if one person finds it acceptable to have mold growing in the bathroom, that shouldn't absolve him of the responsibility to keep the bathroom clean.

The more I think about this question of whether asking my husband to live up to my standard of organization and cleanliness is an issue of control—and my unwillingness to relinquish it—the more I see that the question is not so simple. The issue is not merely how often I want my floors vacuumed; it is whether the work I put into our life is valuable. Emotional labor is not about control; it is about caring. What the question really asks is whether I am willing to completely rearrange the system I have been building since my husband and I first met—the one I designed with great care to keep everyone happy and comfortable— and scrap it, because the prospect of rebalancing the emotional labor in our household is too much to ask of my husband. It puts the onus on me. What am I willing to let go or give up or ease up on to once again keep the peace? What is worth more: his comfort or mine?

Every now and again, I drop the ball on laundry: I do a load and it sits in the dryer for a few days while I am overwhelmed by other tasks. My husband will happily dig out whatever he needs and leave the rest, but it becomes a point of contention if he runs out of workout clothes or my son's favorite pair of pants remains unwashed. It is why my household system usually does not allow for laundry to sit unfinished, at least not for more than a day. It's easier for me and for everyone else if the laundry is folded and put away. It gets everyone ready for the day and out the door with minimal panic over what to wear. From a distance, it may look as if my system of doing laundry daily for one load or every other day for both lights and darks is overkill—born from a desire to be the boss of the household and nothing else. Why does it matter so much? Why don't I just relax? Because I know it inconveniences not just me but others if I let it slide. It matters because it helps me take care of my family with the least amount of friction. There are very few things I do for the joy of control or cleanliness. There is a lot I do to avoid dysfunction and tension.

The idea that women should simply ease up to avoid conflict belies the fact that we do this care-based labor with intention. Certainly, we are capable of compromise, but when it comes right down to it, we are the ones who have carefully considered why we order our lives the way we do. Telling us to ease up is not a favor. It is a misunderstanding of why we undertake emotional labor in the first place.

We don't want to be nags. We just want everything to get done, and it's hard to do it alone. Being seen as a nag is one reason women spend so much mental energy choosing whether to delegate tasks, otherwise known as "asking for help"—which most women don't want to have to ask for in the first place. It's the reason some women take the mental work of delegation off their plate and decide instead to become martyrs to the household work. I've flip-flopped between the two unsavory options in my own life more than once. Becoming the martyr takes the mental work of delegating off my plate but increases my overall workload. Being the nag takes extensive emotion work to get everyone to comply. Some women successfully take alternate paths, like freeing themselves of emotional labor, but that never seemed like a solution that could last for me. I don't want to give up the work of caring. I just want others to care as well.

CHAPTER 4

IT'S OKAY TO WANT MORE

I love my husband, he is the perfect man for me and it was love at first sight, but I would never willingly enter into this state of servitude again," Rufi Thorpe writes in her essay "Mother, Writer, Monster, Maid."[1] I laughed the first time I read this, because I have often joked with my friends that I would rather set myself on fire than be with a man other than Rob. It's not that I don't love my husband, I say. I want to be married. I want to continue on the path I've chosen. And yet, if something catastrophic were to happen, I know with abiding certainty that I would not want marriage again.

I can't help but wonder, why is that? I don't have a particularly hard relationship. In fact, I feel incredibly lucky to have a husband who strives to be a good feminist ally, who has always treated me as an equal, who is kind and funny and smart and does the dishes each night without fail. I feel like my frustrations are disproportionate to my reality. How can I be this frustrated with the people I love when I have it so damn easy?

Rob has told me, time and again, that every time he does the smallest thing wrong, I react with something ranging from frustration to total disgust. I don't even notice it. Or perhaps I do, but it doesn't mean the same thing to me as it does to him. I roll my eyes and huff when he burns the kids' grilled cheese, or forgets an item at the grocery store, or shrinks a sweater in the laundry. It's an overreaction, to be sure, but I can't help but think it's my way of coping with all the emotional labor I deal with alone. I take these moments and spill out the frustrations that have built up throughout the day—because there is so much he doesn't see. He doesn't see me picking up his shoes from all corners of the house and putting them away. He doesn't see me responding to the dozens of emails concerning the upcoming class Christmas party or worrying about the teachers' gifts he doesn't realize are required. He doesn't see me angrily scrubbing the pot of spaghetti he left in the sink to harden. He doesn't see the ways I am constantly maintaining the life that he enjoys, so in those moments when he inadvertently makes my life harder, I snap. It isn't fair to him. I want to stop. But the invisibility of my life makes me constantly on edge.

My less than loving response to minor mishaps leaves me wondering if perhaps I was never cut out for wifehood, for motherhood. When I have such good people as *my* people, I feel as if only a total narcissist could possibly look around a life like mine and say, "But what about me?" My husband does a great deal for me. His help at home, his job, his excellent parenting, his tireless efforts to be the partner I ask him to be—he does all of that for me, and yet I want *more*. It's hard to justify asking such a thing when he's already miles ahead of most men. Why can't I simply be happy with the good man I have?

My grandmother washes the dishes from the family dinner she prepared. I dry and put them away. It's a job the women in the house always undertake after every meal, while the men generally sit and talk on the front porch. This is how it had always been, until I had children. Now my husband is not with the men of the family. He is chasing all three of our children around the garden in front of my grandparents' house. My grandmother sends up a prayer of gratitude on my behalf for finding a man, a husband, a father like Rob. When she brings me back to how good I have it, it's hard to not feel selfish and ungrateful. Even by today's standards, he is an exceptional partner, and my grandmother doesn't even see the tip of the iceberg when it comes to all he does.

"He plays with his kids," she remarks with wonder as we watch them from the kitchen window. *Of course he does*, I think, hardly able to wrap my mind around any other reality—like the one she would have encountered while raising my father and his brother. I love my grandfather dearly, but I certainly wouldn't want to be married to him. I've never seen him wash a dish or cook a family meal, and I highly doubt he ever changed a diaper.

Things have changed since then, much for the better. Even my own childhood was remarkably unlike the generation before. My dad was on board with the newly progressive and involved fathers of the eighties. He drove me to tae kwon do tournaments and Rollerbladed around the neighborhood with me. He once took me and my two best friends on a trip to the Grand Canyon for my birthday, stoically tolerant of our early teen antics and boy talk. He cleaned on the weekends and cooked on occasion. He supported my mother's career, her nights out with friends, her life—much as my husband does for me.

The yoke of parenthood has never rested solely on my shoulders, even during the year I stayed at home with our new baby, unemployed in any other way. I have always had a husband who takes on his fair share of cooking, cleaning, and diaper changes. Was it really necessary, *worth it*, to ask for more? If I think the expectation for emotional labor is low for my husband, I need only look to the past to feel grateful. My version of motherhood looks like a cakewalk when I think about what it would have been like to raise kids fifty or sixty years ago. Yet this is true of so many things in society, and the message that we ought to be grateful for how far we've come is often mixed up with the message that we ought to shut up, stop whining, stop asking for more. We are better off, yes, but that doesn't mean there isn't room for improvement. We can be grateful and still strive for a more equitable relationship. The two do not need to be at odds.

We need to know it's okay to want more from our partners, even when society tells us not to, because that is how progress is made. I cannot say I want better balance for my children when I am not willing to work for that balance in my own life. I cannot say I want equality and continue to put off the hard conversations we need to have about our imbalance. I cannot stand my ground and say emotional labor is valuable, then feel sheepish for "asking too much." Asking Rob to better understand emotional labor isn't a punishment. It's an invitation to better understand what matters to me, what keeps our partnership thriving, and how we can both move forward and do better. It is hard work, yes, but it is worthwhile for both of us. It won't change without our effort.

There is still a lot of careful work I do in explaining the very basics of emotional labor to Rob. It's not because he is some sort of Neanderthal who can't grasp the concept. He is a fiercely intelligent and progressive partner, but the truth of the matter is, he has never had to do this stuff. Emotional labor was not a part of his education. It's not something he saw even progressive men in his circle of peers take on. In fact, he has always been able to look around and see himself as one of the good guys—one of the best. It's not a point I can argue. He is an incredibly involved parent, an attentive partner, and he will complete any task I ask him to do around the house. He strives for an equitable relationship. He supports and respects my work time, encourages self-care, and takes initiative when it's time for the kids to brush their teeth and get ready for bed. His dedication to both me and our family is perhaps the main reason I never brought up the division of emotional labor. I fell victim to the cultural message that I was greedy to want more from a man who was already so good. And I was afraid of being ungrateful.

But wanting more balance, wanting progress, doesn't make me ungrateful, though I can't deny that it sometimes feels that way. Or perhaps more accurately, it makes me feel guilty. Whenever I write about my husband and do anything but sing his praises, even in service to moving us forward and making us both happier, the guilt is there. How dare I ever feel anything but overwhelming love and gratitude for his contributions? I am quick to always add the necessary caveat that my husband is among the best of the best. I make sure his efforts do not go unnoticed. I list them often and praise them in a way that I know is excessive. And yet, I still worry I'm not giving him enough credit. At least not as much as the man in the ice cream shop fawning over his "dad day" would expect of me.

Yet when I think about the imbalance of emotional labor in our relationship, there is no way to ignore that the bulk of this work falls directly on me. He may do more than most men, sure—but that doesn't mean he does his full part. And therein lies the lion's share of our problem. When I compare my husband to most of the men I know, he comes out looking like a Greek god. He is handsome and funny and smart and kind and reads interesting books and engages in meaningful conversations with me and wants to binge-watch the same series as me. I have never met a more engaged father, with such patience for card games and toddler nail painting and coloring books. I can't pretend I hold a candle to his cooking skills, especially when it comes to the perfect rare steak or a home-made platter of fish-and-chips. When he does clean the bathrooms, he does a phenomenal job (good enough, one might suggest, to not hire a housecleaning service). He is attentive to my needs and deals with me at my absolute worst and maintains the most even temper I can possibly imagine, even when I am completely unhinged. Even if the thought of remarrying didn't make me want to light myself on fire, thinking I could find someone who would live up to the standard Rob has set is laughable. No man could ever come close.

But I cannot ignore that if a woman were the subject of that list of praise, it would hardly sound unique. If I cross out "Rob" and write "Gemma" in its place at the top of the list, it becomes utterly unimpressive. Am I attractive and smart and kind and well-read? Yes, I think so. Do I engage in meaningful conversations and binge-watch the best shows with my husband and kill it on the domestic front? Yes. And so do most women I know. I paint toddler nails on the regular. I do board games and card games and fort-building games and lie on the floor when I'm sick and let my kid roll Hot Wheels all over me. I read a whole introductory book on sketching to share a common interest with my son. I can bake four-tier wedding cakes as a self-taught baker. I've made croissants from scratch with homemade tomato bisque to go with them. I not only clean the bathrooms but make the schedule that dictates when the chores get done. And I don't just maintain an even keel when doing emotional labor with my husband during arguments or while navigating the sticky minefield of his emotional state during unemployment; I serve up warmth and counsel to friends and family and invest time in strangers on the internet who find my writing and want to share their stories with me. None of this makes me particularly unique or special. Moreover, it doesn't make me feel like I can hang my hat up at the end of the day and pat myself on the back for a job well done. In fact, I'm far more likely to notice that the bottom of the croissants were a little too browned, and I've snapped at my son after he's asked me to play a card game when I've already played three games in a row and need to move on to my work. I could have responded more generously. I could have done a little better.

"We're not thin enough, we're not smart enough, we're not pretty enough or fit enough or educated or successful enough, or rich enough—ever," Lynne Twist writes in *The Soul of Money*. "Before we even sit up in bed, before our feet touch the floor, we're already inadequate, already behind, already losing, already lacking something. And by the time we go to bed at night, our minds race with a litany of what we didn't get, or didn't get done, that day."[2]

As a woman, making an effort isn't good enough, because we are constantly bombarded with the message that we need to be perfect. At every turn, advertising and media remind us that if only we try a *little* harder, if we just stretch a *little* farther, perfection is within our reach. Our home could be better organized, and here is an article on how to achieve it once and for all. That didn't work? Here's another. There are resources galore on how to be a better parent. Apps to arrange a better carpool schedule. Recipes that are supposed to sneak vegetables into our picky eater's diet. Books on how to be a Zen, or hands-free, or disciplinarian parent. Attachment method. Cry-it-out. The waters start to get murky here, because we have to decide which option is the best and then strive toward the ideal. But at any point in time we tend to know what the "better" version of us ought to be doing, and we push ourselves to the extreme to get to that next plane of perfection. The next version of me is sugar-free and eats more vegetables, plans monthly family dinners with my husband's family, does yoga every day, and volunteers regularly. The better me earns a little more money and has an organized spreadsheet of the household chores so I don't fall behind. It is a chase that has no final destination. We could always do better, and we're caught in the false narrative that we always should.

My knee-jerk reaction to a job well done is almost always that it wasn't quite good enough. My husband's reaction to a job well done is satisfaction. He doesn't live with the constant inner dialogue that he needs to do better when it comes to emotional labor. It's not his job to keep everyone comfortable and happy. The tasks I take on with care do not hold the same value for him. He does not see the organization of a life as anything more than a perfunctory task. I see it as a measure of my love and, furthermore, my self-worth.

Being hyperaware of all the ways I perform emotional labor also makes me painfully aware of the fact that the labor I take on is not the same as what Rob takes on. I realized this most poignantly when we decided to take a new approach to balancing out the domestic labor in our relationship: making a master spreadsheet of everything that needed to be done to keep our family's life running smoothly. It was more than just a chore list. I wanted to see who was thinking about the toilet paper running out, the kids' clothes getting rotated, the school permission slips getting signed. I expected to find him carrying mental tasks that were perhaps invisible to me. I knew there was the car maintenance, yard maintenance, and other handiwork that he took on so I never had to think about it, but as we continued down the list of "things Gemma thinks about" and "things Rob thinks about," the gap between us grew even wider than I expected. The things that fell in his domain were not connected to the daily running of our lives. His mental load involved biannual chores, weekly yardwork, the once-in-a-while projects I nagged him to do (so, I guess, put those back on my list). The one daily thing I had forgotten was in his court was cleaning out the cat's litter box, because it is in the garage, and let's be honest, this one doesn't *actually* get done daily. Everything else was mine. Everything related to the kids, the housecleaning, the appointment making, the trip planning, the holiday hosting, the calendar keeping—the list was seemingly infinite. If it fell within the walls of our house and didn't involve AC or heater maintenance, it was my job to worry about it.

I appreciated the things that were on his side of the list. I certainly didn't want to take on an extensive knowledge of cars or take out the leaf blower in the cold (though I was still the one to remind him of this task from time to time). These tasks contribute to the efficient running of our life, but they hardly take the same daily toll as figuring out what to eat and whether we have the right ingredients and what else I need to pick up at the store while I'm there and when I will be able to make the trip out and which kids I have to take with me.

It's also worth noting that while my husband is particularly handy and good with cars and landscaping, the tasks that fall in the traditionally masculine side of domestic duty are also the most commonly outsourced. A 2015 survey by *Working Mother* found that the gender divide in domestic work for couples in dual-income households was still stuck in a bygone era. Moms were in the majority for scheduling medical appointments for kids, taking time off work for those appointments, cooking, cleaning, laundry, shopping, filling out permission slips, grocery shopping, and tidying, while dads were mostly tasked with taking out the trash, lawn care and landscaping, filing taxes, car washing, and car maintenance. The top five most outsourced chores on the list? Everything in the men's column except taking out the trash.[3]

While there is plenty of opportunity for outsourcing cooking, cleaning, and laundry, it is not an option for many women. But perhaps even more telling is that many women who do have the means for outsourcing choose not to because they feel a greater sense of obligation to "do it all." The home, the kids, the career—you're not supposed to *want* to give any of it up. We feel shame and guilt when we don't live up to the expectations for our emotional labor. It hits us right in our self-worth. The "home control disease" Dufu talks about in her book is real, and deeply internalized. We think that not doing it all means not doing enough. Part of the reason it took twelve years for me to even attempt to seek greater balance in our relationship is because striking a happy compromise seemed overwhelmingly difficult. But another part of the reason is that it didn't occur to me to seek change in the first place. I had it deep in my mind that performing all of the emotional labor in our relationship was what I was supposed to do. It was interwoven with my sense of self-worth. I wanted to fill those roles of good girlfriend, then good wife, then good mother, especially since Rob so effortlessly fulfilled the role of good husband and good dad. He excelled in his position far more than I could ever hope to, because the role of "good husband" and "good dad" requires so much less of men.

So on those occasions when I became fed up with shouldering the bulk of the emotional and mental work in our relationship, I felt like the bad guy for wanting more from my husband. The voice in my head told me I was ungrateful for how good I had it. I was asking too much of him. I was, according to many men's rights advocates online, everything that is wrong with the female gender. But am I really such a horrible angry feminist, a misandrist even, for wanting more help than I already have? Not when I see how much room there is for improvement.

The morning of our nephew's baptism, I knew that despite some light hints, my husband had neglected to get a card or present for the occasion. I was trying to strike the right balance between teaching Rob how to perform emotional labor and giving him the space to figure things out on his own. I decided to do some subtle emotional labor to get him on the right track.

"Is this something we should probably get a gift for?" I asked.

"I don't know."

"Ask your mother," I implored, knowing the answer already.

She of course told him, yes, a gift was necessary, and gave him suggestions for what to buy. A keepsake, a lovey blanket, a picture frame, something commemorative. I gave him examples of what our son had been gifted for his baptism. I told him that a Christian book would likely be a good option, and he looked up a nearby Christian bookstore for hours and location. He offered to go pick out the present and card while I stayed home and got the kids ready. It was a good split. It showed how far he had come from the expectation that a present and card would appear for his brother's child as if by magic.

Yet when he returned home, I quickly flipped through the pages to find he had purchased a book aimed at teaching a child about their upcoming role as a big brother, rather than a baptism-appropriate religious book. I was frustrated and asked him why he hadn't looked in the book before buying it. This was Gift Buying 101. The moment was tense, as he could sense my frustration with him. Beneath my words was another message: *How could you not check to make sure this was a fitting gift? Why don't you care?*

Of course he became defensive. He pointed out how critical I was. How hard my standards are to live up to. We began veering into that dangerous territory where neither of us could hear what the other was saying. I was tempted to throw up my hands and take over the gift buying, but I didn't. After sending him back out to the store to return the book and figure out a better option, I reminded myself that this was his first time buying this sort of gift. While he occasionally picks out the gifts for his brothers and father, gift giving with care is not something he has ever felt compelled to do. Gifts for nieces, nephews, even his mother, often fall on my side of the list. It wasn't simply that he didn't care about his nephew's present. He didn't know how to care about these things. And he should.

Working through the conflicts that stem from an unequal balance of emotional labor in my relationship is difficult. It takes caring deeply, not just about lightening my own load but also about progress toward a better relationship. It's not a topic that will help me gain any ground when I'm angry or at the end of my rope. I didn't help my husband understand anything by sending him back to the store while undercutting his efforts to buy his nephew's gift in the first place. It wasn't until later, when I slowed down enough to explain how buying a gift was an act of caring—one that I have always taken seriously and had now entrusted to him—that we were able to start moving forward. I didn't just want him to get the right kind of gift. I wanted him to understand why the gift was important, why it mattered to get it right. I want him to get better at these things. I want him to care. Not only for my sake, but for his as well.

Emotional labor is essential. It strengthens bonds and creates care-centered structures of order within our lives. As Hillary Clinton writes in *What Happened*, emotional labor is what keeps "families and workplaces humming along."[4] The world would not work with the same level of efficiency, civility, and care if we abandoned it. It wouldn't be a world I'd want to live in. If emotional labor was without value, I would simply let it go. I do not believe it is. Which is why I want my husband to learn how to better hone his skills.

The fact that men aren't expected to perform emotional labor may make their lives easier, but it doesn't necessarily make their lives better. Ignoring emotional labor makes men passive consumers of their own lives. It stops them from being deeply involved partners, fathers, sons, friends. When I spoke with Rufi Thorpe, many things had changed since the writing of "Mother, Writer, Monster, Maid" (for example, her husband no longer leaves his towels on the floor), but there was still the familiar imbalance. "He shows up to a life I've organized," she says.[5] There is so much he doesn't see. So much he doesn't recognize. She wonders if he realizes, if it bothers him, that their children belong to her so much more than they do to him. The way he experiences their life is so different from the way she does.

I don't want my husband to feel as if our children are any less his than mine. Or that our home is less his than mine. I want him to partake in both the keeping and enjoyment of our life, because I truly believe something is missed in simply showing up instead of actively participating. There is a lack of independence in shying away from emotional labor—a lack of say in your own life. Studies have even shown that shirking emotional labor can hurt men later in life. If the spouse who does the bulk of the emotional labor dies, the other is left not knowing how to fully live. They don't have the same bonds with friends. They don't know how to maintain family ties. They often don't even know how to prepare their favorite meals or how to do laundry. They don't know how to take care of themselves, because someone else has always cared for them. Caring more deeply throughout our lives, coming more fully into the human experience, isn't a burden. It's an opportunity.

I don't want to let go of emotional labor. I want to have a partner who shares it and understands it and lives with me in this equal space where he too can appreciate the benefits of caring deeply. I want us each to care for the comfort and happiness of our children and ourselves and one another. Unravelling the cultural expectations that are tightly bound around our identities is not going to be easy work, but I know that it will ultimately create a better life for us. We are working toward understanding the strength inherent in emotional labor, in order to balance it in a way that will allow us both to thrive. That's the endgame. But first we must understand the drawbacks of this type of work if we want to harness its value.

CHAPTER 5

WHAT WE DO AND WHY WE DO IT

In her widely shared acceptance speech at the 2015 *Glamour* Women of the Year Awards, Reese Witherspoon talks about the line she most dreads when reading a script. She explains that there's a moment in many movies where the female character will turn to the male character and utter five cringeworthy words: "What do we do now?"

She repeats the line in a dramatically high-pitched voice, shaking her head and blinking in wide-eyed confusion. "Do you know any woman in any crisis who has absolutely no idea what to do?" she asks the laughing crowd. "It's ridiculous that a woman wouldn't know what to do."

"What do we do now?" isn't a question we ask men. It's a question, most often, that we must ask ourselves. When we're faced with something important, we go into our internal problem-solving mode. We do what emotional labor has taught us to do. We carefully line up all the details, taking in the big picture and all the wide-spreading branches of an issue, and we ask ourselves how to best move forward. We don't simply aim to figure out a solution;

we aim to figure out the best solution. We don't leave stones un-turned. We don't wait for a mistake to be unveiled later and deal with it then. We approach problem solving in a comprehensive and careful way. It's a skill that is all too often undervalued, and it's high time we start recognizing emotional labor outside its role as a burden in our lives. It's a strength as well. It allows us to feel more deeply connected to our lives. It allows us to connect and love with our whole selves. It keeps the world humming along with civility, efficiency, and attention to detail. So our real job, now, is to figure out the drawbacks of this work so we can use emotional labor for its best and highest use—together.

I have been asked many times the inevitable question "What do we do now?" or "How do we move forward?" or "How do we find a balance that works?" in response to unveiling the many frus-trations that come with constantly performing emotional labor. If we are going to move forward to a place where emotional labor no longer drags us down, we need to acknowledge that emotional la-bor is both hard and valuable—and one does not negate the other. Emotional labor is a time-consuming, mentally challenging, prac-ticed skill that manifests as caring, problem solving, and emotion regulation—often all at the same time. We do it at home, at work, and out in the world. Now that we are looking deeply into emo-tional labor, poring over the details and relating them to our own lives, I feel confident we will do what we do best. Those of us skilled in emotional labor will take in this whole sprawling issue and get to work devising a custom solution. We will take great care in finding an answer to the question "What do we do now?"—one that will benefit not just ourselves but those around us as well.

To do this, we must first find the root of our problem with emo-tional labor as it relates to our own lives. Emotional labor has be-come more than a compartmentalized piece of our experience, as Hochschild first described it in relation to work. Instead, it has be-come our way of being. It is woven into the fabric of our lives in ways both good and bad. If it wasn't exhausting, we wouldn't be talking about it. But if it wasn't valuable, we wouldn't be doing it. It's time to harness the power of emotional labor by seizing the parts that make it valuable and fixing the parts that make it so damn exhausting.

While everyone has their own frustrations with emotional labor, as I've talked to hundreds of women, I've noticed three commonalities. They never feel like they have the mental space to solve their own problems because they are so caught up in the minutiae. They never get a break from their role of catering to the needs of those around them. They are never seen, acknowledged, or praised for the emotional labor they perform. The work they are describing is mental, continuous, and invisible. These are the three factors that make this valuable work burdensome.

Mental Work

Creating a life that optimizes the comfort and happiness of those around you is not an easy task, though women may make it look that way. It's not a simple matter of the physical labor needed to keep a household running. It is a lot of mental work, especially when it comes to making choices for others. We are given a wealth of options when it comes to building our lives, and while that may seem like a positive—the option to customize to the point of perfection—it can become overwhelming in a hurry.

Barry Schwartz describes this overwhelm in his book *The Paradox of Choice*. When we are given so many options, the process of choosing is not liberating, it's paralyzing. This is especially true when we are making choices not only for ourselves but also for those around us. "More choice may not always mean more control," Schwartz writes. "There comes a point at which opportunities become so numerous that we feel overwhelmed. Instead of feeling in control, we feel unable to cope . . . [and] figuring out which choice to make becomes a grave burden."[1] Schwartz approaches his book from the viewpoint of a singular consumer, but for women, our job isn't simply to choose the best-fitting pair of pants or the salad dressing we like the most. We are often choosing for the whole family, weighing competing preferences against one another and trying to find the option that will lead to household harmony. We have to find the right doctor and make the appointments for everyone. (Schwartz notes in his research that the burden of choice related to healthcare falls overwhelmingly to women, who are typically the guardians of not only their own health but that of their partners and children.) We help guide decisions on what sports everyone should partake in and arrange the schedules accordingly. We decide when the best time to do homework is. We decide which chores to take on ourselves and which ones to delegate. We make choices constantly, and those choices often don't take into account our own well-being, because we are so outwardly focused.

This is why it's frustrating when someone deviates from the choices we have made regarding the running of a household. When I ask my husband to bring home a certain type of cheese and he comes home with a different type, it is up to me to do the mental work of deciding whether to change our dinner plans or go back out to the store myself, and that choice often comes down to which option will cause the least strife. Were the kids' hearts set on lasagna? Yes. Will it taste the same with sharp cheddar? No. Would asking Rob to return to the store seem too critical? Maybe. Is it easier to transition him into taking over the dinner prep I'm doing or to delegate the store duty back to him?

This constant dialogue of *What should I do to keep everyone happy?* drains a lot of mental energy that could otherwise be used in more productive or creative ways. For years I wondered what had happened to me after college, when I had my first child. Why was it that I could no longer muster up the ability to write fiction, even when I had the free time? Why was I choosing to plop down in front of the TV at the end of the day, wasting my evenings watching reruns of *The Office* instead of feeding my soul with creative work? I wasn't even *doing* that much. When friends asked me what I was up to, I never had an answer. I was at home, deciding what to do with my baby—what the best choice of clothing and food and activities was for us. Worrying over whether he was gaining enough weight, or whether he had died from SIDS every time he was down for a nap. Do I take him to the store or go out later, after my husband gets home? Will the baby be unhappy if I take him out? (Will he poop up the back of his onesie? Almost definitely.) Will my husband feel neglected if I steal off to the store during our precious alone time? Should I breastfeed now or should I try to pump? Should I put the baby in a cute outfit or keep him comfy in pajamas? Even when my days appeared uneventful, I was in my head all the time but rarely thinking about myself in that bigger, deeper way that used to make my life feel meaningful. What consumed most of my mental effort had minimal emotional rewards. It simply left me feeling drained. I finally understood why so many women said they lost themselves after becoming mothers. I no longer had the mental and emotional capacity to tend to my interior life, my creative life, my meaning-driven life. At the end of the day, I had nothing left in my mind to give.

Eventually, I did find a rhythm within motherhood, but it wasn't strictly intuitive. I had to work hard to carve out mental space for my work as a writer, and it's something I still struggle with today. My mind is full all the time. I am still constantly making choices for everyone around me. Worse yet, as my children grow older I am *creating* choices for them to maintain their sense of autonomy and freedom. If I don't want to fight with my daughter about the outfit I pick out for her, I must instead choose two equally appealing options and allow her to decide which makes her happy. (If I let her pick her own clothes, she'll put on a tutu when it's snowing outside.) I can't simply plop breakfast down in front of everyone without protest so I have to present (and be prepared to execute) multiple options: should we have French toast or oatmeal or scrambled eggs with bacon? My husband likes to goad me for being indecisive when I don't want to pick where we go to eat on date night, but the truth is, I don't care. I simply want to be relieved of choice for the moment. When he won't let up, it usually comes down to this: "Where can we go that doesn't have a long menu?" or "Where do I already know what I'm ordering?"

Of course the paradox of choice is not an entirely female phenomenon. In the age of endless options, we are all bombarded with choices every day. On average, we make about thirty-five thousand conscious choices per day, two hundred of which involve food.[2] Choices drag down our mental energy. It's the reason that President Obama chose to wear the same suit every day or why Mark Zuckerberg sticks to jeans and a plain T-shirt. Automating certain areas of our lives leads to greater mental capacity. "To derive the benefits and avoid the burden of choice, we must learn to be selective in exercising our choices," Schwartz writes. "We must decide, individually, when choice really matters and focus our energies there."[3] For women, that's a tall order. We run on the assumption that *all* of our choices are important, not realizing that we can be selective and perhaps let go of some of the details that matter less. That type of prioritizing is exactly what we need if we are going to reclaim enough mental space to make emotional labor work for us, instead of it working us into the ground.

Continuous Work

The choices we make in regard to emotional labor do not stop the moment we walk out the door. Emotional labor follows us into the world, into the workplace, and back home again. Instead of the emotional labor Hochschild described, which could be confined within the parameters of the work shift, the emotional labor we are discussing now lives beyond clear-cut boundaries. When I am out at dinner with my girlfriends, I often glance down at my phone, waiting for a text asking what the kids are supposed to be eating for dinner, or where a certain stuffed animal is, or how to reheat this casserole. Even if that text never comes (it rarely ever does), I am constantly ready to fill the role of household manager, even when I'm not at home. I am the one whose phone number is always listed first on contact forms. I am always on call. I don't get to be fully in work mode or fully in vacation mode, because there is never a time when I can let go of the emotional labor I carry with me. It is hard sometimes to determine where personality ends and emotional labor begins. Am I naturally organized, or am I organized out of necessity, or both? Am I a control freak who revels in ruling the home or simply someone who knows the full weight of being in charge? There is plenty of emotional labor we do because we *want* to. For example, I love planning vacations. Full stop. I love every last detail of it, every decision, every bit of research, even the budgeting and saving that goes into it. I enjoy the mental tasks pinging around in my mind: to check prices on flights, to research beaches, to book reservations. It never feels dull or burdensome to me. But if I didn't love planning vacations—if it became a total drag on my mental space and emotional well-being—I would probably still be the one who did it by default. It has become, like so many other things I do, an expectation that feels unavoidable.

I want to care for others. I want to have a home that runs well. I want people to feel comfortable around me. I know there is value in this work, and so do most women I know. Yet when we burn out and feel resentful, we still find ourselves caring for others, running the show, maintaining the comfort of those around us, because we are expected to fill this role whether we want to or not. We know there is no opportunity for a break or shift in balance when emotional labor becomes too much to shoulder alone. We can have the breakdown, tell our partners we need them to take on more, but it always seems to shift back to the default position where the mental work is still entirely our territory. We're still on call. It's still up to us to ask, to delegate, and to do so in a way that will cause the least amount of friction. It is continuous work, which is the second part of what makes emotional labor so exhausting.

Then there seems to be a never-ending stream of ways we have to use our skills to maintain the happiness and comfort of those around us, no matter what the context. In Joanne Lipman's book *That's What She Said*, she opens the conversation about workplace equality by addressing the notion that women *should* adjust to the male standard—as if they don't do so on a constant basis. The lengths that women go to adapt to the male standard are absurd and still leave them coming up short. "Women already change themselves plenty," Lipman writes. "All of us . . . are attempting to fit into a professional world that was created in the image of men. The way we speak, dress, write emails, present ourselves—we're conscious of how we come across in a culture that's not quite our own."[4] The way we perform emotional labor at work and the way we perform it at home are different to be sure, but it all stems from the same cultural assumptions about how women *should* move through a man's world. We should keep everyone comfortable. We should keep everyone happy. We should be ready to cater to others, always.

The rules we adhere to are not ones we consciously think about. Most of us don't spend our days pausing to think about how patriarchy dictates the way we should behave, react, and live in the world. These things are so deeply ingrained that we hardly notice them at all, nor do our partners. We don't often think about, in the broad sense, how much is on our plate. We come up with excuses as to why everything falls to us, excuses about the way the world works, excuses about our partners, excuses about our own behavior. We accept emotional labor, and the constancy of it, as an immutable part of life. *The Managed Heart* talked about the effects of trying to "clock out" of emotional labor at the end of the workday, but what happens when we can't "clock out" at all? What do we do when it follows us constantly—when we don't get a cigarette break to let it all fall apart for a minute?

We won't get fired if we slip up or don't do our "job," but we will feel guilt that we are not living up to the expectations imposed upon us by society and by ourselves. We know that the home is our domain because everything in our culture tells us that this is where women are in control. (Some have argued that women refuse to give up control in the home because it is still the only place where they feel they have true power, and I can't pretend that doesn't hit home a bit.) I feel annoyed by the dishes piling up in the sink after handing that job over to my husband, not because they won't get done but because they won't get done immediately. They won't get done to my standard. And it can feel like every last detail of how my home runs, whether it is under my control or not, is a reflection on my skills as a woman. Even when we hand over a task, we rarely ever let it go. The emotional labor doesn't end when you pass the buck; it remains until the task is done.

Invisible Work

Of all the frustrations that come from taking on emotional labor, there is one that stands apart. The work being done is invisible. It largely takes place in our minds, it's constant, and no one else seems to understand that we are doing it. It seems unfathomable to me at times that the emotional labor which defines so much of my life remains unseen by so many, especially those who benefit from it day in and day out.

Julie Kimock, a thirty-three-year-old mother of two, says that the invisibility of emotional labor creates a deep loneliness on top of the emotional weight she carries as a military wife. "We sit at home expected to just 'be' without question, recognition, or support. We move and we adapt and we chug along through life knowing that our country comes before our families and we accept the challenge and make the sacrifice and continue to walk alone seemingly unnoticed. We parent alone, we celebrate birthdays and Christmas alone. We hire the property managers, and take the cars to get serviced. We cry alone at nights, lonely and missing our husbands, our partners. We befriend news anchors on the television because some days that will be the only adult voice we hear," she writes in an article for Blunt Moms.[5] She tells me she has to move and restart her family's life every couple of years, finding new doctors and new schools, new playgrounds and new schedules, new grocery stores and new mom friends. It is on her shoulders to create a home that feels welcoming and cater to the emotional needs of her family during transition. She not only takes on this hyperbolic emotional labor but is expected to do so without complaint, or even venting. "There's a culture of grin and bear it here," she tells me.[6] She says the word *dependent* gets thrown around a lot when talking about the wives of military personnel, a term she finds ironic considering how dependent their husbands are on them to hold down their lives when they are away. "We get a lot of comments . . . that we are only in it for Tricare benefits and a minivan, or if you gain weight you are deemed the dreaded 'dependapotomus.'" She says her husband helps as much as he can and offers support, and she knows many military wives are not as lucky in this regard. Still, she gets the feeling that he has long thought this frustrating invisible load she complained of was simply her being crazy. So much of the frustration is tangled up in the fact that her family and culture don't understand and, quite frankly, don't want to hear it.

So many of the women I've spoken with simply want to feel seen. They want a thank-you. They want acknowledgment. They want recognition that the work they are doing is valuable, which is why emotional labor often weighs most heavily on at-home parents. It is hard to have a partner come home at the end of a day that no one has witnessed, only to have all of your work remain unseen by the person you are counting on for solidarity and empathy.

Erin Khar, a forty-four-year-old mother of two who works from home, describes her long list of mental and emotional work as the "behind the scenes." The production doesn't happen without all the work that takes place behind the curtain. Parenting, running the home, keeping everyone comfortable and happy involve a lot of effort. Sure, everyone appreciates it, or at least appreciates the end result, but they don't really see or understand exactly what is being done. Khar says it's an unspoken rule between her and her husband that she is the one who caters to their kids' emotional needs—from the neediness of infancy to the throes of puberty. They both run on the assumption that she is simply "better at this stuff." He understands that she does this work only because she debriefs him afterward, giving him the easily digestible version of the emotional minefields she is navigating. "I find that I am often emotionally exhausted in ways that he doesn't understand because he is not responsible for this type of nurturing," Khar says.[7] It always falls to her, and if she is not available, she notices that her son will seek out her mother or stepmother before Dad or Grandpa. Her son knows it is the women who provide the necessary emotion work in the family, even if he doesn't consciously understand the work going into these interactions.

Of course this emotion work is also in addition to all the other emotional labor that goes into running their family's life. Khar stocks the house with groceries, toiletries, cleaning supplies. She pays the bills. She manages the appointments: medical, dental, haircuts, and more. She handles all the extracurricular supplying, form signing, and scheduling. She buys clothes for the kids, because she is the one who notices when they are outgrowing them. She handles all school-related stuff, because she is the one who checks the backpacks. She does the meal planning, the summer camp sign-ups, and a large portion of the physical domestic labor as well. She describes, as many women do, her husband helping in the home rather than taking charge. He feeds the animals, walks the dog, cleans the cat box, does postdinner dishes and cleanup, and tidies the house. He lets her sleep in on the weekends and gets up with their nine-month-old. The division of physical labor she describes is not all that unfair. But the physical labor is the tip of an iceberg; the unseen work beneath the surface reaches depths her husband and sons cannot fathom.

When it comes to kids, that's simply the cost of parenting. They won't and can't understand all the emotional labor that is going into raising them unless they someday have kids of their own—and even then, it's mostly daughters who have this aha moment. I know I felt it acutely after giving birth to my first child: the overwhelming gratitude for all my mother had done for me, all the things I never saw or understood until I was doing the same emotional labor myself. It was so difficult to spend all day every day catering to the physical and emotional needs of someone who couldn't so much as smile, let alone show any cognizance of all I was doing for them. Which is what made it so much harder, at the end of each day, when my husband walked in and didn't recognize any of my work either. It was so invisible, in fact, that he would take off his shoes and leave them in the living room. He would dump his stuff on the dining room table, hang his jacket over the back of a chair instead of in the closet, get a snack out of the fridge and leave the container on the counter I had just cleaned. The moment my hands were free I would put these things away, knowing that it wouldn't otherwise get done. The tidying after him was almost never mentioned and rarely thanked, not because my husband was rude or expected that I would do these things for him, but because he simply didn't see it. He would feel ashamed when he did catch me hanging up his jacket, apologize, and maybe put it away the next day when he came home, but his behavior always reverted. He'd set something down, and it would magically disappear to the place it was supposed to be, the physical task and the noticing of the task never acknowledged or seen. He seemed immune to noticing the mess and immune to noticing the clean. I always had to ask for things to be done. I could get more help, but it felt like I would never have a full partner who would also notice when things needed to be done instead of being told what to do. My emotional labor would always be shadow work unless I could figure out how to make my husband understand what this invisibility felt like. It's an uphill battle, let me tell you, but it's a worthwhile battle too.

It's worthwhile because I can see that the changes aren't just on the surface. It's not simply that he is noticing more of what needs to be done and doing it. His emotional labor frees up more and more precious mental space for me to do my work and enjoy my life. It's connecting him more deeply to aspects of his life he never realized were lacking. He feels more confident in his role as a father and a partner. He no longer feels like his worth hinges solely on his paycheck. He is truly redefining what masculinity means to him, and it is a powerful change to witness.

In redefining our roles, I can see these obvious and immediate benefits: a full life, a better partnership, a sense of true equality. Yet I see even more benefits on the horizon. As I sat with Cheryl Strayed recording the *Dear Sugars* podcast on emotional labor, she told a story of watching her son sweeping with a toy broom. It is always a fun spectacle to watch our children playing grown-up, mimicking our behaviors with their imaginative play, but this instance in particular stuck out in her mind because when she asked him what he was doing, he answered, "I'm pretending to be a daddy." Strayed said it stopped her in her tracks. It was child's play that spoke to a revolutionary change in our cultural landscape—the kind of revolution that starts within the home. "This is how masculinity is redefined, it's also how femininity is redefined. That's how change is made."[8]

There are so many reasons I want to change the balance of emotional labor in our lives, but the one that stands out is the fact that changing this dynamic will change our children's lives. It will change the future. The revolutionary change I want to see in the world starts here, with us, with our children watching and learning what it means to be true equals. They will not learn their roles in the world from a textbook. They will learn them, first and foremost, at home. What we choose to do now will shape their worldview. What we choose to do now changes everything. I want my sons to be willing and able to carry their own weight in emotional labor. I want my daughter to know that it is not her job to keep everyone around her comfortable and happy. I want us to break the cycle, so all of our children can live better, fuller lives—not just at home but in our shifting world as well.

PART II

EMOTIONAL LABOR AT LARGE

CHAPTER 6

WHOSE WORK IS IT ANYWAY?

On December 12, 2010, I closed up shop at Cache, the retail store where I was an assistant manager, and called my husband to pick me up. My coworker and I straightened the store and took the daily deposit to the drop box in the back of the mall. I tried to take it all in as we walked out together for the last time: the satisfaction of the heavy dead bolt sliding into place as I turned the key, the heady floral smell of the Body Shop, where we often stopped for small talk and lotion samples, the stoned security guards, the blast of cold air we welcomed into our lungs when we stepped out the heavy back door. This was it. I didn't have maternity leave; I had simply worked up until the last possible minute. I had spent the previous three hours of my closing shift in early labor. Rob arrived right at the end of the night to take me to the hospital. I would give birth to my son the next day.

I had spent most of the previous year anxiously awaiting this day: not only the birth of my child but the day I would finally quit retail. I was tired of working with customers who treated me as if I were less than human. Just that night I had a regular client chastise me for sitting on a stool during a contraction, sneering that I wasn't *really* in labor. She remembered what labor had been like for her, and I apparently was not living up to her expectation of what early labor looked like. I was simply being unprofessional, lazy. My pain was an inconvenience for her; it ruined the illusion she had grown accustomed to. She wanted my "normal" lilting customer-service voice and swift help picking out clothing. She expected me to croon about how good she looked as I waited outside the fitting room, stepping into the role of false friendship since she always shopped alone. I had been doing this type of on-the-job emotional labor for years, and I was more than ready to let it go.

Yet the emotional labor of dealing with customers wasn't all I was leaving behind. I had graduated from the University of Nevada, Reno, a mere week earlier, an accomplishment I had long worked toward. In the course of a week, I was going from a life imbued with cultural value as a full-time student and hardworking employee to a life as a stay-at-home mother—a role whose work I would soon realize was entirely invisible and incredibly undervalued. While I may have been treated like crap by customers during my retail years, the culture at large had a lot of respect for me as a student taking on full-time work to make my way through college. In this part of my life, I was often commended for "doing so much." As a mother, I would soon be asked what I did all day.

The isolation I felt in those first few months home alone with the baby was brutal, especially after transitioning from such a full social life. My new life was full as well, more so than before having a baby, but there was no one there to witness or acknowledge the work I performed. The invisibility of the job was maddening, as was the physical, mental, and emotional toll it took on me. I felt at my wits' end merely surviving. I didn't understand why it took so much effort to do so little. When asked what I did all day, I had nothing to show but a still-breathing baby. It took the entirety of my capabilities to make it to bedtime each night, at which point I had nothing left. I had no idea what emotional labor entailed at the time. I simply thought I was going mad.

As time went on, I got better at motherhood. I learned to expertly care for my son, internalized all of his quirks and tastes, educated myself on various parenting styles and chose the one that felt right, upped the ante in how I maintained my home, and more. I read up on pre-K standards and incorporated lessons into our daily routine. I began making elaborate home-cooked meals. I took our meager budget and slashed it further to pay down our debt. I wholeheartedly leaned into motherhood and the keeping of our home. I felt compelled to give it my all because without a paycheck, even from a menial job like Cache, I felt my self-worth plummet. Of course, being a stay-at-home mother was my full-time job, and I certainly felt the toll it was taking on me physically, mentally, and spiritually. Yet no matter how much emotional labor I put forth, it was never revered in the same manner as my husband's job. Despite working harder than I ever had in my life, my cultural standing had never been lower.

My staying at home was a "luxury," according to family members and other moms I knew, even when born of economic necessity and performed to the best of my abilities. My husband's retail job was the "real" work. It was a job with immediately visible social value, a paycheck, and recognition. Creating a life where my family could thrive was important work. Attuning myself to their emotional needs was vital to their well-being. This work was undoubtedly necessary, but it didn't garner nearly as much attention and praise as setting up a new window display of prom dresses at Cache. I had never imagined myself envying mothers who went back to work, but it didn't take long for me to do just that. I could see, as Betty Friedan wrote in *The Second Stage*, that "the real power, the rewarded power, was in that society outside the home."[1] I wasn't going to find that same value as an at-home parent no matter how well I fulfilled my role, because the work I was doing was "women's work"—a type of work we still don't value, and which all too often we still don't even see.

The undervaluing of care-based labor made motherhood hard to enjoy. Logically I knew that the work I was doing in raising children was important. I was on the front lines of forming educated, empathetic, and well-adjusted adults, or at least that was the hope. I also knew, as any primary parent does, that the work was hard. Certainly harder than working retail. In truth, much harder than the creative and intellectual work I do now as a writer. It is a type of work that requires one to draw on a far greater variety of emotional labor-based skill sets. You need to be able to switch effortlessly from one form of care-based labor to another depending on the needs of your family—turning from storyteller to counselor in the time it takes to spill a cup of milk all over your last clean shirt. Emotional labor may not have required training, but it certainly required cultivating, and I was the only one doing that work.

In a way, it made sense to me that there would be some level of imbalance when I was the one at home full-time and my husband worked fifty hours a week. We each had our own full-time jobs, after all, and mine was being the at-home parent. It may not have justified *all* the emotional labor of our family life and relationship landing in my court, but it certainly accounted for why I ended up with a larger portion on my plate. Which is why it was so frustrating and confounding that when my career took off and I began working long hours, making all the money while my husband was at home full-time, nothing seemed to change. Before then, I thought perhaps I was saddled with emotional labor because I had landed in the stay-at-home role by default. What I didn't realize, however, was that becoming a working mother wouldn't solve the imbalance of emotional labor. Working moms are in the same boat, coping with the details in different and sometimes more intense ways. After my husband's layoff, I quickly learned that the divide ran much deeper than the paid hours each of us clocked. Whether I worked full-time outside the domestic sphere, whether I stayed at home, whether I earned more money—none of it mattered. Somehow it would always be my job to do the bulk of the emotional labor, a demand my husband would never face.

When I talk to Maria Toca, she tells me she is on the fence about becoming a stay-at-home mother. She likes her job as a preschool teacher, but working with toddlers day in and day out, in addition to parenting her own three-year-old, is exhausting. Her workday is filled with emotional labor, and her home life is as well. As our two kids play on the floor during our interview, she tells me she's been toying with the idea of stepping out of her career for a while to spend more time with her son, but the trade-offs she might have to make are more than financial. When Toca says she wants to be a stay-at-home mom, her vision is not as idyllic as some working mothers I've known. She understands the toil of caring for kids all day. She knows the amount of work that would go into caring for her son day in and day out without a designated lunch break or someone else to take over, but that isn't what gives her pause.

"I'd like to be a stay-at-home mom," she says. "But I'm sort of scared of the expectation of *being* a stay-at-home mom."[2] Whose expectations? Everyone's. Her Mexican immigrant family is already critical of her "failings" in catering to her husband and child's every need. She feels as if her own expectations for herself might shift. But perhaps above all, she worries that the expectations for emotional labor would also change in her husband's mind. She worries that traditional patriarchal expectations will apply when she takes on the more traditional role in the home.

She mentions a stay-at-home moms' group that she belongs to on Facebook, despite not yet being an at-home parent. She shares, incredulously, that a woman decided to ask the group for advice on how these women keep their partners happy when they come home. The comment section was a flurry of earnest advice: make sure the house is tidied, have dinner ready for him, put on some makeup before he walks in the door. It's the same sort of advice that was given in Reverend Alfred Henry Tyrer's book *Sex Satisfaction and Happy Marriage*, first published in 1936, alongside other gems like only speaking when your companionship is requested and fulfilling your husband's sexual needs while staying silent about any issues you may have. While most of this advice seems laughable and dated, for large swaths of women, the notion that our worth is tied to the happiness of those around us is still steadfast. In fact, some inkling of it persists in even the most progressive relationships.

Toca tells me her partner always cooks for them, and she worries that the expectation might change if she were to stay home. There's so much pressure to do it all when your work is unpaid. Especially with the new world of social media, which shows many bright and shining moments of motherhood (and little of the tantrums, mess, and general horror), the urge to pile more onto our plates becomes unending. I know I have fallen victim to aspirational motherhood more than once, looking at the clean, carefully curated photographs of family life on Instagram and wondering what I have to do to get my life to look like that. More laundry? More white paint? More parenting books? More emotional labor. Much like the suburban housewives Betty Friedan describes in *The Feminine Mystique*, who threw themselves into homemaking to the point of absurdity, moms today have all but turned motherhood into an Olympic sport. I have personally spent hours consumed in failed Pinterest projects, arranged and rearranged home organization systems, baked otherworldly confections for kids' parties, and spent late nights worrying over academic development and school choice. But even during the most intensive years of mothering, I often, if not always, felt as if I wasn't doing enough. Toca says she knows the balance she has now, while working, is probably far easier to manage than taking on the increased emotional labor of becoming an at-home parent, even if her Mexican immigrant family is always nearby to tell her she's coming up short. There's an implication in their "jokes" about her laziness and inability to cook that she's not living up to the emotional labor her partner should be able to expect as a "good man." Their behavior underscores her fear that moving toward a more traditional lifestyle will ramp up the demand for her emotional labor.

"The fact is he gets praise for doing absolutely anything in this household, and I get blamed by family members for expecting too much from him," she says. At least right now she has a job to point to as an "excuse," to alleviate some of the pressure she feels.

She admits there's a layer of guilt that comes with being critical at all, because she does have a progressive partner who does "a lot"—at least in comparison to what her family views as normal. She says her grandmother still does every last thing for her grandfather, fetching whatever he wants or needs so he doesn't have to move unless he feels like it. When she thinks back to her childhood, she remembers her mother cooking everything from scratch, cleaning to no end, getting her and her brother ready for school each morning, and never getting any help from their father, who would come home and sit on the couch. And still, her mother was never allowed to feel like she had done enough. "One time we were having dinner, and my mom had cooked everything from scratch as she normally does. She had worked hard all day, as she normally does. And after being served, my dad said, 'So did you make any salsa or did you warm up any tortillas?'" Toca recalls. "To this day she talks about that incident." Serving others has been her mother's whole life. Her mother recently told her, "It's like someone tattooed me with the words *You have to serve everyone*." That's not the life Toca wants.

She thinks perhaps moving to a new culture (Toca was brought to the United States when she was four years old) helped her break the cycle, but she still admits that she struggles with her partner over emotional labor. "I know I don't *have* to thank him for doing the dishes, but I worry if I don't show gratitude then he might just stop doing them," Toca says. "But when do I get random gratitude for doing something that obviously needs to get done?"

The answer, for most women, is next to never. Despite our growing equality with our partners, there are still wildly different expectations for men and women on the home front—and these differences persist even when women earn an income and are not full-time stay-at-home mothers. Hochschild breaks this down in *The Managed Heart* as a symptom of larger cultural inequality. "An equalitarian couple in a society that as a whole subordinates women cannot, at the basic level of emotional exchanges, be equal. For example, a woman lawyer who earns as much money and respect as her husband, and whose husband accepts these facts about her, may still find that she owes him gratitude for his liberal views and his equal participation in housework. Her claims are seen as unusually high, his as unusually low. The larger market in alternate partners offers him free household labor, which it does not offer her. In light of the larger social context, she is lucky to have him. And it is usually more her burden to manage indignation at having to feel grateful."[3] We're lucky to get help at all. Men are entitled to it.

The reason I spent so long believing that emotional labor was an at-home-parent issue was because it was the only cultural context where this imbalance made logical sense. What is "women's work" (emotional labor) and what is "men's work" (paid labor) are old patriarchal ideas. It's easy, though not right, to justify it by my traditional role as a stay-at-home mom. Or in Toca's family, where her Mexican heritage is at play. But as I talked to more and more women, I saw that the idea of emotional labor as women's work is still pervasive in modern society. While women have spent the past few decades being encouraged to reach for the masculine ideal of success, being told they can become anything their hearts desire in the professional realm, they have not been relieved of any of the emotional labor that waits for them when they return home. The variety of roles offered to women in the workplace doesn't change the fact that emotional labor still sticks to us no matter where we land in society at large. We still don't, as a culture, value this type of work, and we still believe that women should be the ones to take care of it.

Working moms bear the same load as stay-at-home moms, but in different ways. During work hours, their emotional labor shifts to hired help—usually including childcare, possibly housecleaning and other domestic labor. If you want to see how little we value emotional labor, just look at how we fill these jobs when Mom is away. This work is poorly paid and falls almost entirely to women, specifically women of color, which is a critical part of this discussion that is all too often overlooked. "Throughout history, white women have used the labor of women of color to reduce their own domestic burden and free themselves up for corporate and civic pursuits," Kimberly Seals Allers writes in her *Slate* article "Rethinking Work-Life Balance for Women of Color."[4] "Simply put, the labor of Black, Hispanic and Asian American women has raised white women's standard of living. So if we're talking about work-life balance, let's be clear that many white women of means have achieved that balance standing on the backs of women of color." She notes that nearly 28 percent of employed black women work in service industry occupations, work that consistently garners the absolute lowest wages in the country. "Jobs in this broad occupational group often lack important benefits such as paid sick days, according to a report by the Institute of Women's Policy Research," she notes in the article. We may pay lip service to emotional labor from time to time as we talk about the "important job of motherhood," but we obviously don't want to pay well for the actual labor when Mother is at work. While there is certainly much to be said about how our devaluing of service industry labor reflects systemic racism in our country, it is also very telling of our cultural attitude toward emotional labor.

This isn't to say that working mothers get a free pass or have it particularly easy. There is still plenty of emotional labor that working women don't or can't pay for, and that remainder falls to them when they return home. In many cases emotional labor isn't even something we get a reprieve from when we work. The load simply waits for us—and often doesn't do that good a job at "waiting" until we return home. We are always on call should something arise with our children or partners. We still have to be ready to perform emotional labor at a moment's notice by keeping all the details easily accessible in our minds—thus hampering our work and mental space as we try to rise in our careers. Not to mention that working women feel that same perfectionist urge and guilt I had felt so many times as an at-home parent—perhaps even more so because they have less time to "do it all" at home. Working mothers do get more breaks from emotional labor during the workday, but that doesn't necessarily mean the grass is always greener on their side.

Women who work outside the home know this all too well. Interestingly, a 2012 study published in the *Journal of Health and Social Behavior*[5] found that mothers who worked full-time were actually *less* stressed than their part-time or stay-at-home counterparts, but that isn't where the true disparity lies. Being at work full-time alleviated some of the hours of emotional labor experienced within the home, where it tends to be most intense. But the picture for men who worked full-time was where perception was really different. According to the study, men were much happier at home, while women experienced greater happiness at work. The likely reason for this is twofold. Men are saddled with the expectation that they must be the provider, so their stake in the workplace is culturally higher. Home is still their place of refuge, especially since they aren't shouldering much, if any, emotional labor. When women return home, however, we are faced with more work: the work of carrying the emotional labor in our relationships and in our families. It's not that women didn't experience stress at work; it's that they were the only ones experiencing it at home in the form of emotional labor.

On top of this, no one ever asks men if they "can have it all," by contrast to the hundreds of think pieces about whether women can. The question hints at a difficult truth—not only about emotional labor but also about whether or not we "have it all." Is my home up to par? Are my children happy enough? Is my marriage thriving? In our quest to live up to our fullest potential, we want to be not only ideal workers but ideal mothers and wives as well. We feel incredible external pressure to be the *best* mother, the *best* spouse, the *best* career woman we can be, even when we know it's hurting us, breaking us, wearing us down to the bone.

Amy Rosenow is currently working at her own start-up, which—as any entrepreneur knows—eats up every available hour you have. Her schedule is rigid, detailed, and downright intimidating. She wakes at 5:00 a.m. each day to write in her five-minute journal, exercises, has the morning with her two daughters, does a handoff with the nanny, then heads into an intense workday, whether that means working intently on her start-up (which involves, of all things, developing an app to help working parents balance their schedules) or going to watch President Obama speak at the Economic Club. At 7:00 p.m., when her nanny leaves for the day, Rosenow then picks up the second shift at home—doing the childcare, the homework checking, and work that didn't get done during the day—until she ends her day around midnight. In addition to all that, she puts in the vast bulk of the emotional labor in her household, which includes a Sunday session of planning the schedule for the upcoming two weeks for both herself and her husband. She is in charge of the calendar, in charge of travel planning. She is in charge of managing each ball that is in the air at all times, and there are many, from school schedules for her two daughters to when bills need to be paid. It's too much, she knows, for one person to handle, but she has never been able to see another way.

Her husband, a brain surgeon who also works extreme hours and has the slightly more demanding job, has always off-loaded all the emotional labor onto Rosenow. She is the one who has to pick up kids, fill out forms, sign up for everything from school to camp to sports and more. She is the one who sets up carpools, plans meals, does the grocery shopping, attends parent/teacher conferences and doctor's appointments. The list goes on and on.

When asked why she is constantly working, she relays to her daughters that she and her husband work hard so they can go on fun trips and have everything they need and lots of what they want. Rosenow recalls her eldest daughter commenting once, "Mom, those trips are really short bursts of fun, but then you do these really long periods of work." Is it worth it? Rosenow still doesn't have a satisfactory answer to that. She sees the madness of her schedule, says she understands that she is at "the brink of sanity," but at the same time, her emotional labor now seems mild. When she thinks back to ten years ago, when her second daughter was born, her life today resembles something like balance.

In 2008, Rosenow worked as the COO of an investment fund, right as the Great Recession hit. Even while working in the C-suite, Rosenow was always the default parent. The stress of the job was reaching new highs as Rosenow was dealing with new lows in her personal life. Her mother, who lived over a thousand miles away, was dying of cancer and required a great deal of care, which Rosenow took upon herself to arrange. Though she has siblings, the care of a sick parent was dubbed her responsibility as the eldest daughter. It is a position many women find themselves in, no matter how demanding their jobs. The vast majority of unpaid caregivers in the US are women, whether caring for children or for aging parents (often, they do both). A daughter among sons is far more likely to take on this role, regardless of the time, distance, and difficulty involved in providing that care.[6] Throughout her mother's chemotherapy and home care, Rosenow arranged a master spreadsheet for her siblings to organize transportation and care for their mother, along with medical appointments and more. After working grueling hours, Rosenow would hop on a plane each week to take full control of her mother's care. Installing Life Alert? Rosenow's job. Scheduling specialist appointments? Also her job. Sitting with her mother at the hospital? Of course. The emotional toll is one I cannot imagine, not to mention the physical and mental toll of doing all of this emotional labor while pregnant and caring for a toddler. Her mother passed away shortly after Rosenow gave birth, requiring her to travel with a newborn and toddler to arrange and attend her mother's funeral.

Rosenow recalls 2008 as the height of her tribulations in emotional labor. She says it makes her feel grateful for the life she has now, even if it is hectic and frustrating. The emotional labor seems unavoidable and at the same time unbearable. "It's gotten to the point where some forms of planning I used to love, like doing research for trips, have become another item on an endless to-do list instead of a source of joy."[7] Her to-do list has hundreds of tasks left undone at any moment (she can see them all on her app), and she doesn't see an alternative even if her husband wanted to help. "He doesn't have the bandwidth," she says wistfully.

Rosenow, quite obviously, has *created* the bandwidth for herself so she isn't forced to lean back in her career. It's a choice her husband doesn't have to make. No one would dream of asking him to sacrifice his career for the sake of family or better balance. She feels as if she can't even ask him to share some of their family's load. It's on her shoulders to do the emotional labor to find the best balance for both of them, and often that means that the pressure to lean back from family, peers, and the voice in the back of her head is incredible. Would it be easier to deal with the emotional labor if she stopped striving in her career? Almost certainly. But why should she have to? Why should she be the only one asked, *Is it worth it?*

Not everyone has a life quite as hectic as Rosenow's, but most women can relate to the overwhelmed feeling of caring for too many people and not enough for oneself. Emotional labor, in all its manifestations, falls largely to women. Whether it's a newborn or an aging parent, it's women who are expected to automatically defer their careers to take care of everyone around them. To make them comfortable. To make them happy. To worry about everyone else's needs before their own. Given this pervasive bias that women must provide caregiving via emotional labor, it's not surprising that Rosenow may not want to lean back in her career. I am sure she has seen, like so many others, how leaning back turns to opting out and never finding a way back in.

Mothers' inability to reintegrate into the workforce, at least at the same level, was highlighted in Judith Warner's 2013 viral *New York Times* article "The Opt-Out Generation Wants Back In."[8] In the article she profiles a number of women who left high-earning, high-profile jobs to stay home with their children, only to realize the consequence of such a move years later. The women who had left esteemed positions in the workforce were now struggling to support themselves after divorce and finding that their dream jobs hadn't waited for them. Women on the "mommy track" of more flexible work or who otherwise take time away from work to prioritize family pay a huge penalty over the course of their careers. Women with fewer options, like those stuck in the retail jobs I used to work before being edged out by a lack of maternity leave, don't have the option of flexibility. Leaning back is not a choice at all for many women, but opting out of emotional labor doesn't seem viable either. Someone has to do that job, and it's a job that falls to women by default. It seems no matter what we do, whether working full force in a career or devoting ourselves to the care of family, we are all subject to the same dilemmas around emotional labor. We are all expected to do this invisible and exhausting work with no reprieve. We are expected to meet the seemingly endless demand for our time, our mental space, our emotional energy—and do it with a smile, because women are supposed to be "naturally" better at this stuff. But there's truly nothing natural about it. Emotional labor lands in our laps because of social constructs that have ruled unchecked for centuries. And it's not just hurting stay-at-home mothers or working mothers. It's not just hurting women. It's hurting us all.

Emotional labor as women's territory in society is so deeply ingrained that it makes taking on caregiving roles much more difficult for men. It is an issue that Betty Friedan took note of in *The Second Stage*, as men began to experience their own "masculine mystique" of yearning for the fuller life experience they saw women having, while they were still iced out of being fully involved in the domestic and nurturing sphere. "For the real tradeoffs to take place, the sharp demarcation between family and home as 'woman's world,' and work (and politics and war) as 'man's world' will have to be redrawn," Friedan writes.[9] Nearly forty years later, we are still struggling to redraw those lines for inclusivity. We are not only keeping women tethered to these high expectations of emotional labor; we are also keeping men from effectively stepping into the conversation by ignoring the role they could (and should) be playing at home.

John Adams, a stay-at-home father and blogger from the UK, argues that discussing domestic labor and mental labor only as a women's issue is one of the mistakes that has kept us in this long-standing stalemate in the quest for equality. Adams, who wrote "The 'Mental Load' Is Real—but Feminists Are Wrong If They Think Only Women Feel It" for *The Telegraph*, describes the mental load he takes on as a stay-at-home dad and maintains that this is a caregiving issue more than a feminist issue.[10] After all, he is the one who is doing the invisible work of ordering school uniforms, picking out a present for children's birthday parties, emailing relatives, and scheduling things. By ignoring the role many men like himself are beginning to take on, we reinforce the notion that this is women's work, and thus create a barrier for men who might want to take on a more primary caregiving role. I don't think it is right to exclude outliers like Adams from the conversation about emotional labor, but it's important to note the reason he is an outlier in the first place. It requires great vulnerability and bravery for men to step out of the current masculine model and then have to *learn* how to perform emotional labor from scratch as an adult. We don't, as a society, actively encourage men to take on these roles—and we offer little reward to those who do buck convention. Adams is frustrated by the invisibility of the emotional labor he takes on, and rightfully so. The work he is doing is hard and undervalued, and society's refusal to acknowledge that hurts us all. The issue is not strictly personal but also political. "Every time we have an election in the UK there are certain politicians that will start talking about childcare, and it's very often dressed up as a women's issue," says Adams. "Childcare is a massive issue that affects the whole family."[11] Yet framing it as a problem that exclusively affects women makes it easier to ignore politically—and men often don't become involved in the conversation. It's bad news for everyone. The inherent cultural sexism in how we value emotional labor hurts women in far more obvious ways, especially when we are talking about policy. When we consistently refuse to make affordable childcare an option, it's largely up to mothers to take on the emotional labor to make it work at their own expense. But men also suffer from a culture that devalues emotional labor. Where women face pressure to chase perfectionism and take emotional labor to the extreme, men on the other hand face cultural pressure to pour their self-worth into work, leaving the full potential of their lives untapped.

Anne-Marie Slaughter notes this problem with policy in her book *Unfinished Business*, calling for a men's movement of sorts to help men (and therefore women) truly find equality that works for everyone. She writes that while it may be unorthodox to suggest that there is still cultural pioneering to be done by men, "the biggest unconquered world open to men is the world of caring for others."[12]

Vincent Ambo, who lives with his same-sex partner in Norway, agrees with Adams's notion that emotional labor is not a strictly heteronormative issue. He and his boyfriend both work as software engineers, yet Ambo is the one who has always taken on the emotional labor in their relationship. He says he is the more naturally organized and inclined to take on this role in their relationship, but he still finds it frustrating. His partner has indulged in the same learned helplessness many heterosexual men participate in when merging life with their partners.

"He will do chores but only the bare minimum needed for him to do whatever he wants to do right now," Ambo says. "For example, if he needs a cup after the dishwasher ran, and there are none in the cupboard, he will get one from the dishwasher but never empty the whole dishwasher." Of course if Ambo *asks* him to unload the dishwasher, he will, no problem. But he's definitely always the one who has to ask. Ambo figured it was a personality difference between the two of them, but it may go deeper than that.

He is obviously right that emotional labor is not a strictly heteronormative issue on the home front, as Trish Bendix writes in her *Harper's Bazaar* article about emotional labor in her same-sex relationship with a woman. "Though same-sex or non-traditional couples rail against stereotypical gender roles, we often fall into them," Bendix writes.[13] "We live in the same patriarchal, heteronormative society that dictates how partnerships should work, and just because you're both women—or both men, for that matter— this problem doesn't disappear; it simply manifests itself in different specificities or nuances." Bendix writes about her homebound frustrations in much the same way I have described my own heteronormative relationship. "It annoys me when my girlfriend leaves restaurant receipts and gum wrappers all over my desk, without ever inquiring as to how they magically disappear by the time she gets home," she writes. "Or when she alleges we're 'always doing what I want to do' because I'm the one that makes the plans—plans that wouldn't exist without me having made any." Clearly the unfair division of labor can happen in any relationship. Interestingly, though, while many same-sex couples were able to identify with my *Harper's Bazaar* article on emotional labor, there were a great many who did not. On the whole, same-sex couples are far more likely to read an article like mine or Bendix's and have an open discussion that leads to change, or to have had those discussions up front. Multiple studies have shown that same-sex or gender-nonconforming couples divide emotional labor with far more ease than heterosexual couples, who tend to fall into the patriarchal norm without ever giving it a second thought.[14] Perhaps because same-sex or gender-nonconforming partners have already confronted so many gender norms by virtue of their existence, rethinking their roles at home is simply not that big a deal. They don't subscribe to the gender roles dictating that one person should take on all the emotional labor, so they can challenge the imbalance without challenging their very identity. When I spoke with Ambo a few months after our initial interview, he admitted that redistributing the emotional labor in his relationship seemed to be happening with far less friction than my own trial-and-error attempts. It seems to be easier to recalibrate emotional labor when you aren't also dealing with the gendered expectations that plague heterosexual relationships. No one expects Ambo to be naturally better at keeping the house in order or responding to invitations on his partner's behalf. They can tear down and rebuild on equal ground.

The divide in expectations faced by heterosexual couples is part of what sociologists refer to as the stalled gender revolution. A woman who works has to take care of everyone around her, because we still mistakenly assume that emotional labor is an essential part of the female identity. Men who take care of the home and their children are the exception rather than the rule, regardless of who is the primary breadwinner, because we still don't see men in caregiving roles as "natural." As Chimamanda Ngozi Adichie writes in *We Should All Be Feminists*, "The problem with gender is that it prescribes how we *should* be rather than recognizing how we are."[15] As an increasing number of men and women come closer to a fifty-fifty split in their professional lives, the unfair split in emotional labor along gender lines is taking a toll in far more pronounced ways than ever before. Though it's not strictly a heteronormative issue, it is a patriarchal issue, and we need to unlearn these stale roles of who we think *should* take on emotional labor because the answer is *all of us*. Balancing emotional labor in an individualized way that suits our natural strengths is about opening the door to being our truest and fullest selves. Men and women have grown up in the same culture but with different roles ingrained into us, neither of which offers us the fullness we deserve from the human experience. We have to unlearn the roles that don't serve us to move forward together. We have to see how these gender roles we take on harm not simply our relationships but the way we experience life.

CHAPTER 7

A WARM SMILE
AND A COLD REALITY

As a perioperative nurse, Caitlin Mavrakis knows the toll of emotional labor all too well. She describes her job as a "constant balancing act" between the competing pressures of keeping up with the timeline expected by doctors and providing the care that patients expect from her. She tells me about the instant exhaustion she feels when a patient begins to dive into their "life story," and she knows a dressing down will be coming from her boss if she doesn't stick to her rushed schedule. "You want to seem compassionate and caring, but you really don't have the time," she laments. As it stands now, she always faces the threat of getting complaints for not performing the emotional labor that patients expect from her on an impossibly tight schedule. Patients want the warm smile, the home-away-from-home feel, and they're upset when they don't get it. Her very personality becomes a commodity in her work—her wide, bright smile something to which patients feel entitled, regardless of how they treat her.

She finds herself doing emotion work that sounds eerily similar to the flight attendant's deep acting roles observed by Hochschild, but perhaps to an even more intense degree. The high expectation for emotional labor comes not only when working with patients but also when interacting with her bosses. Denigrating comments are par for the course for nurses, who often serve as punching bags for callous surgeons and doctors. In her previous nursing job, she says, she was often yelled at and told she was a terrible nurse. It was simply part of the job, something to be expected. Of course those comments make you want to cry, she says, but you can't. You have to hold it all together while you're being reprimanded and then continue to hold it together as you go in to work with patients. The job is too demanding to allow yourself natural emotions. "You have to make sure everyone is happy, even when you're not," Mavrakis says.

Case in point? The day she got stabbed with a dirty needle. While working as a dialysis nurse, a patient jerked away from Mavrakis, who accidentally stabbed herself with the woman's used needle. At the time, she worked with a population where she regularly saw patients with HIV and other infectious diseases. Her mind immediately rushed to her likely future with AIDS: that she would never be able to have children, her marriage would be over, she would die. That single stab could have destroyed her life, and she didn't even have the freedom to step out of the room and collect herself for a minute. Even in a moment of crisis, her needs were subsumed by the job. She says she will never forget the look on the woman's face after it happened: not one of empathy but of ambivalence. "It was like, 'What's the big deal? Get on with it!' while I'm sitting here trying not to cry, thinking that my life is over." She ultimately had to sit with the patient, pretending nothing at all had happened, for another four hours. She had to make pleasant conversation. She had to remember to smile. She then spent some time cleaning up and about a half hour on paperwork before she was even allowed to begin the testing process to see if she had contracted anything from the used needle. It wasn't until the end of her shift, when she had closed the door to her car, that she was finally allowed to relieve herself of the pent-up fear, frustration, and tears.[1]

Mavrakis says her husband at the time struggled to understand, and while she would occasionally vent to him, most days she would come home, eat dinner, and go straight to bed—where she would often wake in the middle of the night after dreaming of particularly troubling patients, wondering if she had done enough to help them. "I felt mentally and emotionally exhausted," she says. There was so little space for emotional recovery, and such a blurred line between where she ended and work began.

When Arlie Russell Hochschild first coined the term *emotional labor* in reference to the commodified emotion work of flight attendants, she looked into not only what this work entailed but why it existed in the first place. Of course, good customer service is a great way to retain business in the airline industry, but what she witnessed went beyond a courteous demeanor with customers and into much more personal territory. The emotional labor provided by stewardesses was meant to provide a space that felt like home. They were made out to be like hostesses at a dinner party, creating an atmosphere of warmth and security to help nervous customers forget they were on a plane. They had to push their real selves deep inside to don the persona of the flight attendant—the always friendly, always nurturing feminine presence that distracted from thoughts of danger or discomfort.

The work took a toll on the women who performed it, with one noting that she wasn't able to wipe the smile away or cull the incessant friendliness in her real life, even when it felt forced. Others found managing passengers to be a burden, particularly maintaining constant pleasantness while regularly enduring horrific treatment. But most who took on the job excelled at emotional labor, because as women they were well versed in emotion work to begin with. They performed it at home and out in the world; this stage was simply a more dramatized version of a world that had always demanded that they create a space of comfort for those around them. These women were good at jobs heavy in emotional labor because they had been trained their whole lives to do this work, to give of themselves emotionally to please others.

At the time of Hochschild's research, women made up the overwhelming majority of flight attendants, holding down 86 percent of these jobs. In 2014, that number had changed but not in a way that suggests there will be an equal gendered split anytime soon: after more than thirty years, over 75 percent of flight attendants are still female.[2] This trend holds true not only for flight attendants but for service employees in general, especially when those service jobs demand high levels of caregiving and emotional labor. We see an even larger disparity when we look at these jobs through the lens of race, where women of color make up an even larger portion of the emotional labor–intensive workforce.

Service sector jobs that require emotional labor in the form of customer service can become especially taxing for women because they exacerbate the inequality of power in these interactions. Hochschild notes in her research that there is a clear difference between the job of a male flight attendant compared to that of a female flight attendant. While men and women both perform emotional labor in the service sector, that emotional labor is also defined by what we privately expect of each gender. "Women are more likely to be presented with the task of mastering anger and aggression in the service of 'being nice.' To men, the socially assigned task of aggressing against those that break rules of various sorts creates the private task of mastering fear and vulnerability," Hochschild explains.[3] Men are practiced in maintaining authority, women in showing deference. For flight attendants, that means women are often treated in a much more grating manner and have trouble enforcing rules because passengers don't perceive, hence respect, women as authority figures. Not only do men in customer service fields have more natural authority; they also are not expected to perform the same nurturing role of listening to customers, whether for small talk, jokes, or complaints. It is part of their job description, to be sure, but such emotional tasks are not expected or thrust upon them nearly as often. We seek out women to provide these comforts, because they consistently perform the expected emotion work with great skill. Where emotional labor is key, women are always on the front lines.

O ne of the reasons I was drawn to sex work and working as a stripper was that it gave me more agency than other service jobs available," Melissa Petro, a freelance writer and former sex worker, tells me.[4] Petro, who has done extensive journalistic work on sex workers, says this is a common feeling in the field. The other jobs available to women who choose sex work—service sector jobs like waitressing or retail work—place rigid demands on their employees, not only via inflexible scheduling and low pay but through emotional labor as well. "In those jobs, you have to do emotional labor with everyone from your boss to your client," Petro says. There is no right to refuse without risking your job. "Sex workers get to decide if it's worth it. There were some clients who were just too much work, and I wouldn't take them on. In other jobs you don't have that option."

While she was in a position to decide how much emotional labor was too much, Petro says that sex work is primarily grounded in emotional labor, even if the men paying her don't realize it. The men who pay for sex feel entitled to women's time and emotional labor, to such an extent that it doesn't occur to them that they've paid for what amounts to a therapy session with a side of blow job. Much of the work, as Petro describes it, is sympathetically listening to men bitch about their ex-girlfriends. "I love to dance, and that part was enjoyable. The physical work of prostitution wasn't particularly different than nonpaid sexual encounters. It was the emotional labor that was really taxing."

Given that sex work is primarily about emotional labor, is it surprising that the demand for female sex workers is so much higher than for men? In my home state of Nevada, there are nineteen operating brothels but only four legal male prostitutes as of 2013.[5] The reason for the low demand isn't entirely clear, though Petro agrees that perhaps emotional labor has something to do with it (though she also says it's simply much easier for women to have access to nonpaid sexual encounters). The hypothesis is not an outlandish one. Demanding emotional labor from sex workers may not hold the same appeal for women, who are regularly expected to perform emotional labor for others.

A company called ManServants, however, is banking on the opposite. The LA-based service has taken sex out of the equation and hires out attractive male servants to cater to their clients' needs, whether as an escort, a housecleaner, a personal assistant, or a listening ear after a crappy breakup. The men are chosen through an audition process, then trained to build up their emotional intelligence and anticipate the needs of their clients—in short, to perform emotional labor as the crux of their service. In an interview with *The Washington Post*, ManServants cofounder Dalal Khajah states plainly that their service is meant to give women a break from emotional labor—an act that is largely seen as an indulgent fantasy when done by men. "The mental load and emotional labor woman carry is an obvious one to us, as is the need for ManServants," Khajah told *The Washington Post*. "Women almost always get it; it's men that usually follow up with, 'Are you sure there's no sex involved?'"[6]

The fantasy, however, does little to ease the actual burden of women's emotional labor. The fact that women must hire male emotional labor as a novelty act shows exactly how far from societal equality we truly are. The commercials for ManServants are designed to get a laugh, because men so earnestly performing emotional labor for women (in tuxedos no less) is indeed still a joke.[7] I imagine there would be far fewer laughs for a commercial featuring WomanServants dressed to impress and fetching a man a drink or dusting his mantelpiece. There is no power dynamic overturned in that scenario, no flipping of the script we all know by heart. There is no novelty, no "fun" in commodifying the unpaid emotional labor women do every day.

Manservants aside, there are precious few jobs requiring emotional labor in which women don't make up the bulk of the workforce. That is because when men perform emotional labor, it's a joke or exception, not an expectation. It's not a part of their identity, and furthermore, they don't owe emotional labor to the world. Their time and emotional energy and mental space has never and will never be considered a communal resource. Yet for women, this is the expectation. Our emotional labor is supposed to be free for the taking, an altruistic effort we do for the good of those around us. This is a key part of how we justify underpaying for women's work and allow the emotional labor performed both at home and at work to remain invisible, unnoticed, and unrewarded. We're supposed to *want* to do this work, to find it intrinsically fulfilling as part of our feminine mystique. Yet we ignore that the "feminine mystique"— that image women are meant to strive after—is not modeled after our realities. It is modeled to create what society wants and needs us to be. The cold reality is that we build civilization on the backs of women and turn a blind eye when the weight is breaking us.

I grew up witnessing an emotional labor–heavy job in action. My mother has worked as an early childhood educator for over thirty years. She worked as a nanny before I was born, eventually transitioning to in-home childcare, which she still does today. She considers herself lucky as a caregiver, not only because it is her passion but because she lives in one of the few areas where her expertise pays well. She runs her home childcare in a sought-after area of Northern California and earns $70,000 a year caring for a small group of children. The job wears her down, certainly, but it comes with a worthwhile payoff. Most early childhood caregivers are not so fortunate. In fact, the median income for childcare workers is about $10 per hour, and home caregivers like herself can earn even less.[8] I know this firsthand because I tried it.

Before stepping into my writing career, I decided to employ my emotional labor skills as a caregiver like my mother. I had worked in her home daycare as a teenager and knew the ropes when it came to creating early childhood curriculum and working with the schedules of multiple infants and toddlers. I became licensed to run a small in-home childcare where I took care of four children on varying days in addition to my own son, but shuttered my business within a year due to the low pay, the intensity of the work, and the increased labor that came with my own son getting sick at regular intervals. The medical bills outweighed my salary, eventually reaching the point where I could no longer justify keeping my doors open.

The workday itself was over ten hours, with no breaks unless all of the children were sleeping at the same time (which was very, very rare). The skills I employed as a caregiver were both advanced and varied. I studied the pre-K standards to weave learning experiences into the kids' everyday activities. We learned colors with blocks or took stock of the weather for science or counted with Cheerios for math, even before the children were verbal. I took multiple courses on early childhood development throughout the year in addition to the health and safety courses required for my license. I catered to the emotional needs of the kids in my care, created strong routines, kept mental and physical lists to keep our days running smoothly. Yet I made less than a few hundred dollars in a fifty-plus-hour week of childcare. I earned less than minimum wage, as little as three dollars an hour some weeks. Without having a husband who worked full-time, I would never have been able to support myself, let alone my children.

Early childhood isn't the only care-based labor that lands deplorably low on the pay scale, keeping its primarily female workers in dire straits. Most jobs that require emotional labor and caregiving or are related to domesticity (such as maids and other service workers) are dominated by women, women of color especially, and little valued. Even when we are entrusting women with some of the most important work we have in society—caring for the sick, the elderly, the young—we don't value it enough to pay competitively for it, as some countries do. In fact, a 2011 report found that the US ranked 22 out of 27 for teacher salaries.[9] It compared the salaries of educators with fifteen years or more of experience to other college-educated workers. Teachers in the US, on average, made 60 percent less than their similarly educated and experienced counterparts. In many other countries, teacher salaries were on a par with those of peers with the same level of college education—making teaching a choice not only of passion but of practicality as well. In teaching, as in many other care-based jobs, the work requires not only the skills of emotional labor but the sacrifice of salary.

Why don't we pay for work that involves emotional labor when we know it is so necessary to a thriving economy? A simplistic explanation is that caring is women's work and always has been, and we historically do not value the contributions of women. We may pay lip service to women's work within the domestic sphere as important (primarily when we talk about motherhood), but that sentiment doesn't translate into money. Women fulfill caregiving needs in the economy, just as we do in the home—because it's vital, because no one else will do it, but also because we have little choice. Women are pushed into these roles more often by economic necessity than by passion. Jobs requiring emotional labor are women's work not simply because we're better at it, but because we can't obtain entry into other sectors. When we can, we usually do, and the higher we climb, the more likely we are to off-load our personal emotional labor onto women who are paid very little for that work. We don't place cultural value on this work, and it's evident at every level from the low pay we give childcare workers to the dismissal of our skills in the C-suite.

As a society we have consistently valued male skills and traits over those of women. Jobs that are heavily female are some of the lowest-paid jobs in the economic landscape. That isn't to say that there is not a plethora of underpaid male-dominated jobs—jobs that have nothing to do with emotional labor. Farmworkers, food service employees, grounds maintenance workers, and more are also among the lowest paid in the nation and primarily male. But when you look at the opposite end of the spectrum, the top-earning jobs are also male dominated. There is no female-dominated or emotional labor–heavy field that even comes close to the top. Women's work and women's skills are consciously and unconsciously considered lesser—at home, in the workforce, and in the cultural landscape. Indeed, even recent feminist texts such as *Lean In* offer up the advice that women must adapt to the male standard of the ideal worker until we reach a tipping point at which we can enact change. If only it were so easy. With the high demand for women's emotional labor and the low valuation of the skills involved in such work, that tipping point is so far away that our great-grandchildren will be lucky to see such equality. As a society, we are not interested in women's emotional labor skills past their usefulness in keeping everyone comfortable and happy. We don't see it for the valuable work it is.

When Dr. Breanna Boppre decided to spend her graduate studies and career fighting for prison reform with a focus on gender and race, she knew it was going to be difficult work. She was inspired on her path by her father, who had spent much of her childhood in jail for drug-related charges. Visitations with her father introduced her to the problems in the incarceration system that she works against today—punitive crime policies and a lack of rehabilitation programs. Dr. Boppre's research, however, has a more specific focus: the intersection of race, class, and gender in imprisonment or, more simply put, why black women are disproportionately more likely to end up incarcerated. These issues are hard to work through—advocating for rehabilitation and exposing racism in a broken system is an uphill battle—but it's rewarding work for Dr. Boppre. She says the women she has met during her research have had a profound impact on her, reinforcing her belief that the work she is doing is important and necessary. For her dissertation, she conducted semistructured interviews and focus groups with a racially diverse group of women on probation and parole in northwestern Oregon. Their stories, coming both from women of color and white women, illuminated how criminal justice outcomes are shaped by power, privilege, and marginalization through intersections of race and gender. Hence, their experiences were shaped not only by their individual circumstances but also by our social landscape more broadly. Their stories are meant not to fit into a neat box but to expand her view, to help her understand and describe racial disparities in justice outcomes. The end goal of this type of research is to build an awareness of the unintended consequences punitive crime control policies have had on women and their families.

Dr. Boppre's research addressing racial and gender disparities through an intersectional feminist lens is breaking new ground, but not nearly as fast as she would hope—not because the research is not there but because it isn't being recognized. "Value is placed on the traditionally masculine, quantitative approach to research," Dr. Boppre says.[10] Journals want comparative numbers, not the broad view of lived experience. The qualitative research required in her field of study—work that takes an expansive and interconnected view of the problems faced by women of color in the criminal justice system—is considered soft and less valuable. Dr. Boppre even faces setbacks in her personal career because using qualitative research gets her barred from top-tier academic journals, which refuse to publish studies that rely on such methods. Research and care-based involvement do not mix, at least not in the current male-dominated hierarchy of academia.

Yet her traditionally feminine (I might say emotional labor–based) research approach isn't the only impediment Dr. Boppre has faced in academia. It's an old boys' club through and through, and she has seen firsthand the emotional labor required of women in an overwhelmingly male field. She recalls an incident early in her doctoral program, when she challenged a male professor, as a crash course in the sort of deference expected of her in academia. The professor refused to speak to her for the remainder of the semester and lowered her grade without justification. To make matters worse, he was the head of her program at the time. Had she stayed in that field, her chances for success would have been stymied all because of a single interaction in which she didn't offer up the emotional labor expected of her.

While there may not be roadblocks that say, "You aren't allowed to do this work," as there were for women back in the 1950s, there are still a variety of insidious ways in which the professional work of women is undercut by male peers. The power dynamic of having older white men deciding the fate of tenure puts many women in academia at a disadvantage. Not only must they perform emotional labor in their interactions, stuffing down any objections or challenges to maintain the comfort of those lording over the program, but they are also expected to take on emotional labor–intensive roles that interfere with their research. Dr. Boppre says that it is not uncommon for female assistant professors to be asked to chair committees, taking away from the valuable research time that would help them earn tenure. The most common request she sees made of female faculty? Serving as student advisers. It is almost exclusively women who are tasked with the care work for thousands of students, a position that is seen as well suited to those skilled in emotional labor. It's impossible, or at the very least unwise, for women to turn down such tasks, even though it derails their professional advancement. There is no option within this power dynamic that simply allows them to do the work they want.

This isn't a problem solely within academia. While women have made great strides in the workforce, breaking through the glass ceiling in various fields, the gatekeepers of the professional world are still by and large men. In 2014, women held a mere 14.2 percent of the top five leadership positions in the S&P 500. At the very top? There were only twenty-four female CEOs out of five hundred. The problem isn't getting to the very top, it's getting anywhere near there. Without women in the executive pipeline, promotion to the higher echelons of the corporate world is out of reach, in part because of the high expectations for emotional labor men put on women within their field. Women are held to a different standard, one that demands not only professionalism but traditionally defined femininity as well. They cannot speak as directly or make their points without hedging for the comfort of those around them. Their time is eaten up by those wanting to bounce ideas off them, when the courtesy is never returned. Their communality is expected and taken advantage of in a way that detracts from the work they want and need to be doing to break through that next glass ceiling. Women must court favor from male peers and bosses alike in a professional setting, walking the fine line of emotional labor in an all-too-familiar way so as not to upset anyone's ego. Requests need to be cushioned with the male response in mind. Decisions must be justified beyond a reasonable doubt that you could be influenced by your "feminine wiles." Your demeanor is expected to be strong but with a hint of feminine softness, lest you be labeled "unpleasant" or "shrill."

A manual for legal secretaries written in 1974 advised that women be pleasant even under intense stress or when put into uncomfortable situations with the boss: "More executives hire secretaries for pleasant dispositions than good looks. As one of them put it: 'I need a secretary who can stay cheerful even when I get grouchy, work piles up, and everything else goes wrong.'"[11] Even now, when women's roles in the workplace are no longer strictly secretarial, the sentiment that women should be pleasant and "feminine" in the face of male brusqueness is still the entrenched norm. It does not matter if that man is your boss or your peer; there is a societal expectation that women are the ones who need to hold it together and cater to men's emotions, because that is what their status as women requires of them.

In *The Managed Heart*, Hochschild points out that while men and women both perform emotion work, there is always an imbalance. "To have [a] higher status is to have a stronger claim to rewards, including emotional rewards. It is also to have greater access to the means of enforcing claims. The deferential behavior of . . . women—the encouraging smiles, the attentive listening, the appreciative laughter, the comments of affirmation, admiration, or concern—comes to seem normal, even built into personality rather than inherent in the kinds of exchange that low-status people commonly enter into."[12] It seems, from the male perspective, that the emotional labor women perform is something they do *naturally*, not because they have to. Men do not sense the deep imbalance that is so blatantly obvious to the women jumping through hoops to find that perfect balance of leadership qualities and deferential respect that keeps them in the game. The effort is invisible, as it must be to get ahead.

Refusing to perform emotional labor for male colleagues is simply not an option, even today. Women who do not care deeply about how their demeanor and tone affect those around them are quickly labeled a "bitch" or "bossy." Once the impression of unlikability is made, it cannot be undone. If men do not want to work with you—and men hold a great deal of sway at the office—it doesn't matter how qualified you are for a certain job: you won't get it. The fact that people need to like you for you to get promotions is true of both genders, but an aggressive and less emotionally involved man is rarely blacklisted as "overbearing" or a "control freak." He is seen as a strong leader and detail oriented. Emotional labor is still a necessary evil for women to get ahead, but it can redirect a professional woman's valuable time to coddling those around her when she would otherwise be working.

This pressure to be pleasant is women's catch-22 in the professional world. You need to be well liked to move forward, but being well liked often means undercutting oneself to the point of self-sabotage. The expectation of emotional labor hinders women from exerting power in leadership positions or otherwise doing their work without catering to the comfort of others. Then when women do achieve professional success, their likability is almost immediately called into question. Sheryl Sandberg writes in *Lean In* that this sexism-steeped judgment about likability is something she's witnessed firsthand. "When a woman excels at her job, both male and female coworkers will remark that she may be accomplishing a lot but is 'not as well-liked by her peers.' She is probably also 'too aggressive,' 'not a team player,' 'a bit political,' 'can't be trusted,' or 'difficult.' At least, those are all things that have been said about me and almost every senior woman I know."[13] It is presumed that if a woman succeeds she is not putting in the required emotional labor and is therefore selfish or otherwise undesirable to work with. Maintaining high expectations for emotional labor in the workplace puts women in a position where they cannot possibly win, at least not in the same well-liked capacity as men who exhibit similar qualities.

There is no way to the top where you can keep everyone comfortable and happy. This is how women get stuck on whichever rung they land on when they enter the workforce. Though many books have been devoted to the subject of how to get off that rung and climb the career ladder, most methods boil down to adjusting to the "masculine standard" until we can redefine it. Yet this advice glosses over the very real demands for emotional labor faced by women in the workplace. We've been told we can succeed in a world where masculinity is the gold standard but emotional labor is still demanded of women. Success is possible, yes, but should it really be this hard to come by?

CHAPTER 8

TOO EMOTIONAL TO LEAD?

During Bill Clinton's 1992 presidential bid, focus turned time and again to one issue that plagued the American people and his opponents alike: his wife. Hillary Clinton was a career woman long before she met Bill, and instead of letting her work fade into the background as he entered public service, she continued full steam ahead at her law firm, rejecting the ceremonial role of first lady in favor of professional fulfillment. After one particularly frustrating debate, in which Governor Jerry Brown spent most of his time accusing Bill of funneling favorable accounts to Hillary's firm, she punched back. She was fed up.

"I suppose I could have stayed home and baked cookies and had teas, but what I decided to do was to fulfill my profession, which I entered before my husband was in public life."[1]

The context didn't matter; it was the wrong answer. Hillary spent weeks trying to undo the damage, explain her position, drive home the fact that she respected stay-at-home mothers. Still letters from angry Americans poured into *Time* magazine, including one from New Jersey voter June Connerton that read, "If I ever entertained the idea of voting for Bill Clinton, the smug bitchiness of his wife's comment has nipped that notion in the bud."[2] The lengths to which Hillary finally went to squelch the public outcry? She agreed to a presidential first lady bake-off against Barbara Bush to be published in the pages of *Family Circle*. Her chocolate chip oatmeal cookies won the bake-off, and Bill won the presidency, but her comment would never be forgotten.

The infamous quote would follow Hillary Clinton for years, long after her husband's 1992 presidential bid and into her own candidacy in 2016, when her cookie recipe would once again grace the pages of *Family Circle* in the now-traditional bake-off, as it did all those years ago (this time titled the "Clinton family recipe," as there stood to be no first lady). Her career, now decades long, and furthermore her *personality* still worried the American conscience. She was too ambitious, too unapologetic. Her determination to live life on her own terms made a lot of people deeply uncomfortable. The emotional labor she put in to assuage that discomfort was never, and would never be, enough.

Politics has always been a tricky arena for women, who must overcome the stereotypes of being unfit to lead because of their gender while simultaneously having to put much of their femininity into overdrive to keep their constituents comfortable and happy. Making one's way into elected office is, in many ways, a popularity contest. You cannot ignore likability in favor of policy, especially as a woman in what is still by and large a man's world. The higher women rise in leadership, the more emotional labor is demanded of them. By the time you get to the very top, as Hillary Clinton did in the 2016 election, those demands are near impossibly high. At that point you must pick and choose how to perform emotional labor to put yourself in the best possible position. Again: you cannot get to the top and keep everyone comfortable and happy.

As we saw, there were already a great many unhappy people by the time Hillary Clinton decided to make her run for the presidency. She was not feminine enough (with her strict pantsuit wardrobe, she didn't even give us outfits to critique!). She was cold and calculating and much too loud. She wasn't "relatable." Yet on the other hand she was criticized for almost shedding a tear just before the New Hampshire primary in 2008, and certain political pundits without a firm grasp of the sixty-nine-year-old female anatomy wondered if her unpredictable hormones might get in the way of her leadership. She was, in short, too close to the masculine standard for comfort, but still too feminine to be the leader of the United States. In such a no-win position, it speaks deeply to her political aptitude that she went as far as she did.

Hillary Clinton's entire career hinged on her ability to perform emotional labor as she struggled to be the strong, smart political leader while also trying much harder than any of her opponents to be soft, likable, and, of course, less shrill. She admits, in the wake of her failed presidential bid, "Maybe I have overlearned the lesson of staying calm—biting my tongue, digging my fingernails into a clenched fist, smiling all the while, determined to present a composed face to the world."[3] Yet what other option was available? Her male counterparts had no such obligation to manage the expectations of the media and their potential constituents in such a hyperattentive manner. Male politicians in the same ring as Clinton could throw tantrums like my two-year-old and get away with it. Women in politics have never had that option, least of all those as powerful as Clinton. Her political ambitions had to be cushioned in a variety of ways—burying any feelings of resentment, ignoring the obvious sexism, even going so far as to do coffee runs as junior senator for her male seniors.[4] Even those who do not agree with her politics cannot deny that she balanced the expectations as well as anyone could hope in the face of such obvious double standards.

We cannot pretend the difference in expectations is not obvious. In fact, a survey conducted by the *New York Times* in 1979 found that all those surveyed could detect the double standard between men and women in politics. Frances Farenthold, the president of Wells College in Aurora, New York, described the situation in a way that is eerily prescient: "You certainly see to it that you [as a woman in politics] don't throw any tantrums. Henry Kissinger can have his scenes—remember the way he acted in Salzburg?—but for women, we're still in the stage that if you don't hold in your emotions, you're pegged as emotional, unstable and all those terms that have always been used to describe women."[5] The scene Farenthold describes, in which Kissinger threatened to resign at a press conference in Salzburg, Austria, in response to allegations that he was involved in a wire-tapping scheme, seems innocuous in light of the scenes that were par for the course during the 2016 presidential election. What is striking, however, is the degree to which the double standard still exists in how women and men are expected to manage emotions. Nearly forty years later, not enough has changed.

In her postelection book *What Happened*, Hillary Clinton discusses the uphill battle she faced as she tried to balance her responsibility to dole out emotional labor in the public eye with her need to be ambitious and hard-hitting on the campaign trail. She never seemed to find the golden mean that put people at ease. There wasn't that warm, homey feeling when she got on stage—she didn't slip into the pleasant hostess role of keeping everyone comfortable and happy. Neither did any of the other candidates, to be sure, but it wasn't their job. The men she shared a stage with over the course of the election season weren't bound by the same expectations of emotional labor. They didn't have to walk a fine line to be liked. They could ignore or pummel these boundaries as they pleased.

It is no secret that one of the main plagues of Hillary's campaign was the issue of "likability." Before one of her most crucial debates with then-candidate Donald Trump, pundits across multiple news outlets noted how critical a "warm smile" would be. Then in response to the debate, she was criticized for "smiling like she's at her granddaughter's birthday party" by *Atlantic* editor David Frum.[6] Even in the smallest of gestures, it was a lose-lose situation.

There's more than a hint of frustration as she describes the low bar for revealing and concealing emotions for men in politics throughout her book. Male candidates are allowed to yell, to be "passionate" and volatile. It's a mark of their dedication. Women in the same position are not allowed these same flights without a major backlash. Tipping anywhere near yelling means being labeled "shrill," and America has a serious problem with shrill women. Assertiveness turns from a leadership trait to a sign of instability when it is a woman on stage. Attempting to explain her somewhat guarded composure, she writes, "I think before I speak. I don't just blurt out whatever comes to mind. . . . But why is this a bad thing? Don't we want our Senators and Secretaries of State—and especially our Presidents—to speak thoughtfully, to respect the impact of our words?"[7]

The truth is, what she describes here is not unique to the campaign trail, as I've discussed before. Women are skilled at controlling their language, at thinking before they speak. It's a way to protect ourselves and ensure that we keep the peace. This is one area of emotional labor that many men are also skilled in. It's not a requirement for them in the same way, but it's a skill that can easily be honed and used to their advantage. A man who thinks before he speaks to best manage the emotions of those around him is methodical and careful. That composure Hillary describes, when not scrutinized under the lens of womanhood, may well be an advantage. Just look at Barack Obama.

President Obama was an incredibly composed leader; whenever he spoke, it was with a great deal of care. He seemed to have a firm understanding of the weight of his words and wielded them wisely. He was allowed pause without being criticized as cold and calculating. He was allowed the occasional tear without being labeled emotional and unstable. He was able to care openly without the same yoke of scrutiny. The same could also be said of his first presidential opponent, John McCain, who still garners respect from both sides of the aisle for his careful words and political moves. We love a man for his composure yet distrust a woman for the same.

Managing the emotions of those around her (or failing to) was not the only emotional labor on the campaign trail. In fact, Hillary Clinton spends a lot of time in *What Happened* recounting the emotional labor she performed not only in the public arena during her 2016 presidential run but in private as well—with her family, with her friends, with her staffers. Being the person who cares about all the details and the people affected by them doesn't go away, even when you're campaigning to become the next president of the United States. "I make sure everyone has eaten, that my staff is wearing sunscreen if we're at an event in the baking sun. When reporters who traveled abroad with us got sick or injured, I made sure they had ginger ale and crackers and would send the State Department doctor to their room with Cipro and antinausea drugs."[8] While she admits, in relation to emotional labor, that many things were taken off her plate by paid help (for example, she hasn't gone to the store for an emergency milk run in decades), she is still the one in charge of emotional labor on the home front as well. "I'm the one who schedules family visits, vacations, and dinners with friends. Bill has many positive qualities, but managing the logistical details of a household is not one of them."[9]

While Clinton obviously laments the unfair demand for emotional labor that is placed on women, she also sees, as most women do, the value in this type of work. She sees that women are the ones doing constituent outreach, phoning in, writing letters, organizing workshops, coordinating efforts. "We're not just the designated worriers in our families; we're also the designated worriers for our country."[10] It is high time we start valuing that effort as an essential trait. We are not merely worriers but warriors of caring.

The value of emotional labor and the skills we employ in keeping those around us comfortable and happy are not simply of value in the home or in caregiving roles. The level of care and attention to detail (as well as the big picture) that a woman's lens often brings to the table is invaluable in business negotiations, national politics, and household politics alike. Using the skill set of emotional labor wisely at all levels is simply good business. Caring leaders are good leaders. Their teams, their citizens, their peers are more motivated to work for them. Their attention to issues that extend outside their own concerns makes them exemplary. Their problem solving is more comprehensive, more attuned to the larger picture. We should want those at the top to be deeply invested in the comfort and happiness of those below them, moving us all toward a better place.

Women's experience with emotional labor makes them adept problem solvers. We are trained to always look at all of the different parts that are in motion and then carefully consider the choices that will put us, and those around us, in the most advantageous position. This skill translates directly into business, where women's interconnected viewpoints can give valuable insight into how to best move forward and keep all parties happy.

In fact, a 2016 study from the Peterson Institute for International Economics found that increased gender diversity in the highest corporate offices led to a 15 percent increase in profits.[11] By leaving women out of these positions, companies are hurting their bottom line—not simply because they leave out 50 percent of the world's talent, but because the vastly different perspective of that other 50 percent adds tangible value. Yet in spite of the link between female executive board members and higher profitability, nearly 60 percent of the 21,980 firms surveyed had no women on their boards whatsoever, and more than half had none in C-suite positions. The largest increase in profits was found when there were more women in the C-suite, followed by women on boards. The results also found that female CEOs had little effect on the overall performance of firms, underlining the importance of increased female representation as opposed to getting one lone woman to the very top.

Still, those lone women are not without their share of positive attributes. A 2012 survey conducted by *Harvard Business Review* found that female leaders, despite being in the minority, scored higher than their male counterparts in nearly every category that defines exemplary leadership. They scored higher in all "nurturing" leadership fields as expected, such as team building, inspiring and motivating, developing others, and collaboration and teamwork. However, they also scored higher in other areas, such as taking initiative, driving for results, strong communication, and problem solving.[12] When you think about the emotional labor women perform in private, these skills should really come as no surprise. We have to be expert delegators—noticing and effectively solving problems in the home through careful communications work. We must always take the running of our lives into our own hands: if we don't take the initiative to plan the vacations, sign up the kids for summer camps, or decide on the weekly menu, who will? We are incredibly adept problem solvers, creating masterful systems of organization to keep our families' lives running smoothly despite varying and competing schedules. We nurture relationships, taking time and emotional effort to make those around us feel comfortable and happy. And we hold ourselves to the highest of standards, driving for results that are above and beyond expectations both at work and at home as we seek to "have it all."

It's worth noting, however, that the margins were relatively small between male and female leaders. At the top of the list when it comes to taking initiative, women rate about 8 percentage points higher as effective leaders, but the large majority of these leadership traits give women a 2 to 6 percent edge over their male counterparts. I don't think these results prove in any real way that women are necessarily better at their jobs than men, or that the female way of doing things ought to be the new best way. What it does show, however, is that there is relatively equal value in the skills that men and women bring to the table. There is, therefore, untapped value that we are not taking advantage of when we leave women out of the equation or tell them to adapt to the male standard to achieve professional success. It is time for us to start valuing the skills of women—a skill set deeply linked to our experience with emotional labor—on a par with those of men to move toward greater success in the global economy and the domain of culture. We must allow women to use these skills for their highest purpose rather than as a way to keep offices pleasant and comfortable. And that starts with recognizing emotional labor skills for the leadership qualities they truly are.

Just like in our private lives, where the emotion work of fathers and husbands is lauded as progressive while women doing the same work are simply working at baseline, we face a similar battle for equal valuing of traits, most notably in leadership roles. In fact, the very traits that are praised in male leaders are often given a negative connotation when applied to female leaders. Men who employ emotional labor are thoughtful, caring, organized, team players. Women who perform emotional labor are nags, control freaks, perfectionists, worrywarts, doormats. Our tasks can be the same. Our approaches can be the same. But the way we view them through the lens of gender makes them anything but equal.

In 2003, an experiment was conducted at Columbia Business School to gauge how students perceived leadership in relation to gender. Researchers presented students with a case study about real-life entrepreneur Heidi Roizen, a successful venture capitalist who had leveraged her outgoing personality, as well as her large personal and professional network, to get to the top. But half of the students received the case study with a different first name: Howard. The students were then polled on their first impressions of Heidi/Howard. Students respected the accomplishments of both Heidi and Howard, but there was a disconnect in how they responded to them personally. Howard was well liked. Heidi, by contrast, was selfish and an undesirable colleague.[13] Men can get to the top without offending others along the way because their accomplishments belong to them. Women, however, are subject to the expectation that their efforts should always be communal—always catering to those around them instead of working for their own success. Therefore, when women succeed in a leadership role they are viewed as having "a perceived deficit in nurturing and socially sensitive communal attributes," as the Heidi/Howard study showed.[14]

Therefore it is unsurprising that the dearth of women at the top persists from the C-suite to every level of government. In the United States, women hold a mere 20 percent of positions in the House and Senate, and that number is an all-time high.[15] Most of the world's countries have never had a female leader. According to data from the Pew Research Center, Americans have various opinions on why women have such trouble getting to the top both in politics and in high-powered careers: women are held to higher standards, they are dealing with a society that isn't ready to consider their talents, and they are still expected to maintain an exceptional work-life balance.[16] These issues stem from the imbalance in emotional labor between genders in both the public and private spheres. They are also issues that legislation could help rectify to some degree. It makes sense, then, if we want to see substantial change in how we value emotional labor across the cultural and economic landscape, that we should rally for more diverse representation in government. Yet, as many female politicians have found, the demand for emotional labor is especially high for women in government. There are two starkly different standards for the emotion work demanded of men and women who hold office—persistent aggression and force on one side, nurturing and deference on the other. If women overstep their bounds even slightly, unable to walk along the razor-thin line demanded by the world of politics, they are severely criticized and risk their continued success.

I am not here to argue politics or to say that Hillary would have won the 2016 election had she walked the fine line of emotional labor more carefully. That is neither my area of expertise nor my interest. There were many more factors at play than her commentary on cookie baking or her much critiqued smile or laugh. However, I do think it's worth noting the double standard in politics regarding how we define leadership for men and for women, and how those expectations limit women. Because, in truth, the expectation that women should constantly perform emotional labor to keep those around them comfortable and happy has consequences beyond the perception of our ability to lead the world or our stalled progress in personal relationships as we continue to lead on the home front. The demand for women's emotional labor includes being told to make ourselves smaller and quieter, to not disrupt—even, indeed especially, when criticizing men who have wronged us.

The demand for emotional labor keeps women from speaking up when problems arise, because we do not have the same ground to stand on. We cannot criticize a male boss, a male peer, a male partner, a male *period*, without having our integrity questioned, because we are disrupting the comfort of those around us. We are breaking the social rules. When we do not give the deference expected from us at home, it can lead to a fight. At work, to a career setback. But out in the world, on the streets, while walking home at night, it can lead to much worse. When we aren't employing emotional labor to gain ground in our relationships or to get ahead at work, we are using it to survive.

CHAPTER 9

WHAT QUIET COSTS

M e too."

It was a sentiment I heard often as women reached out to me to share their experiences of emotional labor. "Me too." This is my story, my mother's story, my sister's story, my best friend's story. Then, shortly after my article went live, those two words went viral in the wake of Harvey Weinstein's damning exposure as a sexual predator. Actress Alyssa Milano resurfaced #metoo, the grassroots movement started in 2007 by youth activist Tarana Burke as a way to let young women of color know they were not alone in their sexual harassment and abuse. The revitalized campaign across social media stated that perhaps the world would understand the full weight of sexual harassment and assault if every woman who had experienced it were to simply write those two words and put them where everyone could see: on the internet.

For days my Facebook and Twitter feeds were filled with those two words. I posted them myself, mentally recounting stories I had only told my closest friends. *Smile*, a man had told me just days earlier as I walked home alone. I cannot count the number of times a stranger has stood in front of me, demanding that I perform the most basic kind of emotional labor for them: *smile*. Nor can I quantify the sense of unease I've felt walking away from those situations, looking back over my shoulder, hurrying along my way. And *smile* is the innocuous one. There have been so many far worse: the ones who follow you, who threaten you, who touch you. Of course I had experienced sexual harassment. Hadn't every woman? I almost didn't post #metoo. It seemed such an obvious thing to share, like stating the sky is blue. Yet the cacophony of voices raised as the movement grew made it loud and clear that this message was necessary to break the weighty silence so many of us have lived with for so long. The Associated Press reported there were over twelve million #metoo posts, comments, and reactions on Facebook in less than twenty-four hours.[1] Quiet had been costing us a lot of hidden pain.

I was taken aback by the stories women willingly shared, not because they were unfamiliar, but because they were so raw and emotional. They lay themselves bare in order to be seen by other women who would understand and believe them. These stories were also placed in plain view for all men, creating a moment that allowed those who truly want to be allies to reevaluate what they had always viewed as normal in our culture, and what their ignorance had cost us. There were stories of rape and abuse. Stories of childhood horrors and male friends who had betrayed their trust. Stories of teachers, colleagues, relatives, strangers putting these women in situations ranging from uncomfortable to traumatizing. All of these stories, I noticed, had a common theme: emotional labor.

The expectation of women's emotional labor, the demand for women's emotional labor, seriously contributes to rape culture. Men can feel emboldened to cross one line, and then another, because of the very real expectation that women will not do or say anything to disrupt their comfort. When it comes to sexual harassment, women have to employ emotional labor to anticipate the reactions and manage the emotions of their abusers, no longer because their priority is to keep the peace, but because it is essential to their safety. It's a dangerous cycle in which the demand for emotional labor enables rape culture, and rape culture reinforces the demand for emotional labor.

When women face sexual harassment, we approach the situation the same way we approach all emotional labor: with the question of what will keep others comfortable and placated. What will prevent anger, assault, retaliation? What can I do to mitigate the damage that is already being done to me? Caring is taken out of the equation as we deal with the immediate need for self-preservation, whether it be the preservation of our career or our safety. The burden placed on women is then further exacerbated by the fact we are entangled in a culture where men don't learn the emotional labor tools that would help mitigate toxic masculinity. The blame, the problem solving, the peacekeeping—it all falls to us.

Dr. Robert Bogosian, author of *Breaking Corporate Silence*, says that many factors rush through our minds when sexual harassment arises in the workplace. "Defensive silence is rooted in fear," he says. In our internal dialogue, we are working out the consequences, because we know we will be the ones to bear them. "'I could lose my job. I could be labeled. I could be ostracized. I could be marginalized, and I can't afford to have any of those things happen to me.' So the best way to stay safe and survive here is to keep my mouth shut."[2] That defensive silence is what is going to keep everyone comfortable. It's how we don't rock the boat, don't get blamed, don't get labeled. He says labeling is particularly fearsome for women—being portrayed as a bitch, a complainer, a whiner, a liar serves to isolate the victim further. So we look around us, see that this is simply the accepted culture, and live with it. *Everyone else seems okay with it, so I guess I should be too.*

What Dr. Bogosian describes is a "culture of tolerance." It's the predetermined forgiveness that sets the precedent for bad behavior. Instead of condemning sexual harassment, we portray it as a part of a man's accepted personality. "Oh, that's just Harvey." "Come on, he didn't mean it like that." "Lighten up, he's like that with everyone." It's the "boys will be boys" attitude, all grown up. These dismissive remarks then lead to a culture of silence, where it's common knowledge that harassment is something we don't talk about here. The behavior is normalized, and the damage is trivialized—which is exactly what rape culture is. This leads to a severely toxic work environment that foists a great deal of emotional labor and emotional stress on the women who must endure it. As one victim of Charlie Rose recounted in *The Washington Post*, "You know if you don't behave a certain way, there's someone else behind you."[3] The stakes are higher for the person with the lower status, which is why women rise to meet the expectations for their emotional labor. Their livelihoods, indeed their lives, depend on it.

While Dr. Bogosian's area of interest is corporate culture, the pressure for women to accommodate sexual harassment can be even harder to overcome in service sector jobs that demand emotional labor. Dr. Bogosian talks about the "rock stars" of each industry, who are generally exempt from accountability, like restaurateur Ken Friedman, whose sexual misconduct went unreported for years because of his status in that community. Trish Nelson, a former server at one of Friedman's restaurants, told the *New York Times* that even after she finally quit following years of harassment and a frightening incident of sexual assault, she didn't dare come forward. "I was terrified to tell anyone why," she said. "Ken bragged about blacklisting people all the time. And we saw it happen."[4] When you go lower down the rungs, it doesn't take much status or money to create a toxic culture of tolerance. A waitress or clerk is outranked by nearly everyone on the job, making her a target for sexual harassment to a degree women in the C-suite rarely experience. Yet both women must use their skills in emotional labor—either surface acting that everything is fine or going into the deep acting of convincing themselves that this doesn't really bother them—in order to make it through the day.

This self-preserving display of emotional labor is one most women are intimately familiar with. Even if we work in environments that don't tolerate harassment, we cannot be entirely shielded from the world. Nearly all of us have, at some point, been put in the uncomfortable situation of sizing up the danger involved in responding to a lewd comment yelled on the street. Do you smile when you're told to smile? Do you keep walking as if nothing at all happened? Do you dare to speak up and break the code of silence? We use our skills in emotional labor to figure out the appropriate response, because each situation is unique. While it's often tempting to confront street harassment, we have all heard the stories of women who were brave at the wrong moment. You don't know which man is going to shy away, shamed by a rebuke, and which is going to follow you home.

When I spoke with Melissa Petro, she could not recount the number of times she had been approached in cafes by men who wanted to encroach on her personal space, her time, her emotional labor. She recalls one moment in particular, when she was sitting on a park bench with a friend and they were approached by a stranger who sat down and inserted himself into their conversation. After a few minutes, her friend turned to the man and said plainly, "We don't want to talk to you." She was shocked not only by her friend's "impolite" behavior but by the fact that the man actually left. *You can do that?* Petro thought. Then of course she remembered that you *can't* just do that. At least not without a level of risk that outweighs the potential benefit of reclaiming your time. She says that despite the strong example of her friend, she still indulges men who feel entitled to her emotional labor, because that politeness gives her a sense of security. "If nothing else," she says, "it gets me through my days without being called a cunt." It's the path of least resistance, the one with the least psychological stress. This practiced form of emotional labor is one she has no doubt honed over the years, as many women do. We are not born with an innate knowledge of how to handle ourselves in these situations, but we all learn in time.

As a young girl, I was always fierce. I would sharply back-elbow boys who made grabs at me in the school hallway. I once publicly shamed a group of boys in a crowded mall for looking me up and down and calling me a "sexy little mama." There was, in those situations, the safety of many peers and adults nearby. The danger was minimal and the recourse empowering. I didn't understand why more girls didn't simply fight back like I did. At least I didn't until the Halloween when I was fourteen.

A group of friends and I met up to trick-or-treat in one girl's gated community. It felt safe enough: there were maybe ten of us, plenty of streetlights, lots of kids out on their own. We weren't far into the night when a group of older boys began following us. We had all noticed, moved quickly from one street to the next, before they began yelling at us to come with them, asking us what we were so scared of. I don't remember what I said. Some trite middle-school insult? Maybe a "screw off"? One of my girlfriends looked at me with horror.

"You can't say that!" she yelled before pulling on my hand to run. I don't know if the boys were running yet, but her movement was instinctual, born from knowledge of the world I didn't yet have.

They were chasing us, and they were fast. I can still hear their shoes beating hard against the pavement as they gained on us. I couldn't look back. None of us could. We were lucky to have a head start, but we had to split into smaller groups, darting down any open pathway we could find. I ended up in a group of three, not knowing what had happened to the rest of the girls as we huddled in the bushes near the community pool and watched the boys run on. Had the others gone that way? How would we find them again? In what condition would we find them?

I don't know how long we stayed hidden, crying. It felt like hours, though it probably wasn't. We eventually found everyone unharmed. We were lucky that night. It wasn't until I was older, until more terrible things had actually happened to me and those I loved, that I realized how lucky I had been.

I learned after that night not to tempt fate. Now when I walk down the street, even with my children in tow, I feel compelled to smile when I'm told to. I know when to make eye contact and when I can get away with keeping my head down or acting distracted. I learned, in time, the safest ways to manage the emotions of those harassing me while keeping my fear under wraps. It's a self-preservation tool. But even the most skilled employment of emotional labor is often not enough.

This is why when the best efforts fail and sexual assault occurs, we look to the victim, not the perpetrator, for explanation. In the large majority of rapes—those perpetrated by someone the victim already knows—we ask if she was leading him on (indeed, if her emotional labor went too far into intimate territory). We ask what she did to stop it from happening (could she have walked the fine line more carefully?). We ask what she was wearing (was she playing the appropriate role in her appearance?). We scrutinize the emotional labor performed by the victim, because it is more socially acceptable to criticize the behavior of victimized women than it is to criticize men who are criminals. It is this aspect of rape culture that makes victims so hesitant to speak out about their experience in the first place.

There are many problems in coming forward after assault, as victims know all too well. They are often not believed. The justice system fails them. According to the Rape, Assault, and Incest National Network (RAINN), for every 1,000 incidents of rape, only 310 are reported to the police. A mere 57 of the reports lead to an arrest, and only 7 of those result in felony charges, with even fewer actually serving their full sentence.[5] Time and again the "bright future" of a rapist is held to be more important than the pain of the victim, as in the case of Brock Turner—the promising young rapist whose potential swimming career was worth more than his victim's physical and psychological damage. After being indicted on five charges of sexual assault and rape, he was sentenced to only six months in jail, ultimately serving just half the paltry sentence. For all the horrors and demanding emotional labor the twenty-two-year-old victim, "Emily Doe," endured in bringing these charges, it seems woefully inadequate that justice was served in such a small portion.

Too often, victims are told it's "not the right time" to talk about this. In the case of Eric Schneiderman, an outspoken advocate for women during the #metoo movement, women were discouraged from speaking out about his physical abuse, thereby dethroning a man who was an "ally" to the greater cause of women's equality through his work. One of Schneiderman's former girlfriends recalled telling a number of friends about his abuse after she ended their relationship and being told he "was too valuable a politician for the Democrats to lose" and "to keep the story to herself."[6]

Even if a victim of assault doesn't come forth publicly, coming forward to family and friends can open up a Pandora's box in terms of the emotional labor expected of the victim. In cases of familial abuse, they're told to consider how it will hurt the family if they publicize their abuse. They are reminded time and again that it is their job to regulate their own emotions and consider their impact on those around them, including their attacker.

Laura grew up in an abusive home. Her training in emotional labor started early, and the stakes were high. She had to hide the abuse she endured at home because she didn't want to cause her abusers pain by revealing their actions. As she grew older, she found herself drawn into controlling and abusive relationships but once again hid the abuse because she couldn't answer the question "Why do you stay?" She eventually ended up hiding abusive relationships from her children, trying to spare them the pain of watching their mother suffer abuse but also so they wouldn't inherit these roles for themselves. "All of the guilt, shame, pain, and embarrassment, it's all always been my responsibility to hold it," she says. "I carry a box of violence, trauma, and pain around with me at all times, filled with the problems of other people so that they don't have to hold it."[7] Having to hold on to all that pain and keep it under wraps so that others can be comfortable means she doesn't get to process any of it. She says people often refer to her as tough or stoic, but in reality, she puts on that face for their benefit. "I don't want to feel what it feels like to cause that pain to others, even when it means protecting my abusers. I haven't found another way to survive yet."

Perhaps it should come as no surprise that women often stay in abusive relationships or cover up past abuse. They have been conditioned to put the comfort and happiness of others above their own; in cases of abuse, this conditioning mixed with fear leads to silence and acquiescence. It is also easy to become "comfortable," in a sense, with a specific pattern of emotional labor in an abusive relationship, rather than deal with the amped-up emotional labor and danger of leaving—a danger that could be life threatening. Over 70 percent of murders in domestic violence cases occur *after* the victim has left. Leslie Morgan Steiner, author of *Crazy Love*, a memoir of abuse, says that this is the final step in the abuse pattern because the abuser at that point has nothing left to lose. In her book she describes the aftermath of leaving her abusive husband after he attempted to kill her: double-checking that she had locked the door, then finding him standing outside her apartment window on many nights after filing a restraining order. Anything could have happened.[8]

Steiner's popular TED talk, "Why Domestic Violence Victims Don't Leave," touches briefly on the frustration of people constantly asking, "Why does she stay?"—as if it is a passive choice, one that isn't carefully weighed each day, each moment.[9] As if all of your emotional energy isn't spent in trying to prevent the next outburst. She retells in her memoir that her then-fiancé had gone into a rage on the first night in their new apartment. Instead of leaving, she questioned how she could have changed the outcome—how she could have better performed emotional labor in an attempt to curb his violent behavior. "Was Conor scared that we were moving in together?" she writes. "So afraid that he'd lash out at me like this? Why hadn't I been calmer? I could have, should have, laughed it off. Told him I loved him more than any man on earth."[10] It wasn't until years later that she understood the truth: that there was no line she could toe carefully enough to prevent the abuse from happening. Nothing she did made him beat her. Nothing she did could make it stop.

She also recounts the emotional labor of keeping the terrible secret and the guilt she felt upon telling her best friend that her husband hit her—how she didn't want to burden anyone with that knowledge. She found herself so preoccupied with caring for others, both her abusive husband and her loved ones, that she lacked the perspective to see how all this emotional labor might, eventually, literally kill her.

Reema Zaman, author of the memoir *I Am Yours*, says that she stepped into her abusive relationship because it felt familiar and stayed for much the same reason. She grew up watching her mother, a strong and intelligent woman, cower before her father, whose anger was unpredictable and intensely aggressive. She says her mother took on all the emotional labor in the household, including fielding her father's outbursts, and she learned to do the same. "Through it all, my mother was continuously forgiving, kind, patient, compassionate, quiet, nurturing, acquiescing, fearful, deferential, and docile."[11] So was Zaman, when she was married at twenty-five to a gorgeous, charismatic man eleven years her senior. Her childhood had groomed her not only to be attracted to toxic men but to become exactly the sort of woman they loved.

She knew how to perform emotional labor well, as any woman in an abusive relationship must. It's the only way such a relationship can thrive. Yet as much as she gave, her husband was always ready to take more, to deplete her to the point of exhaustion, while simultaneously taking steps to further bind her in the trap of abuse.

"Physically and emotionally, my husband had managed to move us far away from our friends and family," Zaman says. "He demanded so much of my energy that I didn't have any emotional resources left to invest in other people. I lost contact with relatives and friends. We lived in upstate New York, tucked deep into a small town, so remote that we didn't have cell reception." She handed over her earnings to her husband every week. She took heed of all the things he didn't like about her, changing everything from the way she made the bed to how she dressed and did her makeup. "Our relationship 'worked' because I knew exactly how to tend to his temper, how to move around him as he raged through the world, how to calm him using words, sex, distraction, humor, and food, how to put out fires he lit constantly with his sister, mother, friends, and bosses."

Even women who aren't in abusive relationships bring this skilled and careful mind-set of emotional labor into relationships. While we may not be walking around on eggshells, we still walk a fine line when it comes to interacting with our partners. We quickly acclimate to our partner's behavior patterns and strive, as we've learned, to keep the peace. Though many men argue that they do the same, it doesn't come with the same intrinsic motivation. As Margaret Atwood poignantly put it, "Men are afraid women will laugh at them. Women are afraid men will kill them."[12] Our tempered responses, at their core, always carry an undercurrent of self-preservation. We are living in a world that is not ours to roam freely, and we know it.

For many women, though, we are concerned less with danger than with frustration. We don't want to rock the boat, to derail our days, to put out any more emotional labor than is absolutely necessary. While the emotional labor we put into our interactions is not fear-based, it is still self-preserving. We already expend a great deal of mental energy to keep everyone comfortable and things running smoothly. So when it comes to points of conflict, it often makes more sense to tiptoe around the problem than face it head-on. That's part of the reason it took me thirteen years to broach the subject with my husband. It simply wasn't worth it until I reached my breaking point. For me, it was a seemingly innocuous blue Rubbermaid storage bin in the closet. For Zaman, it was the day she realized she could never bring a child into their abusive relationship.

It seems like, both at home and in the world, we are all beginning to reach that collective breaking point. The overwhelming support for the #metoo campaign and the seriousness with which we are now handling allegations of sexual harassment and abuse are heartening. These changes suggest that we are ready to move forward and take a hard look at how and why inequality persists. It is time for us to stop using our emotional labor in ways that do not serve us or only serve to maintain the status quo. It is time we look into how we can shift the balance of emotional labor to help us, as well as those around us, lead better lives. It is time for us to value women's skills and labor and voices.

"This year, we became the story," Oprah said, referring to women and the #metoo movement in her stirring Golden Globes speech as she accepted the 2018 Cecil B. DeMille Award. "For too long women have not been heard or believed if they dared to speak their truth to the power of those men, but their time is up." It is a hopeful statement—perhaps premature, but it resonated. In the wake of seeing so many powerful men publicly damned—Harvey Weinstein, Matt Lauer, Louis C.K., Charlie Rose, Ryan Lizza, and many more—their demise no longer seems impossible. If their time is not up, it is at the very least dwindling as we ride this new wave of feminism into the unknown future—a future that Oprah can see in the distance. She concluded her moving speech by painting a picture of the world that young girls today can look forward to. "A new day is on the horizon, and when that new day finally dawns, it will be because of a lot of magnificent women . . . and some pretty phenomenal men fighting hard to make sure that they become the leaders who take us to the time when nobody ever has to say 'me too' again."

CHAPTER 10

FINISHING THE FIGHT

In 1957, Betty Friedan, soon to become one of the most influential leaders of the feminist movement, conducted a survey of her former classmates from Smith College for their fifteenth reunion. What she found was that many of these promising young women were now leading lives that they found unfulfilling, their skill set from college vastly underused in their new lives as housewives. Friedan began interviewing other suburban housewives, curious as to why so many of these bright, healthy, college-educated women were unhappy with their lives even though they were living the so-called American dream. They had the house, the husband, the kids, the comforts of modern life, and yet they were plagued by a frustration that was hard to describe, a frustration that Friedan began calling "the problem with no name." This issue became the catalyst for her book *The Feminine Mystique*, which is credited with ushering in second wave feminism.

None of the women Friedan interviewed could quite put a finger on what was wrong, especially since they were living in a culture which told them that lives as housewives and mothers were supposed to be a foolproof path to womanly fulfillment. Friedan noted that when these housewives described the problem with no name, it simply looked as if they were recounting their days. "Her day is fragmented as she rushes from dishwasher to washing machine to telephone to dryer to station wagon to supermarket, and delivers Johnny to the Little League field, takes Janey to dancing class, gets the lawnmower fixed and meets the 6:45. She can never spend more than 15 minutes on any one thing; she has no time to read books, only magazines; even if she had time, she has lost the power to concentrate," Friedan writes.[1] She argues throughout the book that the feminine mystique—the culturally perpetuated ideal that all women can and should find fulfillment through being a mother, wife, and housekeeper—was producing the problem with no name. Women were throwing themselves into housework and kids' extra-curriculars, chasing after the fulfillment the feminine mystique promised them, yet they were still suffering what appeared to be a massive identity crisis. They felt as if they didn't exist, or as if they only existed as wives and mothers and had no shred of their own identity to lean on. These housewives didn't know how to voice their frustrations, finding that "if she tried to tell her husband, he didn't understand what she was talking about. She did not really understand it herself."[2] It sounds, honestly, much like the problem I experienced when I tried to explain to Rob the frustration of being the household and emotional manager for the family. I didn't have the vocabulary to directly address all the emotional labor I was doing, and I couldn't yet see how it was about so much more than the physical work of domestic chores. Perhaps it was part of the same frustration felt by women in the early 1960s: emotional labor masked by the far more obvious culprit of the feminine mystique.

Friedan never puts a name to the "problem with no name," though I suspect emotional labor is a large part of it. She only offers the solution that women need more stake in the world, that they need to become more fully human by using their skills and intelligence to experience fulfillment. While she did note that "basic decisions as to the upbringing of children, interior decoration, menu-planning, budget, education, and recreation do involve intelligence,"[3] she didn't spend much time delving into the emotional and mental toll of such work. She assumed, and other family-and-household experts agreed, that the bulk of women's time was being taken up by the physical domestic upkeep of the home. If anything, emotional labor was the bright spot in a housewife's life, because it used her skill set and capacities in a way that waxing the floors did not. In any case, it wasn't deeply explored as a more important path forward was forged. *The Feminine Mystique* is largely regarded as the book that "started it all" for the women's liberation movement of the 1960s and 1970s. Women began to step more fully into their lives, into their careers, into choosing family when it worked for them, and the old feminine mystique was thought to be mostly vanquished. Women had arrived.

Yet part of the original problem with no name—the frustration born from emotional labor—persists decades later. If we were underchallenged and underwhelmed in our roles before, we are now challenged and overwhelmed to an equally stifling degree. We did not, in fact, vanquish the old feminine mystique. The ideal of the perfect housewife and mother may have changed a little over the years, but these roles did not disappear or become obsolete. Instead they were added to the new roles women were taking on in the world and in their careers.

Women now have to contend with the male standard of the ideal worker in the workplace but are still expected to fill the role of the devoted housewife and mother in a fraction of the time. All of the emotional labor, most of the physical domestic labor, and whatever other competing priorities we have outside the home are all our domain. And instead of fully recognizing the overwhelm and demanding change, we have bought into the new feminine mystique that women can and should want to "have it all." We can have the family and the career. We can live up to both the ideal mother and ideal worker. In theory, it sounds like the best of both worlds, but in reality, having it all means having entirely too much on your plate. Comedian Michelle Wolf pokes fun at the ridiculous notion of having it all in her HBO special "Nice Lady" (2017), saying that having it all is a terrible idea—no one leaves an all-you-can-eat buffet feeling like they made the best choice. She also makes a strong point that men don't have this same yearning to "have it all," or even have a lot. "Men don't try to have it all," she says. "They're just like 'I've got a job and a sandwich, I'm good. My wife says if I behave for another year she'll give me a section of the garage where I can sit. . . . I love sitting.'" It's a joke but also an obvious contrast to the woman who feels pressured to have it all—the type of woman who wouldn't dream of sitting and relaxing—because there is no one there to pick up the slack while she takes a breather. Men don't try to have it all, not only because they don't feel the same societal pressure for perfection, but also because women enable them to "have it all" without working for it. Men can have the successful career and the beautiful family, because women make it possible through their emotional labor. They don't have to yearn for "it all" because it isn't missing. That balance is taken care of for them, by women who are striving to have it all.

Which is why when Darla Halyk wrote a lengthy Facebook post about her frustration with emotional labor, she confronted the misguided notion of "having it all" head-on. "The mentality of women 'doing it all' is not only propagated by males, but females alike," Halyk writes. "When I was growing up, both of my parents had full-time jobs. Careers, in fact. My mother was a successful bank manager, yet when she arrived home she still cooked and plated my father's meal. No one did that for her. She did it with love, she wanted to take care of him, but regularly she was exhausted. No less tired than any man in her position. Yet she was assumed to come home and feed her family. Expected to clean 'her' house, only to be told she wasn't worthy of the title on the deed. Sometimes she wanted her husband to take care of her. To plate her meal, or fold her laundry. Most times she wanted to be respected and appreciated. This I know because I have lived my mother's life. I have catered to the men I love. Not with regret, but often with repugnance."[4] She describes her life growing up with gendered chores and a mother who took on all of the emotional labor while her father got to be the "fun" parent. She saw firsthand the effect it had on her mother, who was exhausted and depleted, a feeling Halyk now relates to all too well. She ends her observation with the statement "I can do it all, but all of it is not mine to do." The post went viral within days, with *Metro* running an article that called Halyk's statement a new feminist anthem.[5] Yes, we can do it all, but we need to question whether we should *want* to do it all—indeed, if all of it is really our responsibility to do.

Why is it always my responsibility to notice when something needs to be done? To delegate out that work or do it myself? Why is it on me to have the conversation over and over again, to bring up emotional labor and to guide my husband through it—an act that takes a great deal of emotion work as is? The fact that women continue to perform emotional labor without any semblance of balance or reciprocation translates into a deep gender inequality that is hard to shake, and we cannot change this dynamic alone. We need to start sharing this load with our partners, to have them truly understand what sharing emotional labor means, in order to move forward. We need them to become the partners—the feminist allies—they claim to be, by taking up the work themselves. How much of an ally is he, really, if I am constantly doing all the heavy lifting for him?

I don't expect my husband to intrinsically understand emotional labor in the same way that I do, but I do expect him to put in the work to understand it better, to ask the right questions when he is unsure, to *want* to work on it for himself, for our relationship, for our kids and their future relationships. If he does not, the constant demand for my emotional labor is going to keep us running in circles forever. We'll never make any real progress until men willingly take on the role of allies and begin talking to one another about how to make emotional labor work in their relationships. Because if there is one thing that comes from the cultural demand for women to shoulder the bulk of emotional labor, it is this: it maintains the status quo. It keeps men comfortable and maintains both their position of power and their passivity. They can make small changes here and there—do a bit more laundry, take on dinner duty, or wash the dishes—but all of the emotional effort still lands on us. We have to do the patient explaining, use the soft tone of voice and the cushioned responses. We have to make sure we don't come across as ungrateful for the efforts they *have* put forth. We have to make sure our partners do not feel attacked or blamed. While women have made great strides in the past century, the work remains incomplete in large part because of the demand for our emotional labor. It is why so many women, even today, hesitate to label themselves feminists: they are worried about the connotation more than the actual meaning of the word.

I was one of those girls in high school. I so strongly associated feminism with the image of angry women who hated men and family and high heels and pie baking (and I made a mean apple pie) that I actively denounced feminism. I reveled in being told I "wasn't like other girls," in being one of the elite "cool girls," an attitude born of deeply internalized misogyny. I didn't realize that feminism was simply the belief that men and women should have equal rights—that it was a pursuit of giving women the right to choose the life that works for them rather than abandoning and denouncing anyone who wore makeup or wanted to stay at home with their children. Yet even after I understood the simple universality of the concept, it was still a difficult label to adopt. I found that bringing up any subject that might fall under the umbrella of feminism required careful navigation and lots of emotional labor, especially when men were involved in the conversation. I felt as if I constantly had to prove that I wasn't an "angry feminist," that I didn't fall into the group that refuses to do emotional labor and is therefore ignored. For my voice to even be considered, I first had to prove that I was quiet enough, calm enough, reasonable enough to be considered.

The demand for this type of emotional labor inhibits and undermines change, because the arbiters of what is "reasonable" in these interactions are those whose power is being challenged, namely men. Our anger threatens to upend the status quo, so we are not allowed it. Our opinions cannot be too forthright, too extreme, because they interfere with the comfort of others. This demand for emotional labor stretches far outside the feminist movement as well, enforcing the status quo in a similar but even more intense fashion in more marginalized groups, where there are tiers of power to consider—and many more voices telling them to stay quiet, calm, and conscious of who holds normative culture in their hands.

As a disabled person, Alaina Leary finds herself regularly performing emotional labor in all of her relationships. She lives with Ehlers-Danlos syndrome, a genetic connective tissue disorder that she explains as endlessly complex; because there's connective tissue all over the body, EDS can impact multiple parts of the body. She is hypermobile ("Meaning I can naturally extend body parts beyond what people typically can, but this is painful and causes my joints to erode"). She has poor coordination, and she bruises and injures easily. She has chronic pain and exhaustion similar to the brain fog and fatigue experienced by people with chronic fatigue syndrome or fibromyalgia. Her muscle tone is poor, and her posture suffers. And when she isn't explaining all this to inquisitive journalists, friends, and family, she is doing an immense amount of emotional labor to avoid bringing attention to her disability. "There's so much labor that even goes into making plans and hanging out with someone,"

Leary says. "It's usually on me to figure out if an event or activity will be accessible for me and a lot of behind-the-scenes detective work (scoping out an event location, seeing how far it is from public transit, seeing if there's a parking lot nearby, trying to figure out how much standing it'll require or how long lines will be, checking out info on seating, looking up detailed menus for anything involving food). I have to do preparation up until the point we hang out."[6] If she doesn't plan everything perfectly, she risks being in severe pain or not being able to make it. All the while she works to shield those around her from all the emotional labor she is performing to simply move through the world. "I don't want to make the hangout all about me and what I'm dealing with or my accessibility needs." She finds herself worrying about being "too much work," a problem she says stems from internalized ableism. She knows she lives in a world that isn't set up to accommodate her or even be accessible to her, so she feels the need to overcompensate, to prove herself in a way, and she relies on her advanced emotional labor skills to do so. "Even my best, most well-intentioned nondisabled friends don't understand what my life is like," she tells me. It's her job to educate, to perform the emotional labor, so that her friends, family, strangers, the whole status quo can remain comfortable while she does all the heavy lifting.

Naseem Jamnia also finds themself doing a great deal of emotional labor, simply for existing as someone who is trans nonbinary, especially with their family. "I am always deciding not to explain or get into it with my family, because experience has taught me that it's just not worth it," they say.[7] Their mother occasionally tries to understand, but Jamnia says that when it comes right down to it, she just doesn't *want* to understand. "I tried to talk to her about using my pronouns—in Persian, there aren't gendered pronouns to begin with—and she just fell back on how she's always mixing up pronouns anyway, so why does it matter?" says Jamnia. "It matters because she thinks of me as her daughter, as a girl, and I think of myself as her child, as someone agender." Being trans nonbinary is easier with friends and strangers, Jamnia says, because it doesn't come with the same history or expectations that are present in their family dynamic. While everyone deals with emotional labor expectations within families, dealing with gender identity and the nonbinary pushes it to an entirely different level. Jamnia says that it has become increasingly frustrating as they have become conscious of how much emotional labor they put forth every time they are with their parents. "I am totally drained whenever I'm with them. I'm aware of what I'm doing, of the energy I'm putting in that they don't even appreciate or realize. Our relationship stays the same because I do what I can to not rock it. It's less exhausting for me to keep things the same than it is to try and change them."

Asking for equality, pointing out obvious racism and other injustices, cannot be done without exhaustive emotional labor, not to mention negative impacts. In fact, one woman I interviewed for this book asked that her name be redacted because even talking about the emotional labor she endures as a black woman might hurt her as she builds her platform and business. A mother of three, she explains that emotional labor impacts her far beyond her personal relationships or the management of her home and family—it is woven into almost every area of her life. She regularly has to field or engage with ignorant and downright racist questions, or faces white people's expectation that she will do the work of educating them on topics of race, when they are fully capable of educating themselves. She is expected to be able to absorb microaggressions and act as if nothing is wrong. She is subject to having her lived experience denied by those around her ("Are you sure that racist thing that you're describing was really about race?") and again is expected to self-regulate and pretend as if this isn't enraging.

She tells me about a recent excursion to a state park with her kids and elderly mother. They had stopped for a few minutes while her mother stayed in the car. When she returned to the car, an officer approached her about not paying the eight-dollar parking fee. She pointed out that the car was still running, her mother had stayed with the vehicle, and they had only been stopped there for a few minutes. It was a valid argument, one I'm sure I would have made in the same situation, but I would never have to expect what came next: the officer put her hand on her gun. The story itself is horrifying enough, but then she told a white friend, who sided with the cop, insisting the interaction had nothing to do with race and denying her reality as oversensitivity.

"I have a million stories like this," she tells me. "Eventually you stop telling these stories. You get tired of having to justify whether or not it was racist. If I looked like my neighbor, if I was a little white lady with glasses, with three little kids and my seventy-five-year-old mom in my minivan at 11:00 a.m. at a state park . . . if I was blond, she would not put her hand on her gun."[8] It's frustrating, she says, when you live in a world where people deny your life experience to maintain their comfortable view of the world.

Emotional labor isn't just demanded of her either. It is even worse when she sees how a certain deference is demanded of her children. She recalls going to a community pool in a white neighborhood and having to explicitly tell her kids that they couldn't be too loud or too rowdy—basically, too kid-like. "You can't be a kid in the way that a white kid gets to be a kid," she says. "Not only do I change my own behavior, but I change the behavior of my kids. I'm limiting them." She has to. She says this comes from her understanding that when white people talk about behavior in relation to black children, it is coded language that justifies racism. She and her kids have to make sure that everyone, especially the white people around them, is as comfortable as possible. "At the end of the day you walk through life in a body that people have deemed threatening. Just your very existence is threatening." She has to put forth inordinate amounts of emotional labor to counteract that, and that labor is rarely, if ever, recognized or valued.

While the emotional labor of women of color is regularly abused, their experience with increased emotional labor poises them to lead change and problem-solve with absolute excellence. Rhiannon Childs is a community organizer for the Women's March in Ohio and works on the advocacy side of Planned Parenthood. Currently she is preparing to take some of her organizational expertise into her local elections while advocating for women's reproductive rights. She is, without a doubt, excellent at what she does, despite only moving into advocacy work after the 2016 election. She previously worked for twenty years in the healthcare field and has a military background serving in the US Air Force. She tells me she was spurred to reshape her career by the election, which resurfaced so much of the misogyny and racism she had experienced in the military. She noted that the sexism stuck out in a big way on the campaign trail. "It was startling to see that one of the most powerful women in the world [Hillary Clinton] was experiencing some of the same things I had been silent about and hadn't confronted myself when I was young."[9] Now she is done being silent. She cannot let her daughter grow up in a world that tells her she isn't good enough, cannot let her relive her own experiences.

Childs's success can surely be attributed to a variety of life experiences and personality traits, but her experience with emotional labor as a black woman is chief among them. She knows how to bring light to the blind spots of those around her. She has a deep understanding of how to empathize with others, as well as what she describes as an almost innate ability to be considerate and understand other people. "That is why we so often say to trust and center black women," Childs says. "We face so many different layers of oppression. We understand. We understand most perspectives and adversities. We don't miss anything. We don't miss a voice. As an organizer, when I'm planning something I think of *everyone*. There's nothing that gets past me. There are so many things we think of that other folks do not." The world may demand her emotional labor regardless, but using those skills in her advocacy work is a way Childs says she is able to reclaim her time.

Emotional labor is more than just a problem within personal relationship dynamics about who leaves their socks on the floor and who picks them up. The fact that emotional labor was ignored by the women's movement has not simply hindered progress in the domestic sphere. We have held back equality on all fronts by not addressing emotional labor and the power imbalance created when one side is expected to do all the work, including the work their allies *should* be doing themselves. Childs tells me that while she often does the emotional labor of educating others, there comes a point where she cannot do the work for them. "I can't bring you all the years that you've missed. I can't keep going backward. You need to catch up. You need to learn and educate yourself," she says. It's a point Ijeoma Oluo makes often in her book *So You Want to Talk About Race*, repeating that if you still don't "get it" and have no black friends willing to offer up more of their emotional labor to you, then google it. Your question has likely been answered plenty of times already. It reminds me of the many women whose partners didn't want to read my *Harper's Bazaar* article, instead asking for it to be explained to them: "Give me the easy-to-process *Reader's Digest* version of the problem." That's not how change happens. We should be able to expect more from our allies; we need to be free from hand-holding every once in a while so we can use both hands to work toward progress ourselves. Taking on your own share of the load is not easy, but for progress, for equality across all planes, it is worth it. It is necessary.

So where do we begin? How do we address emotional labor and the inequality it upholds when one side or one person is expected to carry all of it in perpetuity? I cannot answer that definitively, but I find myself drawn again to Betty Friedan, who decided to revisit what was left behind in her later book, *The Second Stage*. "The questions have to be asked personally before they become political,"

Friedan writes. "Both men and women have to confront the conflict between their human needs—for love, for family, for meaning in work and purpose in life—and the demand of the workplace (and, I would add, world) as it is structured today."[10] She looks back to the home, back to the parts of the feminine mystique that were left intact as the feminist movement fought forward, and sees the ways in which the personal must change before the political is accomplished. The reforms in our culture, in our politics, in our workplaces are all necessary and actionable, but only if we are first willing to make the necessary changes at the personal level. We need to learn to value this work in our own lives. We must start with our children, our partners, ourselves to create change.

PART III

THE PATH FORWARD

CHAPTER 11

NATURE VERSUS NURTURE
Are Women Really Just Better at This Stuff?

My husband and I grew up together. I mean that both literally and figuratively. We met in high school and have spent all of our formative teen and adult years together. Where this could have led to a relationship that struggled to mature, we went in the opposite direction and grew during that metamorphosing time, comfortably transitioning into what I consider an incredibly progressive relationship. While nurturing a relationship from childhood to adulthood comes with its fair share of struggles, there are also distinct advantages. One of the most notable advantages is that we had the unique opportunity to build our relationship roles from the ground up. We didn't have time alone to get stuck in our ways, and we hadn't been molded by past relationships (unless we want to count my *very* serious middle school boyfriend, with whom I made out on school field trips, held hands in the hallway, and never went on an actual outside-of-school-functions date). Rob and I brought neither baggage nor knowledge to our relationship, a combination both thrilling and precarious. We knew very early on that building a life together would require flexibility and openness to compromise, and when I look back over the fourteen years since we first met, I'd say we've rolled with the punches fairly well. We have been together for the building of a home and a life, from the one-bedroom apartment we leased during college to the large family home we own now, complete with three kids, a dog, and a cat. We did all of that side by side, openly communicating along the way. Or at least I thought so. But why, then, were we still caught up in an imbalance in how we ran our home, how we took responsibility, how we spoke to each other? Where did the divide in emotional labor come from, and why did it take me so long to really see it?

When I talk to my girlfriends, my mom, my aunts, my grandmother, all of them understand exactly what I'm talking about, while my husband struggles to grasp it. Even those women who haven't previously heard the term *emotional labor* need only hear an example, like the frustration of telling your partner where a basic household item is kept as if he were another child in your household, and the light bulb immediately flickers on. *That's relationships. That's men. That's the patriarchy. That's life.* They aren't entirely wrong in these assessments. It *is* a part of heterosexual relationships, interacting with men, the patriarchy, life in general. But there's a specific frustration that arises from the careful self-regulation of feeling, management of emotions, and micromanagement of other people's lives that strikes a particular chord. *That*, I tell them, *is emotional labor.*

Every woman I know recognizes this work, but there is skepticism and downright disbelief when I suggest that the dynamic could ever change. "If I don't do it, it won't get done." I've heard this countless times from countless women, word for word. (I'm fairly certain I've said these words while venting with girlfriends too.) There is a deep distrust that even the best partners won't "get it," that they not only *won't* do what we do, but *can't* do what we do. There is this notion that even if men were willing to take up more emotional labor, they simply wouldn't understand how to—that we are hardwired so differently that there is no hope for balance. Both men and women are conditioned to believe this myth. *Women are just better at this stuff.*

I've looked at my own relationship and wondered at times if that is true. After growing up together, starting our relationship with as blank a slate as anyone could ever hope for, we still unwittingly fell into this pattern. Did I naturally take over because I was born better at this stuff? It seems a fair question to ask. After all, aren't I more naturally organized? Better at noticing what needs to be done? More attuned to the emotional needs of our children? Maybe not. When I ask Dr. Michele Ramsey how much of emotional labor is nature and how much is nurture, she's quick to respond that she thinks it's almost 100 percent nurture.

"Children understand gender roles by the age of three, both in terms of what they're 'supposed' to be doing and what they're not supposed to be doing. We know that from birth children comprehend a lot more than most people assume, and most children are exposed to a lot of media content (or to other children who've been exposed to a lot of media content) and so they learn the gender role stuff very early." She says some women will disagree, saying their toddler sons are "naturally" drawn to trucks while their daughters are drawn to dolls, but this is simply ignoring how early those gendered messages creep into their consciousness. Kids get these messages everywhere: family, friends, media, religion, education—it's inescapable. We model the behavior that is familiar to us, and all of us have grown up in a culture that tells us emotional labor is women's domain.

Pauline Campos is a first- and second-generation Afro-Latina American whose father was an immigrant and her mother US born but raised in Mexico. Growing up, emotional labor wasn't a concept she was consciously aware of. Women performing this role was simply the way it was. If she understood it at all, it was through the colloquialism "Si el esposo es la cabeza, la esposa es el cuello" (If the husband is the head, the wife is the neck). The saying pokes fun at the notion that men are in charge when women are the ones who really run the show. Yet if there was one thing the women in her family didn't control, it was the unquestionable gender roles they were expected to fill. The eldest of five girls, she recalls how she and her sisters were expected to wait on any man who came to the house. When a date would come to pick up Campos, one sister would get him chips and another would pour him a drink. "If he needed a refill, my dad would signal to one of my sisters like one of his customers at the restaurant he and my mother worked at to refill his water or pop or whatever it was he had been drinking while waiting for me to get ready."[1]

She says her father never once changed a diaper, and she had a baby on her own hip from the age of eight, often waking up her younger siblings and getting them ready for school to give her mother a break from the constant and exhausting work of running the home. "It's just how things are done," she tells me. Even now, she has trouble recognizing all the emotional labor she does in her own relationship with her husband. She says it takes putting on her "third-party goggles" to see the invisible labor that has become second nature because of the way she was raised. "I still find myself surprised when my husband steps in to clean or give me a break from parenting—like he's doing me a favor and not just being my partner in parenting," Campos says.

Most all of us, in big and small ways, have been conditioned to accept emotional labor as our lot in life. I watched my mother run our home, plan our meals and birthday parties, take us to doctors and dentists, send birthday and Christmas cards to every extended family member. I remember her being the one to lie in bed and listen to me talk at night. I remember her relentlessly trying to break through the emotional walls I put up as a teenager. I recall her ironing everyone's clothes, and helping her fold and put away everyone's laundry when I was old enough. I didn't notice the mental load she carried, but I knew she was the one to go to if I needed something, be it a misplaced sweater or a running list of snacks in the pantry. All of these small things were quietly absorbed, day after day, year after year. I looked to my mother for the type of behavior that would be expected of me in the world, and to my father for the type of behavior I could expect from a partner. In my dad I saw a man who shared in the domestic labor of the home, who brought home flowers "just because," who was always ready to be the "fun" parent, but who was never the one *in charge* of the emotional labor. My mother was the one running the show, giving direction, facilitating the fun without the recognition. I didn't notice these things outright, but I can't pretend they didn't inform the way I now run my home and family and relationship.

Yet there is so much of my upbringing that I have been able to undo. While I didn't have a particularly problematic childhood, I was raised to think that *feminist* was a dirty word and watched everyone around me tout traditional gender roles as the gospel. For the most part, however, my husband and I have been able to move past these stagnant roles and into a relationship that is markedly different than that of our parents, just as my parents had markedly different relationships than those they witnessed growing up. Yet emotional labor remains a constant from one generation to the next. Even when we talk about it with our partners, it doesn't seem to change. It's a constant we see in so many relationships across so many cultural and societal boundaries different than our own. This can lead to a sense of inevitability, a misapprehension that the division of emotional labor between men and women is somehow predestined, even biological. It can be hard to accept that culture could so entirely convince us that these are our natural roles without there being some truth to it. But the deeper we look, the clearer it becomes that in emotional labor, nurture trumps nature at every turn.

Initially, in researching and thinking about different part-nership models that might light a way out of the emotional labor quandary, I set out to look at matriarchies. But it quickly became evident that my logic was flawed. Flipping the script and focusing on cultures in which women run the show was not going to address the fundamental problem of imbalance; it would simply reverse the roles. Only an egalitarian structure would lend that critical insight about how the hell we get out of this mess. This led me to anthro-pologist Barry Hewlett's research on "the best dads in the world": the men of the Aka tribe.[2] The Aka Pygmy tribe consists of around twenty thousand people who live a hunter-gatherer lifestyle that isn't without gender but certainly bucks what we would think of as traditional gender roles. Hewlett found the Aka to be the most egal-itarian parents of any people he had ever studied. The roles of men and women are interchangeable both at home and on the hunt, with men slipping effortlessly into caregiving roles without micro-management of any kind, and women often outperforming the men when they go out to hunt. Everyone in the Aka tribe seems to know what needs to be done and how to do all of those jobs without being told. Even, perhaps especially, when it comes to parenting.

While we may be wedded to the idea that mothers or other fe-male allo-parents are the most natural nurturers for a child, the men of the Aka tribe turn the biological debate on its head in how they raise their children. Hewlett noticed during his stay with the Aka that male breastfeeding (or at least using the nipple for com-fort) was a completely normal way for men to comfort their babies when the mother was away. It wasn't unusual for men to gather for a "guys' night" and drink palm wine while cradling infants to their chests. Hewlett found that Aka fathers were within arm's reach of their children 47 percent of the time—more available to their children than any other fathers in the world. There is no stigma attached to men slipping into the role of primary caregiver, because there is no preconceived notion among the Aka that women should "naturally" assume that role. Intimacy between father and infant is the norm, just as intimacy between mother and infant is. Which begs the question of where we got our Western ideas about what is natural in the first place.

Indeed, when I ask most women about the emotion work that goes into their relationship with their children, they assume they have a slight edge over their partners. They have stronger intuition, a better ability to pick up on moods and disturbances. They are more attuned to their children's needs. They "naturally" have greater gentleness and compassion for those around them, or so they think. But science doesn't back up the biological claim to compassion or nurturing. Emma Seppala, science director of Stanford University's Center for Compassion and Altruism Research and Education, describes broad research finding that women and men have equal capacities for compassion but may express it differently because of the way they are socialized. "Compassion is natural and no gender differences have emerged across [various] studies," Seppala notes in an article for University of California–Berkeley's *Greater Good Magazine*. "While women's expression has culturally evolved to be expressed through nurturing and bonding behaviors, men's compassion has traditionally evolved to involve protective behaviors that helped ensure survival."[3] Men are socialized to associate masculinity with aggression, emotional suppression, protection, and breadwinning. Women are socialized to associate femininity with emotion work, caring, nurturing, child rearing, and deference. It's obvious, then, why emotional labor is much easier for women to bring into their lives and identity, even though men are equally capable. It's nurture. Not nature.

While certain cultures can show us proof of how harmoniously and naturally an egalitarian society can handle emotional labor, they don't show us how to implement such a model in our own lives. The Aka live outside of Western influences, free from the centuries of deeply ingrained conditioning we are all a part of, whether we want to be or not. Becoming aware of this conditioning is one thing, but reversing its effects is quite another. Yet there is one modern example we can look to for guidance: Iceland.

While many Nordic countries have become more egalitarian societies in recent decades, none have done so at quite the breakneck pace that Iceland has. It has been labeled the most feminist country in the world,[4] but it hasn't held that spot for long. In fact, it's only in the past decade that Iceland has truly turned from its macho Viking culture into the egalitarian utopia it's touted as today. Though there is obviously some contention as to whether they have feminism down to a science, it's hard to argue that there isn't something to learn from a country that boasts a low gender wage gap, the best working conditions for women, and a parliament where women currently hold 48 percent of seats alongside a female head of state. The country also has some of the most generous parental leave policies in the world, which both mothers and fathers take.

Much like the US, Iceland was hit especially hard in the global recession of 2008, and it was obvious to its leaders that government needed to change if Iceland was going to get back on its feet. But as Joanne Lipman notes in her book *That's What She Said*, there was a notable difference in the way each country dealt with the fallout. "In the U.S., the men who crashed the economy remained at their posts. In Iceland, the men were sent to jail. Women replaced them. Two of Iceland's three banks named women as their new presidents. The entire Icelandic government resigned, right up to the prime minister."[5] The wave of discontent following the economic crash spurred a large change in parliament as Iceland elected its first female prime minister, Jóhanna Sigurðardóttir, in 2009 (if you want to talk about someone skilled in emotional labor, Sigurðardóttir is both openly gay and a former flight attendant). She quickly went to work, implementing a quota of 40 percent for women on corporate boards. She made sure that spending on men and women in the country did not slip into an imbalance by implementing a new sector in the Finance Department called "gender budgeting," which ensured that all budgeting decisions were made with equal rights in mind. She helped ban strip clubs, introducing legislation she says was aimed at decreasing human trafficking, and legalized gay marriage during her time as prime minister. Her agenda was feminist, obviously, but she says tackling gender inequality would not be possible without the understanding of men. "[Men] have to realize that equal rights are not merely a 'women's issue,' they concern each and every family and the whole of society," Sigurðardóttir relayed in an interview with the Women in Parliaments team. "If a woman is treated badly in some way in the labour market, for example if she is being badly paid, her entire family suffers. If welfare-issues are not high up on the agenda, then it becomes a huge social problem that harms children, the aged, the disabled and, thus, most of society."[6]

Iceland steadily climbed up the ranks and has been sitting at the top of the World Economic Forum's best countries for women for ten years running. Though the country is now operating under a new prime minister, Katrín Jakobsdóttir, it is still making strides forward, recently implementing a law that makes it illegal for companies to pay men and women differently for the same job. If a company cannot demonstrate its fair wage practices, it faces fines of up to $500 per day.[7] Lipman, in her quest to figure out what makes Iceland the best place in the world for women, found that while all these statistics helped it rise to the top of the list, it was the notably different attitude of Icelandic men that really set the country apart. In fact, she found that most Icelanders *didn't* consider themselves part of a feminist or egalitarian utopia. Men didn't believe that women had made it to a place of equality, though they hoped to see that change. They also didn't see themselves as persecuted by the strongly feminist agenda of the past decade. Indeed, they viewed many American men as weak for this precise reason. By contrast, Icelandic men's machismo was intertwined with a commitment to equally shared power. Most men she spoke to felt confident in claiming the title of feminist, and it is this spirit of solidarity that seems to be catapulting the country forward. Men and women both want to see a more equal society, and both are ready and willing to fight to make that a reality.

It may be hard to imagine a political overhaul that could lead to the swift change in gender equality that Iceland has seen, but if we can shift our personal views—the false narratives that have long held us in this stagnant imbalance of emotional labor—it is possible that we could see such a change on the horizon. If both men and women can get over the notion that it is nature, not nurture, that holds us in these roles, we can come together to harness the power of emotional labor and make this valuable skill set work for us all. That means we as women need to stop tethering ourselves to the idea of our own natural superiority in emotional labor and accept that our partners may be able to acquire these skills just as well as we have, perhaps better in certain areas. We need to trust that they will succeed instead of assuming that the moment we let something go and hand it over it will end in disaster. It probably will. It almost definitely will, but with enough time and space and perspective, it will get better. For this to happen, men need to stop feigning incompetence and learn these skills, even if it doesn't come "naturally." They need to recognize the work their partners are doing and rise to the occasion. We all need to own emotional labor as our responsibility as adults, regardless of our gender. That's how we fix this imbalance.

I know, because I am now living on what I consider to be "the other side." My husband and I have balanced emotional labor in a way that works for us most of the time. Right now, I am writing this while he is at his parents' house with all three of our children. When I returned home from the library after spending the morning on research, he had packed them up all on his own. The laundry was folded and put away. The dishes were done. The house was tidy. Moreover, I did not micromanage any of this. I didn't leave him a to-do list. I didn't send any reminders of what the kids would need for the day. I didn't have a hand in any of it. I didn't have to ask.

Perhaps I should rewind for a moment here to fill in the gap from how I last described my husband: taking off for a bike ride leaving the house looking as if a food-toy-clothing volcano had erupted inside it without his knowledge. Or perhaps I should rewind even further, back to how before that day, I had thought he was changing his ways—because he was. It was me who wasn't. He *had* been taking over more and more during my increasingly hectic workdays. He was figuring out how to get the kids to school and make sure everyone was fed and doing laundry and cleaning here and there. He may not have had the same masterful system of organization that I had, but he was managing. He was getting things done. I was grateful, but if I'm honest, I was also often frustrated that things were not being done my way. Some things simply weren't getting done. His emotional labor efforts seemed sporadic, and I couldn't figure out why. So I tried talking with him—at him, really—about it. I followed up my thank-yous with suggestions of how he could do better. I tried implementing new systems for us every other week, from rotating chore charts to author Tiffany Dufu's "Management Excel List." He didn't seem particularly interested, and my frustration grew. I assume his did too, even though he kept a tight lock on it.

The truth was, I was constantly looking for ways to change his behavior and perspective, because I assumed that his behavior was the heart of our problem. I assumed that women were really the only ones who had these skills and that I could effectively teach these skills to offset some of my mental and emotional workload. If nurture was the reason for the seemingly stark differences between our aptitudes for emotional labor, that simply meant I would have to "nurture" my husband to become more like me. To think like me and problem-solve like me and do emotional labor just like me. After all, I was so damn good at it. I had such an efficient system when I was the sole person in charge. It wasn't like he could make up for three decades of different socialization all on his own, right?

Basically, I oscillated between two modes: figuring out ways to get Rob to adhere to my expectations and waiting for him to fail. I needed to "fix" us before this book came out or else I would be a total fraud. I asked him how he thought we could make it work, and he said he didn't know. He couldn't figure out what he wasn't getting. So I would implement a new social experiment–type solution and then wait for the inevitable disaster. That second part, the expectation of failure I thought was invisible to him, wasn't. He could feel my lack of confidence in his ability to take up emotional labor in the same way I did. He knew, at some level, he was right in saying that what he did would never be enough. Because unless he did everything in the exact same way that I did, I was always going to find something to pick at, something to do over. I would always give some indicator that he didn't have what it takes.

He was changing everything he felt was under his control—I could see that. I thought I was changing too, by having these open conversations with him and coming up with these solutions, but I wasn't. I was trying to change our relationship dynamic, our balance of emotional labor, without ever having to change anything about myself. I hadn't yet looked into the way my own perspective, my own ideas, were holding us back. I hadn't examined my own biases: that I would always be better at emotional labor, that my way of caring and nurturing was always—naturally—the best, *that Rob couldn't master these skills on his own.*

It seems unreal to me now that I was subconsciously holding on to that last one. I had done the research. I knew that men were more than capable of taking on emotional labor without someone holding their hand through the process. Single dads rise to the occasion when there is no partner to do the job for them. John Adams, the dad blogger from the UK, was never instructed by his wife on how to best manage their home. No one socialized Vincent Ambo, the Norwegian software engineer, to take on the emotional labor in his same-sex household. What made these men so different, so much more capable than my husband? Maybe it was as simple as not being married to me. They didn't have anyone looking over their shoulder, waiting for them to fail. They had the time and space to develop competency in emotional labor, something I had been withholding from Rob without a second thought.

I would like to be able to say that I came to this epiphany and then changed my ways, but that wouldn't be anything close to the truth. The truth is I got overwhelmed and couldn't keep up with the micromanagement. I locked myself in my office, wrote for whole days, read for whole nights, and didn't have the energy for once to care about the way the laundry was folded. I wasn't doling out tips on ways Rob could be more efficient with the running of the home while I was in work mode. I ignored the mess. I let it all go to hell. It was hard and it sucked and I was angry a lot of the time. I spent many days feeling like a fraud, wondering if I would get to the end of my book and have to make some half-hearted attempt to pretend that what I was writing had any worth whatsoever. I felt like I was pretending that something had changed when I was every bit as frustrated as when I began.

Then one day, I came out of the office and noticed the house was clean. Not sort of clean. Not clean in a way that is good for Rob but doesn't meet my standards. It was clean and under control. Not perfect, but damn good. Then I realized that I hadn't done any meal planning for over a week, that today was grocery shopping day, and that we would have to scramble to put something together for dinner. I opened the fridge to gauge the ingredients left, only to realize that the shopping had been done without me making a list or a plan. I began walking myself backward through the past week: When was the last time I did laundry? Checked homework?

Reminded him to pack bedding for preschool? Asked for something to be done? I couldn't remember. Rob had fully taken over when I wasn't around. In fact, he had taken over *because* I wasn't around— and I don't simply mean out of necessity.

The truth is that my constant meddling and unintentional undercutting were exactly the things holding Rob back from taking on emotional labor with confidence. He knew I didn't have full faith in him, and that mistrust led to self-doubt. He needed to figure things out on his own, to have the time and space to come to grips with his competency, before he could feel confident in taking on the emotional labor that had so long been my domain. He had to see for himself that he could rise to the challenge without me waiting in the eaves, silently (or not so silently) judging his performance against my decades of experience. Now that he knows his capabilities, we can work from a place of equality and decide what balance works best for us. That balance neither looks nor feels the way I thought it would, but that is because I am still working to change my own behavior and perspective. Though it is hard to fight my internal biases, I do not believe that women naturally have a skill set that is superior to men.

Men are also subject to the same false message women perpetuate: that men just don't get it. They could never do what we do. They don't have the natural skills necessary to take over emotional labor. When you hear about your incompetence often enough, it starts to sound true. Most men would never suggest that their partner's way is anything but the best, because they know that's a recipe for disaster. They know they are stepping onto our turf, and we rarely give up any of our ground to let them explore emotional labor for themselves. So many men fall into the mind-set that they are naturally bad at these things. They were born bad at folding laundry and noticing when the paper towels are running low. They were born clueless about cooking and cleaning and calendar keeping. They were born forgetful of dates and immune to buying birthday cards. These are character traits, true incompetencies, completely unchangeable. Lies, lies, lies.

We were all born with a similar aptitude for emotional labor, but only half of us were trained in it as we grew up. That's not for nothing, and it's why, on the surface, it appears that women are naturally better at emotional labor than men. But these skills can be learned and honed. So long as we are willing to work together to create space for one another's progress, there is no reason why men can't rise up and claim emotional labor as their territory as well. They may, with time and practice, find the value in it as it opens a new side of the world to them, a new human wholeness that can help them feel more connected to their lives.

Despite my endless frustrations, I have seen how worthwhile it is to lean into the issue of emotional labor rather than ignore it. While Rob and I are nowhere near a perfect balance, we are getting ever closer to that moving mark—not only because of my knowledge of emotional labor but also because of his perspective and understanding. I think we will find our best solution if we are willing to blend the power that both men and women bring to the table. It is a conversation we must invite men into if we are going to truly find and change our blind spots and root frustrations. But we must first get rid of the power imbalance, our assumptions, and our biases, so we are listening to one another from a place of equality. And we need to know how to talk about it.

CHAPTER 12

TALKING ABOUT EMOTIONAL LABOR

Joni Edelman is no stranger to the concept of emotional labor. The editor-in-chief of the feminist pop-culture site Ravishly has written on the subject multiple times, rehashing the frustrating details of being the person in charge of emotional labor in her home: What it looks like day to day. What it looks like during the holidays. What it looks like, god forbid, when she emerges after being debilitated by the flu for weeks. She tells me of the all-too-familiar feeling of lying in bed, fever-ridden and barely able to move, wondering about things like who will clean out the refrigerator and who is going to make the appointment for the dog to go to the vet (answer: her, when she's well enough to stand). Illness doesn't simply put stress on her body; it puts stress on her mind, heaping dread on top of an already unsavory situation. She says this is a stark contrast to her husband's experience when he is sick. He lies in bed and gets to actually rest and recover. He knows he will be taken care of, and that everything else will be taken care of too, without even giving it a passing thought. He doesn't have to worry about a mountain of tasks that will be waiting for him when he is well again. That's because tasks don't exist for him unless he is asked to do them. He fears getting sick only because it is uncomfortable. She fears getting sick because it means more work. Their experiences are so fundamentally different that it makes talking about emotional labor difficult, even seemingly impossible. When I ask her what her conversations about emotional labor look like, she's quick to respond: "I'm frustrated. He's defensive. Almost without fail."[1]

She says there are two things that most often contribute to the stalemate. First, he feels like he does a lot (compared to other men, mind you, not compared to her). Second, he feels like if she needs the "help" that badly, she should simply ask him to do more. That's the one that always makes her furious, because he doesn't understand that asking is work. It's actually a huge part of the work. Cue the fighting.

The emotional labor that goes into working through moments like these rather than shoving the problem aside for another time is intense. For all our cultural conversations about men being less emotional and more levelheaded, women usually have to do a whole lot of tiptoeing around men's feelings while trying to get our point across. Bringing up the emotional labor you have put into a task gets immediately translated into an attack on your partner for not pulling his weight. It's judgy, shamy, bitchy. It often leads men to a knee-jerk reaction of jumping on the defensive, listing all the things of value they do and implying that you are ungrateful for bringing up any unfair division of emotional and mental labor. Too many men believe there is a strict dichotomy between being a "good" partner and being a partner who has room for improvement, even though these two truths can (and do) live side by side.

Or you may hit the brick wall of "I don't know what you're talking about." The concept is foreign and tricky for many men to grasp, because it has never directly affected them. Instead of exploring this new notion of emotional labor, they want to deal with the fight we're having here and now. The fight about the blue Rubbermaid storage bin left in the closet. The fight about always having to be the one to arrange for childcare and after-school activities. The fight about how to load the dishwasher. The fight about things that seem stupid and small because one person is looking at the big picture and the other is homed in on the last straw. Avoiding the snags of "But I do so much" or "I don't know what you're talking about" takes time and effort. It's often easier, in the moment, to say, "Why bother?" Having the conversation is frustrating. Not having the conversation is frustrating. It comes down to choosing your poison. Either keep plugging away with the emotional labor that overwhelmed you in the first place or take on the emotional labor of having a conversation with your partner, which may or may not land you right back where you started.

Women tend to fall into a vicious circle when it comes to talking about emotional labor. We get overwhelmed and finally bring it up by asking for help. Then we get tired of asking, because delegating is a managerial job that requires a lot of brainpower. And we must also pay close attention to *how* we ask for help, always keeping a sunny disposition and taking into account the emotional state of the person we are interacting with; it's often easier to just do things ourselves. So we start taking on everything until we reach the next breaking point, and then we have another frustrating fight over emotional labor—somehow never reaching the root of the problem. Ad nauseam.

We have to find a way to disrupt the cycle—to get through the conversation with clarity, so we can continue moving forward together instead of circling around back to the start. Talking about emotional labor takes emotional labor, but the only other option is keeping things the way they are now. The overwhelm we feel from taking on all of the emotional labor is not going away unless we consciously work to change the balance in our relationships. It's a challenge, to be sure, but one that we are perfectly poised to deal with. After all, we've been practicing for this our whole damn lives.

It's also worth considering that for many men it's simply an awareness problem. Lots of men strive for equitable relationships, but we simply haven't had the language to talk about this problem before. This subject is an intrinsic part of my experience as a woman but still incredibly foreign to my husband, because he's never had to do this kind of work or acknowledge it. He was raised with a vastly different set of expectations when it comes to emotional labor, and in many ways I have reinforced those expectations throughout the thirteen years we've been together. I never disrupted the system, never delved into the problem of emotional labor myself. Learning this stuff from scratch as an adult isn't easy—nor is it easy to explain to someone who has never experienced it. I think that is why we so often hit snags in the conversation about emotional labor. We are approaching the conversation from two fundamentally different places: intimate knowledge on one side, unintentional ignorance on the other.

When I had the meltdown in our closet on Mother's Day, crying over a storage tub that needed to be put away, I didn't do a great job articulating my problem with emotional labor. I blamed Rob for not getting it right, as if he were purposefully burdening me with all the emotional labor in our relationship, when in truth he had no idea what I was talking about. Of course, there was progress too. I finally put into words that I didn't want to have to ask Rob for help anymore. Putting that particular frustration into words was life-giving.

While that moment of clarity was a game changer for me, it was not exactly the same for Rob. I hadn't cushioned the conversation with gratitude for all the things he was doing, and what he heard was "You are not doing enough." So naturally he wanted to point out all the tasks he performed. He got up in the night with our toddler. He was currently scrubbing the bathroom. He did the dishes every night. He completed any chore I asked him to do. He never complained when I went out with my girlfriends, always held down the fort and took care of the kids. He would even take them out into the world to run errands from time to time when I needed (and asked) him to. Why on earth wouldn't that be enough?

When I look back at that argument, I can see clearly that we were talking about two completely different things: physical labor on one hand, emotional labor on the other.

When we had both calmed down, we came back to the conversation. I tried to explain the mental load and why delegating was such a big deal. I tried to explain how the mental and physical work of running our home and our lives compounded in such an exhausting manner. I wanted a partner with equal initiative. I couldn't continue to delegate and pretend that we were maintaining an egalitarian, progressive relationship. Divvying up the household chores when I still had to remind him to do his share was not enough. That still left all of the emotional labor as my responsibility, and *that*, I told him, was what needed to change.

He still didn't totally get it, but like I've said, he's a good partner and he *wanted* to get it. So he gave me the help I was asking for. Little did I know, but I was still asking for the wrong thing—still missing the mark in a big way.

Why We Need to Stop Asking for Help

Monisha, a mother of two, tells me a story that is intimately familiar. The stress of her day-to-day emotional labor is tough enough on its own, but it compounds to the extreme when she takes on the invisible elf-work of the holiday season. She describes to me the process of ordering family Christmas cards and all the boxes that must be checked. First, there's choosing the perfect picture, sifting through family photos to find the one that is just right—everyone smiling, looking at the camera, flattering angles, or at least as close as you can get to that ideal. Then the actual card must be chosen. For some it can't be too religious, or too silly, or too this, or too that. The address book has to be updated, and you must carefully consider who may need to be added to the list from the previous year. You have to track name changes, address changes, divorces, deaths. Then there is the actual sending of the cards. The envelope licking. The stamps and address stickers to be bought. The little bits of personalized writing required in each card. It's an exhausting process, and the task is only one relatively small blip on the Christmas radar.

She also describes the holiday shopping and considering what *everyone* wants—not just her own two daughters or her side of the family, but also her husband's side of the family and their kids. What should we give the mail carrier and teachers and neighbors? What gifts should be from Santa? What gifts should be from the parents? If we're spending Christmas away from home, how do we transport Santa's gifts? Both sets of grandparents come to her to ask what the kids want for Christmas and what she and her husband would like, and perhaps she could throw in some ideas for other nieces and nephews and daughters-in-law while she's at it. Monisha says this often leaves her in the difficult position of giving away her best gift ideas and having to start brainstorming again from scratch.

"This ends up equating to literally hours of thoughtfulness," she says. "Thoughts about what other people want or need or would like, and then giving it all away."[2]

She delegates some gift wrapping to her husband, plans holiday get-togethers with the help of the other sisters-in-law. But my goodness, she could really use some more help. I can't help but laugh when she tells me all of this. It sounds exactly like my life up to this point. I ask her if she (like me) is also the "decoration organizer" who knows where every last nostalgia piece must be displayed for the season, with a system for putting everything away at the end of the holidays.

"Naturally," she says.

The harried holiday mother is a role I know all too well. (I also have the added joy of planning my son's mid-December birthday, as well as planning for my nephew's and dad's Christmas birthdays.) For the most part, I enjoy a lot of the holiday magic making. It's joyful work. I want to do it. But I've also long wanted a partner who would help me with this work. Just a little help. Why couldn't we make that work?

It only recently dawned on me that this sentiment was exactly why our conversations kept going in circles, making things better for a little while and then reverting back to baseline after a few weeks. I would tell Rob I needed *help*. I would even tell him that I needed him to help without me asking. Then he would think of ways to help me. He would work on noticing the things I usually handled as a way to lighten my load. He packed for our day trip to the pumpkin patch. He did a full load of laundry. He called his mom to babysit when we needed her. He asked me for a list and did the grocery shopping. He would do really well for a while, but when I started to seem less stressed, he'd step off the gas. He only helped when it looked like I needed help. And a lot of the time, I didn't look like I needed anything. I am so used to doing this work all on my own that I create the illusion of being 100 percent fine with being in charge of all the emotional labor, even when I'm not.

The root of the problem was that I was asking for the wrong thing. The truth is that I don't need "help"—I need full partnership. There is a difference between the two. Helping means "this is not my job." Helping means "I am doing you a favor." Helping means "this is your responsibility." Helping implies that the helper is going above and beyond, while the responsible party is falling behind. Why is only one of us responsible for our shared life? Full partnership, on the other hand, means not having to delegate and micromanage. It also means significantly shifting our perspective on who is expected to do what—who is expected to be in charge. It means turning away from the idea of help entirely and taking on responsibility in an even manner. It means dismantling the hierarchy in the home, even when I desire that control, because what we need more than my perfect system is for us to be on even ground. We need to be clear about what we are asking when we initiate the conversation about emotional labor, because "help" isn't it. "Help" is a bandage on a broken bone. We need a total reset. And that doesn't just mean changing our partners' perspectives; it means changing our own too.

I wrote in my *Harper's Bazaar* article that I wanted a partner with equal initiative. It was true in a sense. What I didn't write was the extended version of that truth: I wanted a partner with equal initiative to do everything exactly like me, someone who would take my strident standards and execute them step-by-step in the manner I had grown accustomed to. I wanted more of a compliant assistant than anything else. That was the "ideal" solution, because it didn't require that I deal with my own issues—those of perfectionism, control, subtle biases, and social conditioning.

Asking for full partnership instead of "help" means both parties have to work. But that doesn't mean simply meeting halfway in completing the physical tasks that keep everything running smoothly. It's challenging the notion that our way is the best way. It's facing the biases and half-truths we believe in—like our partners being incompetent without our step-by-step guidance, or the myth that we are born with an organizational gene and a need for clean countertops (I'm still hesitant to fully discard that one, but I'm working on it). We have to look for our blind spots, to accept them when they come into the light. We have to work to change ourselves. It's only fair if we expect our partners to do the same.

Start with the Big Picture

On a cold March morning, long before Mother's Day, I opened the curtains in my bedroom and looked out into our backyard. A familiar resentment flooded my system as I pulled on my coat and boots and stepped out onto the frosty grass, iPhone in hand, to take pictures of poop. There were mounds of it everywhere. Fifteen frosty Labrador dumps to be exact, and I angrily took pictures of all of them. My fingers were numb, but my hot rage kept me going. I took a panoramic photo of the poop-laden yard. I started taking close-ups of each one. Yes, I was wasting a lot of time, considering that all of this poop needed to be cleaned up before the babysitter arrived. No, that didn't stop me. Thankfully the photos took too long to load, and the text message I had planned on assaulting my husband with so early in the morning never arrived. It wasn't one of my proudest moments. And it really wasn't a great way to bring up emotional labor.

The point I was hoping to make (in a very aggressive manner) was that I needed Rob to notice things like this. He had spent the whole previous afternoon in the backyard tuning up his mountain bike, and I had assumed he had taken care of this job. The point was supposed to be that I should be able to make that assumption. He should notice the obvious things that need to be done without me telling him to do them. He should take that initiative.

When he arrived home later, I went the slightly less aggressive route of telling him I needed a heads-up if he wasn't going to do the dishes or clean up the dog poop before the babysitter comes in the morning. He knew what I meant was: you need to do these things, damn it. He went straight on the defensive. He forgot this one thing, this one time. Why didn't I just ask him to do it if it needed to be done? Why was everything he did never enough? *Why do I need to ask you to do everything? How does pointing out this problem negate all the other things you do? How is that even relevant? Why am I even trying to have this conversation again?*

It's hard not to get stuck in the weeds when we're approaching the conversation about emotional labor, because it is almost always triggered by something small. The dishes that were left in the sink overnight. The RSVP that never got answered, despite your "nagging" reminders. The mess you came home to after going on a business trip. There are a million small things to pick apart. A million small problems to be solved. Put your clothes in the hamper. Stop leaving the cap off the toothpaste. Call your sister on her birthday. Don't make me remind you to do everything. Make your own appointments. Put them on the calendar. Don't wait for me every time the baby needs a diaper change. You can feed him too. Take the initiative. Do this. Don't do that. Maybe men aren't so far off base when they come away from conversations about emotional labor feeling attacked.

Whether we mean to or not, talking about emotional labor can often come off as a personal attack in our partner's point of view. Even when we're being careful with our words and tone, as we so often are, we are still talking about what *they* need to change. What *they* are doing to cause this. What *they* could do better. However, when we try to pull the conversation away from the details and into the broader context of emotional labor, our partners often lose the thread. They don't see the connections that we see. They don't understand what we're talking about.

When we're talking about the big picture in this context, we're usually focusing on the interconnected ways emotional labor affects us in our relationships and lives. That's hard for many men to understand because they've never experienced it. They don't see how emotional labor drains our personal resources—our time, our mental energy, our emotional resilience—in a way that not only prevents us from leading the fullest version of our lives but in fact enables our partners to cruise through their lives at our expense. Instead they see our resentment and assume it is simply tied to them forgetting a minor detail: the dishes, the vet appointment, a single ingredient or two at the store. They don't see our emotional labor as a whole—as we do. To them there is no clear connection between sorting the mail and keeping the calendar and doing the laundry and making the shopping list, but we see the party invite that we need to open immediately and make sure to RSVP and put it on the calendar, then ensure everyone has the right clothes ready and the gift and card are bought in time. One task leads to an avalanche of other tasks that need to be done, because we put each task into a broader context, whereas men often compartmentalize each single task as unrelated to any other. They don't see why we're overwhelmed by the mental load. They don't see why their behavior needs to change. They don't see why this is such a big deal.

It's not that the concept of emotional labor is too big for them to understand, but perhaps we're not putting it into a big enough context. If we want to see change, we need to look at an even bigger picture before we bring it back to the personal. This is a cultural problem that requires cultural change, and men can and should help us lead that change.

When things finally started to shift in our relationship, it wasn't because I had hammered home the importance of keeping the kitchen table cleared. It was because we had finally had a few real and productive conversations about emotional labor, ones that didn't revolve around the minutiae of everyday frustrations. We had finally started to talk about how this imbalance didn't start with either of us doing something (or many things) wrong. It started with the way we were each raised, the cultural expectations we had absorbed, the subtle societal messages we hadn't realized were working against us. Viewing our imbalance as part of a larger cultural problem resolved the issue of personal blame and allowed us to each examine the baggage we were bringing to the table. Now we can slowly unpack each piece, thereby ensuring we don't pass it on to our children.

In looking at the big picture, our kids were the biggest part that my husband was instantly able to wrap his head around—and looking toward our kids' futures can also be a better way to talk about emotional labor now. When I say, "Let's change this dynamic for our kids," it takes on a larger purpose than making my life easier or making Rob a "better" partner—though these are also worthy purposes. Without kids, our reason for changing the imbalance of emotional labor would be first and foremost the health and happiness of ourselves and our relationship. These things matter greatly, but I can't deny that the accountability of parenthood makes it easier to check ourselves, because we know our behavior is shaping our children's understanding of the world. We are role models for our kids, and we want to model the kind of behavior that will make them all successful, happy, well-adjusted adults. I want both my sons and my daughter to have the skills of emotional labor. I want them all to have partners who are truly equal, who understand them and work with them to create a life that makes them both feel fulfilled. I don't want my son's eventual partner to be the one reminding him to call me on my birthday. I don't want my daughter to feel like it's her job to delegate all the housework to her partner. Or vice versa. I want them to live in true partnerships, and I want them to know what that looks like. And if they decide not to partner, I want them to have the independent and vital skills of emotional labor for themselves. I want them to live the fullest versions of their lives, and I want them to learn how from us.

Looking at the big picture helped open new doors to communication, so we no longer keep stubbornly fighting in the same place. We are starting to recognize our patterns and learn from them. It doesn't mean it's all smooth, effortless progress. We still struggle. We still get frustrated. But more importantly, we still move forward. Starting with the big picture helps us both better understand the small stuff without getting stuck on it. We can talk about shared standards because we know our standards differ as a result of the culture we were raised in. We can grow because we've explored the roots of our problem.

C hanging the way we talk about emotional labor can lead to progress, but it's important to keep in mind that in the end, we can only change ourselves. This is why we so vitally need men to be active participants in this conversation, to be fully invested by bringing their perspective and their solutions to the problem as well. For men who want to be allies, who want to get to a truly equal partnership, who want to understand and address emotional labor: I'm glad you're here. We need you if we're going to have any hope of changing the cultural tide.

But also, can we have a little chat real quick?

There are so many good men I know who want to be a part of the solution, and because of those good intentions, they really don't want to be cast as part of the problem. The culture is the problem, not the individual, right? Yet at some point, each of us also needs to take personal responsibility for how we've contributed to a culture that devalues emotional labor and then places the bulk of it on the backs of women. Whether you meant to or not, whether you intended to or not, you're a part of the problem by default. That doesn't make you a bad guy or an asshole. We're all products of our culture and the way we were raised. We all have our blind spots. However, we also all have the potential to challenge our internal biases and deeply ingrained habits. We're all capable of change. And the change we need from men first and foremost is a willingness to really see us and hear us when we tell you how emotional labor is affecting our lives. We need you to give us the space to talk about emotional labor without demanding more emotional labor from us. Now more than ever, impact is going to count so much more than intention.

We aren't having this conversation because we want to be nags. We're talking about emotional labor because we believe you can help us change the culture. If we didn't believe that, we'd keep talking about it among ourselves, and we'd keep getting nowhere fast. We need men to understand emotional labor, to understand our perspective, and to help us work toward a balance that will be better for everyone. This is not a one-and-done conversation; rather it must become a dialogue where we can talk about each other's blind spots without jumping on the defensive—where we can bring deeper understanding to each other's experiences and work toward a more satisfying relationship.

I am no longer talking with my husband about emotional labor only as an act of desperation, delivered when I have finally reached the end of my rope. I am continuing the conversation with him as an act of faith. I am trusting him with my story, trusting that he will see me and value me and understand my lived reality better. I am trusting that he will be strong enough, vulnerable enough, to share his truths with me, and bring me to a deeper understanding of his lived experiences as well—because I know our actions stem not only from our love for one another but from our understanding of one another as well.

CHAPTER 13

CREATING A CULTURE OF AWARENESS

I can't do this anymore," I said.

I had just snapped at one of the kids for some small infraction and could feel explosive anger roiling inside me. I was *done*. It was a feeling I had known before. It was a feeling I would know again.

"Can't do what?" Rob asked me.

"I don't know." I looked around, noticing all the things he clearly didn't see. The mess piled up on the kitchen table. The kids getting into a fight I'd soon have to resolve. The mental to-do list that stretched to eternity. "All of it," I said.

His reaction was part frustration, part panic. Was our marriage in trouble? Was I getting a late round of postpartum depression? Was I upset that we had moved? Was I regretting my whole life in some sort of early midlife crisis?

No. No. No. No, not really. I kept grasping for words, but I didn't have the language to describe it. I had so much to express but an inadequate vocabulary with which to do so. And the silence was obviously making Rob jump to more and more worst-case scenarios. So I settled on a half-hearted explanation that made me feel frustrated for even bringing it up.

"I'm just overwhelmed, I guess. It was a hard day."

It wasn't even true. The day hadn't been that hard—not harder than normal, at least. The only thing that was different was that on this day, I had reached the end of my patience, another moment of sheer overwhelm knowing that "all of it" was going to be on my plate forever. How was I supposed to put that into words my husband would understand? I didn't have an answer. I was unaware of the term *emotional labor*. Unaware of the term *mental load*. Unaware that my situation was not at all unique—that, in fact, this was one of the most universal frustrations women feel the world over.

I am aware now. And I am not alone. We are collectively coming into a space of cultural awareness surrounding emotional labor, coming into a space of understanding where we can start working toward change. We now have the language to put emotional labor into words. The concept is no longer an abstract frustration. It is no longer a problem with no name. We can see it clearly from the minutiae to the big picture—the crescendo of overwhelm that has defined so much of our lives. We can see the value we bring into the world through our emotional labor. We can see the points of frustration that diminish reward: the mental exhaustion, the invisibility, the constancy of this work. And already, there are many of us who are seeing progress by virtue of being able to see emotional labor for what it is.

Brigid Schulte writes extensively about how the cultural landscape shapes personal dynamics in her book, *Overwhelmed: Work, Love, and Play When No One Has the Time*. She tells me the whole point of her book really is to show us the water we're all swimming in so we can make better decisions both individually and culturally. While the term *emotional labor* had not yet evolved into the comprehensive term it is today at the time when she was writing her book, her research made it possible for both her and her husband to examine their roles in regard to emotional labor—and to realize that he was capable of making summer camp arrangements for the kids and that she could have him take the kids to the dentist without feeling like a bad mother. "It's better now because we have a language where we can talk about it," Schulte tells me. "Whereas before we would always get stuck. I would get mad at him, he would get defensive, and we would get stuck there. Now we're sharing this part of our life."[1] They're both aware.

Much of our cultural awareness up to this point has focused on what emotional labor entails, but to more fully comprehend what serves us and what does not, we must look beneath the surface to see the root of the imbalance. We are still holding on to many half-truths and myths about emotional labor that are keeping us in a stalemate with our partners. If we look at the issues with emotional labor only on the surface, we are going to be treating symptoms without getting to the source of our pain. This is where the work is not just on men to step up to learn and adapt, but for women to dig deep and understand our own ingrained issues with emotional labor as well. There are behaviors and thought patterns we need to change within ourselves. Change starts, as always, from within.

I had to realize that my social conditioning set me up to perform emotional labor in a very specific way: the "best" way. This way strives not only for the comfort of those around me but also for an unattainable perfection. It envisions an existence so streamlined that I will someday break the barrier and feel freedom *because* of my emotional labor. If my calendar system were perfect, our busy family schedule wouldn't be a source of stress. If I found the best possible way to plan and prep meals, I'd never be frustrated by the question of what is for dinner. If I stuck to the perfect cleaning schedule, it would hardly take any time or energy to keep things spotless. If my home were perfectly organized, there would be no suffering. The problem is that perfectionism never delivers on these promises; it just adds more emotional labor to our plates.

Much of my adult life has been a constant, exhausting pursuit of the best possible solution to the mental load and emotional labor. I delve into the research offered in parenting books and blogs to help me cope with my children's emotional plights. I make time for date nights and downtime to keep my marriage healthy. I read so many articles on minimalism and home organization I could probably teach a college-level course on how to declutter a closet. I track my time in thirty-minute increments to maximize my productivity (seriously, the spreadsheets I could show you . . .). I yell at my phone to remind myself of random to-dos while I'm driving. I am always trying to find that sweet spot where all this effort will pay off in perfect peace. As author Gretchen Rubin puts it, I'm looking for outer order to lead to an inner calm.[2] Effortless emotional labor: I'm beginning to realize that perhaps the final destination doesn't exist.

This isn't to say that the way I perform emotional labor has no logical or aesthetic purpose. My intricate systems of organization, my approach to conflict management, my strident standards were all honed to ensure that those around me were happy and comfortable. But that's not the whole truth. I honed them in this particular way because I've been striving to meet an impossible standard— sold to me by the same system that told me all the emotional labor should land on me in the first place. My aspirational life and the way it manifests in my emotional labor isn't an internal drive. I'm motivated by the cultural idea that women are meant to be perfect and that anything less than perfect makes me less than worthy. So I keep reaching and reaching for perfect, and I get better and better at emotional labor. But just because my method works and works well doesn't mean it is the best and only way.

Rob was able to figure out a way to keep everyone happy and comfortable, without any guidance from me, when I gave him the space to do so. He did so without striving for perfection, without second-guessing himself, without wondering if his way was the best way. His standards are not my standards, because he has not been taught to expect domestic perfection from himself. He approached emotional labor without any baggage: good enough was good enough. While we still struggled to find a happy medium in our standards of cleanliness and timeliness, after watching him take the lead I was ready to reevaluate which of my standards were objectively best for us and which were products of my perfectionism.

I had to give up a deep-seated belief that my way was always the best way; otherwise I couldn't have the real conversation we needed to have about emotional labor—the conversation that goes beyond our personal relationship and into the cultural discussion of why we were stuck in this pattern. The conversation that seeks understanding rather than "winning" the fight. We both took on the roles that were presented to us, the roles that made sense to us because of the culture we were raised in. We cannot create a new culture without first understanding the one we aim to leave behind.

The culture that women need to shed isn't the one that devalues emotional labor. I think it goes without saying that we'd readily accept having our emotional labor praised and valued. It's more on men to change that side of the equation. What women need to abandon is our perfectionist striving, which leads to control issues and a false narrative that no one else could do what we do. It's a narrative that undermines and infantilizes men, preventing them from ever trying to do more than offer "help." We need to realize that our issues run so much deeper than a desire for control, because we obviously struggle with the push and pull of wanting less control, then taking it all back against our better judgment. We want our partners to take on more emotional labor, but we hesitate and thwart ourselves, because their way isn't our way. It isn't perfect. It never will be.

Our partners could do what we do, given enough time and practice. What we do is exhausting, yes, but it isn't impossible to learn. Given step-by-step instructions, perhaps a quick glance at my thirty-minute time-log spreadsheets, Rob could definitely do exactly what I do. There's a reason he doesn't want to, though, and it has nothing to do with laziness or incompetence. The degree to which I perform emotional labor doesn't make sense to him. It only makes sense to me because I'm still stuck believing that my worth is tied to things like putting a well-balanced meal on the table or never losing my temper with my kids or keeping my closet well organized. He takes note of what is necessary, while I take note of everything. When I go on a "noticing" bender, where one task leads to another, then another, then another, I'm like a woman possessed. I get angry that Rob is sitting on the couch not noticing things like the dusty floorboards or a few small specks of toothpaste on the bathroom mirror. I act as if him relaxing for any amount of time were a personal affront meant to infuriate me. Look at all the things I'm doing! Look at all the things I still have to do! I'm angry not only because he isn't caught up in the minutiae, but because I cannot seem to free myself from it even when I want to. I can't sit on the couch and read while there is a pile of laundry to be folded. I struggle to feel like I've had an accomplished day at work if the house is a mess. These are feelings I have to change if I want to better prioritize my use of emotional labor.

We need to become aware of our impulse to take over, an impulse still driven by a culture that encourages us to "have it all" and do it all. We need to challenge the notion that our way is best, that we are inherently better at emotional labor, in order to allow room for change to occur. When we know better, we can do better— and knowing the root causes of why we keep such a stronghold over emotional labor is key to understanding how to do better. We've helped create this imbalance, and we are thus perfectly poised to dismantle it. But we cannot do it alone.

Just as women need to stop comparing themselves to the impossible standard of "having it all," men need to stop using comparison as an excuse for not changing. For most progressive men, it is easy to look around and feel superior about how they are good feminist partners. But are they? Are they going above and beyond "helping out" and taking full and equal responsibility in a life that has, up to this point, been paved by the work of a partner? I can already hear the rebuttal, "But I do a lot!" and I'm going to have to ask, "But do you really?" Do you go above and beyond physical labor? Do you do things without being asked? Do you notice all the things your partner does for you, for your kids, for your extended family, for friends? Do you give as much praise as you get? Do you do a lot compared to other men, or do you do a lot compared to your partner?

Progress is not perfection, and coasting barely above the crap heap of mediocre dudes doesn't make you a feminist hero. Yes, it is terrible that some other dads you know refuse to "babysit" their own kids. No, that doesn't mean you are beyond rebuke or improvement.

I will admit that the bar for fatherhood and partnership has been raised considerably for men in progressive relationships in recent years. I am lucky to be married to a man who consistently rises to the challenge. Yet for all the high hurdles he clears, he still fumbles over the relatively low bar set for emotional labor. So what gives? What internal myths and biases are keeping men from stepping up and owning emotional labor on a par with their partners?

The most obvious, most pervasive internalized myth I encounter, even in my own relationship, is men's belief that emotional labor is not their job. Anything that falls in the domestic realm, in fact, is not their job. It's their partner's job. They're just helping. Even the best and most self-aware men fall prey to this line of thinking because it is so commonplace in our culture. The workload men have started to take on in the home has increased considerably from one generation to the next, but the way this work is framed in men's minds hasn't progressed at the same rate. Men feel like exceptional partners for doing less work than their partners, because they subconsciously believe it is not theirs to do.

This subtle misogyny isn't always intentional, but it is always harmful, and I don't just mean for women. When Rob was laid off from his job, it quickly became apparent that taking on a larger portion of the emotional labor was frustrating for him. It wasn't simply that it was hard to learn these skills as an adult (though that was certainly part of it). He struggled to feel like his days held meaning, because the work he was doing was, well, mine. *Women's work. Not real work. Not valuable work.* When he told me that it felt like the work he was doing wasn't important, I bristled.

"You're doing exactly what I did for years. You're raising our kids and keeping everything running. That's like saying that all those years I spent at home doing the job you're doing now wasn't worth anything."

"You know that's not what I mean."

"I know, but what's the difference? Why should it be enough for me but not for you?"

"I feel like it's not enough, because I should be working."

"But we don't need the money."

"But I need to work."

He didn't really know how to put it into words, but I could see what he meant. Being a stay-at-home parent and doing all the emotional labor in the home could be enough for me because that followed the cultural script we both knew by heart. I also had the freedom to work, whether from home or in an office, and that too fell within the realm of cultural acceptability (so long as I still took on all the emotional labor, of course). For him, there was only one path, the path of the ideal worker. He was supposed to be the provider, the breadwinner, the protector, because this was the role laid out for him from childhood. Paid work had always defined his worth, and without that anchor he felt adrift in a world where he struggled to determine his self-worth. This was his home. These were his kids. But this life had been made by me. It felt like it was never meant to be fully his.

He needed to move past the notion that emotional labor was not his job and not his place so he could feel confident taking on the new role. He then had to wrestle with the value of emotional labor. This work is not paid, for one, and it is often invisible. He wasn't used to doing a job that wasn't rife with praise and recognition. He wasn't used to taking on responsibility in our relationship instead of offering help and expecting gratitude. Owning this role is not easy for him, because it goes against the grain of what we've been taught about masculine and feminine worth. It takes a secure sense of self to step outside of these prescribed roles and do the job society says is not yours to do.

The current model of masculinity does not value emotional labor, but it's time to change that. "It seems strange," Betty Friedan writes in *The Second Stage*, "to suggest that there is a new American frontier, a new adventure for men, in this new struggle for wholeness, for openness to feeling, for living and sharing life on equal terms with women, taking equal responsibility for children— the human liberation that began with the women's movement. Unlike the American hero of the past, the new frontier liberates men from the isolating silence of that lonely cowboy."[3] It is time for men to be part of the emotional labor conversation, to find their place and their skills in this domain, not only for their partners' sakes but for their own as well. There is value to be gained for men by stepping more fully into their lives rather than simply accepting the life being built around them.

Todd Adams, cohost of the *Zen Parenting* podcast, realized this when he came back from a weekend trip with some college buddies twelve years ago. When his wife, Cathy, asked about his trip, he realized he had little of substance to share. They golfed and drank beer but hadn't had a single conversation of depth during the whole weekend. He could say the guys were doing "awesome" but couldn't describe what was actually going on in their lives in any detail. He wasn't connecting with them in a meaningful way.

"Cathy will go out with her girlfriends, and two hours later she'll know everything that's going on in their lives," he says.[4] He realized in that moment that he was missing out and wanted a little more of the connection he saw his wife having, so he began a men's group where guys could meet up and have an authentic conversation once a month, a mission that eventually blossomed into a full-fledged men's coaching career.

Now, as a certified life coach, he focuses his work on supporting men in discovering healthy masculinity and developing more conscious relationships. What this means, quite often, is working on being vulnerable enough to participate in their relationships and lives in a more fulfilling way. This is why, he says, the men in his groups are the exception and not the rule. Being vulnerable is something men are taught is a weakness rather than a strength. It takes a lot of confidence and bravery to admit otherwise, but the payoff is so worth it.

"I tell my guys: This is your life. These are your kids. This is your wife. Step up and forget about your fragile male ego," says Adams. Why would you want to keep living on the surface level of your life when there is so much more to enjoy?

Men who are not engaged in emotional labor are in many ways living the same sort of half-life that women were living just a few decades ago. Without a stake in the domestic realm, without emotional connection, without responsibility for their own lives, their worth hinges solely on their career status—what else holds value for them in the world as we know it? Because society tells them it is not their place to be vulnerable and connected, many men don't pursue the well-rounded life that women strive for. They settle for less where it matters most, because we tell men that their worth is linked not to who they are but to what they do.

If men and women can both push back against the cultural messages we have been conditioned to believe our whole lives, we can all start living more fully, connecting more fully, understanding each other more completely. It is not merely an issue of women needing to off-load their burden onto someone else. In fact, I don't know a single woman who truly wants to let go of all her emotional labor. We don't want to become disconnected from that part of our lives. Emotional labor is too vital for us to simply let it go. What we need is for more people to understand and harness the power of emotional labor. What we need are partners who fully comprehend our lives, who can offer solidarity from a place of understanding, and who are equally engaged and responsible for co-creating a life with us.

CHAPTER 14

OWNING OUR WORTH

Before I get to Stephanie Butler's home in Reno, Nevada, she sends me a text warning me that she might not be presentable, and I assure her it is all right. Butler has a newborn, and I remember well those early, unkempt days of motherhood (to be honest, I still have a lot of those days, even with the baby stage behind me). When I arrive, she is sitting on the couch feeding her three-week-old son. I ask her how the transition from one to two kids is going, and she tells me he is not the easiest baby. He keeps spitting up, and she has no clean bras left. She and her husband bought two baby swings, one for upstairs and one for downstairs, and he won't go to sleep in either. He fusses if he's not being held. He wants to eat all the time. This period right here is round-the-clock labor and sleep deprivation, especially with their four-year-old daughter to contend with as well. She settles into the couch, relieved when he falls asleep on her chest after his feeding. She had been worried he would fuss throughout our conversation, and she would have to console him the whole time. Even though her husband would be back soon, this work would still fall to her.

"My husband's not a baby person," she tells me.[1]

He is looking forward to having them develop into more fully functional human beings so he can interact and play with them, but for now he focuses his energy on other aspects of their household. He doesn't come home and play with the kids or take the baby from her arms to give her a break. Instead, according to Butler, he gives her balance in different ways. During my visit he returns to the house with a full load of groceries, putting them away in the fridge and going about his household responsibilities. He cooks and does a good deal of cleaning. She has never once done his laundry. (He was in the military and is incredibly particular about the way he likes his shirts folded.) While she does have to delegate certain things, like vacuuming and scrubbing the toilets, he takes care of the visible surface work without being asked. He notices, for the most part, when things need to be picked up and put away. He makes the bed. He cleans the kitchen. He tidies up as necessary. He is clearly not the husband who comes home, changes into sweatpants, and cracks open a cold beer, but he's also not the husband who takes over the emotionally heavy work of newborn care either. I don't know what to make of Butler's contentment with this arrangement.

Even as she reveals how their balance works, I can't help wanting to get back to the beginning of our conversation. My eyes must have widened like a deer in headlights when she told me her husband was mostly hands-off with their two kids. It took a lot of strength not to blurt out, "But how do you *live* like that?" The newborn period is a struggle even with a fully engaged and committed partner. If I hadn't had the opportunity to thrust our screaming infant into Rob's arms from time to time so I could go cry in the bathroom, I don't think I would have survived. Yet sitting here in front of me is a woman who is doing the feeding and soothing and constant holding, mostly on her own. Although Butler looks tired, there isn't a hint of resentment in her voice as she talks about her husband or about taking on the brunt of motherhood.

"It makes me feel valuable," she says. "The emotional labor I do makes me feel like I'm bringing something important to our relationship."

She tells me she sometimes thinks about what it might be like for him if she were to die. She knows without a doubt that the grief wouldn't be the only difficult part. Picking up the emotional labor she does would also be a serious burden. I wonder internally if perhaps that's not healthy. Shouldn't both partners know how to take on this work? Should we really wait for tragedy to strike before picking up these skills?

For her, taking on the bulk of kid time, even during these early years, is simply another way they each play to their own strengths. She *wants* to relieve him of this intensive time during parenting because she is better at engaging with their kids, better at being patient with them, better at caring for them in a nurturing way—no doubt virtues of her Christian upbringing. She also wants him to keep doing the budget and dealing with the insurance and doing his own laundry. She's not looking to balance out the emotional labor in her relationship. She accepts, indeed seems to enjoy, that this is the way it is. The way it *should be*, at least for them.

She tells me about the first night in the hospital with their new baby boy: how she was up and down with him all night, how hard it was to get him to latch, how she had to be by his side every time the nurses came to unswaddle him and take his vitals, how even in those first few hours the work was overwhelming. At one point during the exhausting marathon of being in the recovery room, her husband turned to her and said, "You're such a good mom." She says it's moments like that, moments when she feels the deep and unshakable value of her emotional labor, that make it all worthwhile. And though these moments of visibility are few and far between, she never forgets that the work she is doing is important. That's why, she says, emotional labor doesn't bother her.

Butler's interview rolled around in the back of my mind for months. I couldn't make sense of it. How could it simply not be an issue for her? She clearly saw the work she was doing. She felt the exhaustion. But she didn't harbor resentment. She didn't *want* change. How could she not be bothered by having a partner who didn't pick up his share of the emotional labor—who didn't even pick up the baby most days?

Eventually I would find that Butler wasn't alone in this type of "emotional labor doesn't bother me" attitude. When I came across Jennifer Lois's research, I saw that there were women who, though obviously burdened with more than their share of emotional labor, didn't seem to find it burdensome. In her book *Home Is Where the School Is: The Logic of Homeschooling and the Emotional Labor of Mothering*, she interviews dozens of home-schooling mothers, many of whom didn't see the need to rebalance the emotional labor in their relationships even though all of the emotional labor and domestic work landed on them. The reason, Lois explained, came from the intersection of Christian faith and tempered expectations. "The more conservative home-schooling mothers would be willing to accept that *this is my role as mom. This is my duty. This is what God wants me to do*," Lois tells me. "The Christian faith helped them manage their feelings of stress."[2] There was a feeling of purpose behind their emotional labor, and that, coupled with the unquestioned expectation that they would not receive help from their partners, allowed them to "manipulate their feelings" so that emotional labor did not weigh on them so heavily. I wonder if trying to find balance is something they never even think to do, or if they simply know it's not worth challenging, because they know their partners. For many women, Lois says, "if you define motherhood in a way that expects you're going to have an equal partner, then you're going to be disappointed."

I know she is right. I've heard from these women firsthand. For all the women who reached out to me to say that my words on emotional labor helped their partners understand their world, there were many other women who found that my words crystallized their feelings of isolation in their partnerships. Their husbands refused to read the article, just as they will refuse to read this book. What are we supposed to do when our partners won't change? How are we supposed to move forward when no one acknowledges our work but ourselves?

I kept coming back to these questions, plagued by the many stories of women whose husbands refused to recognize their emotional labor as real work. I thought about the 2015 MetaFilter thread on emotional labor, and how a whole section was filled to the brim with women lamenting the fact that they knew their partner would never read through those experiences, would never even attempt to understand them. We all have to start where we are, and it's important to acknowledge that not everyone will have the support of a partner who is willing and ready to enter into this conversation about emotional labor. So what is the answer? How can we find contentment in the face of imbalance? Must we manipulate our feelings to find peace? Do we have to let it all go? Is there a happy medium to be found when you see emotional labor for the work that it is and your partner does not?

I'm honestly not sure there is a true balance to be found when one partner refuses his share, but I do believe there is room for progress no matter what base we start from. Even those of us with partners unwilling to change can always change ourselves.

When I wrote my *Harper's Bazaar* piece, I wasn't looking for a "solution" to emotional labor or seeking to provide one. I simply wanted my emotional labor to be valued and validated. I wanted to feel seen. With every share, every "like," every woman who reached out to me, I received the connection and understanding I had been longing for. Then eventually I received the same at home, where it mattered most.

I wrote a follow-up article about the changes we made in our household regarding emotional labor—the way my husband was suddenly taking on tasks that had always been my jurisdiction, and was doing so *without me asking*. I nearly cried when I went to get dressed one morning and found my favorite pants folded and put away in the closet—pants that I had neither washed nor dried nor folded. I felt a surge of love upon finding that the nearly empty milk carton in the fridge had been replaced without my delegation. It wasn't that these tasks were burdensome—the physical relief was minimal. I had performed these jobs my entire life, and most of the time, they didn't weigh heavily on me.

What struck me wasn't the act itself but the fact that these tasks were no longer invisible to my husband. I knew, as he took on the planning and the noticing and the details that usually fell in my domain, that he was finally seeing me completely for the first time. He was gaining a new understanding of my life and priorities. Perhaps that was all I wanted from the start. I wanted to feel seen. I wanted to feel valuable. I wanted to know that the emotional labor I performed each day was *worth something*.

But what if I had a different type of husband—the kind who refused to acknowledge not only my emotional labor but the fact that this work exists at all? What if I wasn't a writer by trade who could heal the wound of wanting to be seen by putting my words out into the universe? How do we deal with emotional labor when we're the only ones who see it?

I found myself thinking, yet again, back to my interview with Stephanie Butler. Her perspective was formed from a very specific Christian worldview, but there was something to her words that I couldn't ignore. *Value.* She had talked about it time and again in our interview. Despite having a husband who didn't take on emotional labor, despite living in a world that doesn't acknowledge emotional labor as valuable work, she never lost sight of the deep value of her work. I have spent a whole book's worth of time arguing that emotional labor is valuable, that it should be valued by our partners and society and the larger culture, but there's another, more important part of the equation.

We have to start valuing emotional labor within ourselves.

When no one else acknowledges that this work is valuable, when the mental load remains invisible, when the work is thankless but still necessary, we have to find a way to pause and appreciate the emotional labor we are performing. We have to know with unshakable certainty that this work has worth, because if it didn't, we wouldn't be doing it. If this work were not keeping the world humming along—if it were not keeping our families knit together and our friendships strong and homes efficient and our children comforted—we would not be doing it. There exists the noxious but persistent idea that women waste their time worrying about things that don't matter. This couldn't be further from the truth. We all get stuck in the weeds sometimes, but by and large, we concern ourselves with the details because we know it makes the world around us better.

We perform emotional labor because we care, and the things we care about are important. That statement does not hinge on whether your partner remembers to make the vet appointment you asked him to or whether you married a man who changes every diaper or one who sits on the couch ignoring the smell of poop. The worth you bring to the table when you undertake emotional labor isn't tied to anyone else. See it and own it and value it.

Our emotional labor is an asset. It allows us to be deeply and fully engaged with our lives, with our home, with our kids, with our friends and family. Emotional labor goes beyond simply keeping things running; it keeps everything connected—from our social bonds to our systems of organization. Our skills in emotional labor allow us to see the big picture in every situation, to navigate the world in a way that helps us and the people we love feel grounded and secure. Emotional labor is not a burden to be shirked but rather a powerful skill set that can be harnessed to make our lives and the lives of those around us better.

Author and happiness expert Gretchen Rubin talks a lot about the intersection of happiness and emotional labor in her books as well as her podcast *Happier*. While many of the habit changes she discusses in *The Happiness Project* and *Happier at Home* revolve around taking on *more* emotional labor (celebrating holiday breakfasts, creating memento files for your children), nearly all of the habits she discusses involve reframing emotional labor so we can see the true value in it. She shows how performing emotional labor actually makes our lives better rather than weighing us down, because it gives us a deeper connection to our lives. Through her personal "happiness" experiments, she makes a compelling case for not only performing emotional labor but enjoying it. While not all of us may be keen to put more on our plates—like, say, sending out weekly group emails to family members or planning yearly vacations with our in-laws—for some of us that kin work can lead to deeper connections and, yes, deeper happiness. But before we start feeling bad about all the things we *should* be doing (and enjoying, no less), it's important to note that reframing isn't the key ingredient in Rubin's secret sauce. Seeing the value in the emotional labor we do is important, but having clarity on why we perform emotional labor is the key.

She identifies clarity as one of the primary strategies for habit formation in her book *Better Than Before*, saying that *clarity of values* and *clarity of action* are the two types of clarity that support making change. "The clearer I am about what I value, and what action I expect from myself—not what other people value, or expect from me—the more likely I am to stick to my habits," Rubin writes.[3] This advice applies not only to creating habit change but also to becoming clear on our priorities with emotional labor. So much of the emotional labor we perform is wrapped up in societal and cultural expectations. We're expected to pick up the slack for our partners. We're expected to keep our homes as clean as a 1950s housewife despite working full-time. We're expected to send out the Christmas cards, even when we don't care about them. We're expected to keep track of everyone's schedule instead of expecting independence and shared responsibility. We're expected to live up to impossible standards—and worse yet, we internalize these expectations, which don't make sense for us personally. We expect the impossible from ourselves without considering our true priorities. Valuing our emotional labor needs to include setting boundaries for it as well.

One way or another, this work is essential. You'll either crash from the sheer overwhelm or carve out time to get clear on your priorities. I'd personally suggest the latter. If you have too much emotional labor on your plate and your partner is unwilling to lean into the conversation, have the conversation with yourself. Ask yourself what parts truly serve you, and which do not. Which parts of your system are shaped around perfectionism, and which truly benefit you and the people around you? What do you want to drop? What would happen if you let go of these things? What do you want to prioritize? Where can your clarity of values and clarity of action meet so you can make the most of the emotional labor you put forth? None of us can do it all, but we can choose the things we want most and do those things well. You don't *have* to make dental appointments for your husband. You don't *have* to be everyone's constant reminder. Everyone's responsibilities do not have to become yours simply because you are the one who has grown up trained in emotional labor.

"Daring to set boundaries is about having the courage to love ourselves, even when we risk disappointing others," Brené Brown writes in an article for *O, The Oprah Magazine*.[4] That risk, especially when it comes to emotional labor, is very real. People are likely to be disappointed when they can no longer rely on you to keep their lives comfortable. Yet if you truly value your emotional labor, you'll need to be okay with a little bit of fallout and prioritize yourself anyway. It's not an act of spite: setting boundaries is not about punishing those who don't take on their share. Setting boundaries isn't about others at all. It's about you. It's about making sure that your time, mental space, and emotional energy are being spent in ways that align with your values and priorities. Emotional labor always serves a purpose, but it doesn't always serve you.

We must not only see the value of our emotional labor but show ourselves that we value it by setting strong boundaries and making sure we are performing emotional labor in a way that doesn't leave us feeling overwhelmed, undervalued, and used. This is, first and foremost, for our own health and well-being, but I also believe that valuing our own emotional labor can pave the way for change we didn't believe possible. Even if those around you don't see emotional labor as work, handing off that responsibility might change things. When others realize they cannot rely on you for their emotional labor needs, they will have to figure out their own priorities. They will have to either take on that work or live without that comfort. I'm not suggesting we do this as a vindictive way of saying, "I'll show you how much work emotional labor is." It's creating space so we can change the balance on our own terms.

We need to create space so that both men and women can experience the power and value of emotional labor. We may think that our micromanagement is an act of love, and it often is, but it also robs those we love of the opportunity to step fully into responsibility for their own lives. They need to create their own systems, their own connections, their own priorities instead of wandering through a life that has been created around them. We need to stop modeling martyrdom and start modeling boundaries—no longer allowing emotional labor to overwhelm us but rather harnessing those skills to make our lives more fulfilling. While we often think of emotional labor as purely serving others, we can use its skills to better care for ourselves as well. We can ask ourselves, "What would make me comfortable and happy?" just like we consciously and subconsciously do for those around us. Plan for relaxation, carve out time in the schedule for activities you enjoy, invest in relationships where you know you'll get as much emotional labor as you give. Plan the holiday party if it brings you joy and fosters connection (but maybe let go of some of the perfectionism if it stresses you out). We can prioritize the emotional labor we want to put forth and shed what doesn't serve us. We can do this not just in our personal lives but in the world as well. We can leverage the skill set of emotional labor in the workplace instead of letting the dominant culture tell us our way isn't best. Caring about the details gives us an edge. Delegation is our strong suit. Keeping everyone's comfort and happiness in mind as we view the big picture inspires innovation. If others can't or won't see the value in that, it is their loss, not ours. But for our part, let's lead into the future knowing the worth of our work—knowing exactly when and where emotional labor best serves us and those we love.

CHAPTER 15

FINDING BALANCE

As my work with the book picked up, my husband's job search hit a wall. He had spent hours upon hours applying for jobs, almost none of which were panning out as we headed into the holidays. It was time for the pendulum to swing into his corner, and I told him so in no uncertain terms. I was ready for a trading-places scenario—for once I was going to be the one who filled the role of ideal worker while he shouldered the emotional labor. I explained that having the house be a total disaster when I was working wasn't something that I could overlook or put out of my mind for a few hours. I couldn't write with a clear head if I knew a pile of unknown horrors was waiting for me on the kitchen table. It stressed me out knowing that once one shift ended, another was waiting for me. I also couldn't have him come talk over meal plans with me while I was in the middle of work, or ask any other questions about what to do next while I was on the clock. I needed him to do some real emotional labor—and that meant figuring it out without my guidance and delegation. It was a steep learning curve but one we both knew he was prepared to master.

He did exceptionally well taking on the brunt of emotional labor, as I've said before. Without my constant micromanaging, he was able to find his confidence and start feeling competent in this new role. I still asked if he had checked this or done that, but after a few weeks of realizing the answer was always "yes," I stopped worrying that he needed my guidance and focused on my work like I said I would. Rob became the only one checking homework and making sure school lunches got packed and meal plans were made and the kids were picking up their belongings (and he was picking up his own). He wrote all forty of our Christmas cards when I was too burned out to do them. He was the only one calling and texting his parents for most of the month. He reminded me of things that were on the calendar, even when it was on the wall a few feet from my desk. I hadn't planned on off-loading so much to him; it simply happened. I would end my work hours and fall onto the couch to read more research books, while Rob was the one making dinner and then cleaning up afterward.

Then I noticed one afternoon when I took my lunch break that he seemed really far off. He was there but not really there. I figured I knew what was wrong—that the job hunt was getting to him or he was suffering an identity crisis, but that wasn't at all what he described when I asked him what was wrong.

"I feel like there's something I need to be doing, something I've forgotten, and I can't figure out what it is."

He had sent our daughter to school with freshly laundered bedding for her cot, packed a lunch and snack for our son, done the laundry, and cleaned the house, and he had reached a lull in his day. There wasn't anything, at least not anything important, that he was forgetting. He was bogged down by the mental load, though, and couldn't seem to think straight. It was a feeling I knew well: the nagging sense that I couldn't sit down or relax for a moment because there was always *something* that needed to be done. It's the creeping anxiety that gnaws at you when you're the only one carrying the mental load for the family. You're afraid of something falling through the cracks, because you're so tapped out from trying to make sure nothing falls through the cracks. The anxiety wasn't a revelation to me, but the fact that it was happening to Rob and not me was eye-opening. This wasn't what I wanted for either of us. When I examined where we were at the moment, with me devoted to my work and nothing else, I also found myself feeling untethered to my life. When I was solely focused on working, letting everything else fall away, I was irritable and unhappy much of the time. There was a distinct emptiness when I wasn't tending to any emotional labor at all. My life no longer felt rounded and whole. Neither of us was living in a way that made us feel fulfilled.

"It takes trial and error," Betty Friedan writes in *The Second Stage*, "to work out the practicalities and the real tradeoffs, with men and women now sharing work and home responsibilities, instead of replacing the dreary realities of one with fantasies of the other."[1] In other words, it takes a lot of conscious effort to get past the fantasy that the grass is always greener on the other side and start tending the soil where we are. We have to figure out how to balance emotional labor through trial and error. We have to accept that we aren't going to get it right the first time no matter how clear we are in our intentions. I understood the lesson in theory but was still learning it firsthand.

Trial. Error. Back to the drawing board.

Letting go completely is tempting at times, certainly, and sometimes it can even be necessary, but it's not a great solution in the long run. It's simply trading one warped imbalance for another. When I reconnected with Karen Brody, the author of *Daring to Rest* who gave up emotional labor completely, she told me that eventually she did take some of it back—not because she had to but because she realized that there were parts of emotional labor she missed. She missed the connection with family and friends. She missed the satisfaction of helping co-create a life. Living a life when you have no part in making it is easy, but it isn't fulfilling. Stepping away from control in the way Brody did for the two years she spent writing her book is also not for the faint of heart. It's something most of us wouldn't even want to try. "You have to be okay with things not getting done at all," she tells me, and that attitude doesn't resonate with most women.[2] The only reason I've been able to let go at all is because I have faith in Rob's capabilities now. I know things are going to get done, and I know I'll pick up the things he forgets. I've spent too long creating this life to let it all go to hell.

Yet I did envy how Brody's method gave her clarity when she came back to pick up certain pieces of emotional labor after her time away from being the "cruise director" of her family. "I certainly didn't have high standards anymore," she tells me, laughing. She was fully done with the micromanaging and worrying over details. What she was left with, after everything else was stripped away, were high priorities. She knew which pieces of emotional labor were worth her time and energy. She knew which parts of emotional labor were worthwhile to her. "I'm not taking on things just to take them on," she says of her poststrike life. "I'm willing to go out of my way only for things that matter to me." She decided to reinstate her yearly Hanukkah party and open her house for gatherings after her son's soccer games. She values things that foster community and conversation, and she puts her energy there. It's a clarity she doesn't think she'd have without giving up all the emotional labor for a while.

But who says you have to drop it all to find those priorities in the first place? Most of us aren't interested in diving off the deep end and shedding all of our emotional labor, but that doesn't mean we can't reevaluate our priorities and find a better balance. A crisis or sudden change can give you clarity, but you can also tease out that clarity without shock therapy. You simply have to know what you are looking for. You have to get clear on what really matters to you, to take those emotional labor problem-solving skills and apply them to yourself.

"The time to find your priorities is there," Tiffany Dufu, author of *Drop the Ball*, tells me when I ask her how she managed to become so clear about her mission, her priorities, her sense of self. "You can spend that time stressing and being angry and telling yourself really negative stories, or you can decide that you want something different—that you want to create a new reality for yourself. The hardest part about dropping the ball, at the end of the day, is that it is your decision." You have to decide what stays and what goes. You have to decide what is worth it. If there is anyone who makes these decisions with clarity, it's Dufu. I've never encountered anyone with such a strong sense of who they are and why they are here on this earth. If you ask her what her priorities are, she can tell you without skipping a beat: advancing women and girls, raising conscious global citizens, and nurturing a great partnership with her husband. She says once you're clear on what matters most to you, it becomes easy to figure out what to do and what not to do—and she's certainly living proof. When she approaches emotional labor, she has a single question that helps her decide if it's worthwhile: "Is this my highest and best use?" It's beyond the simple question "Is this worth my time?" It's easy for us to argue our way into murky waters there, because women tend to undervalue their time and skills. A 2014 study from Babson College found that female entrepreneurs, despite being the ones in charge of payroll, still paid themselves a salary of only 80 percent compared to male entrepreneurs who had graduated from the same Goldman Sachs Small Business Program.[3] Similar studies have found this repeated time and again; we have trouble determining how to value our time and skills, because society consistently undervalues them for us. That is why we must become clear on our priorities, on what the highest and best use of our time is, if we want emotional labor to really work for us.

Of course, this won't look the same for everyone. Everyone has his or her own idea of what a fair and equitable relationship looks like according to personal circumstances. Striking the right balance of emotional labor is going to look different, even for people in similar situations. There is no perfect formula across the board for working partners without kids, or one stay-at-home parent and one full-time worker, or single parents, a work-from-home parent with a part-time working partner, or any other combination. And because there is no single formula, there is also no single conversation that can change our current dynamic. It will take time, adjustment, trial and error to find what works best for us—so it's vital that we are clear on our sense of self and our priorities first and foremost.

I knew spending time with my family was a priority, which is a large part of why I tried so hard to streamline our life. Same for my work. The more efficiently we were able to live, the *more* we were able to live—at least that is what my perfectionism told me. Rob's standards? They're based in necessity and convenience (which is better than some men, whose standards are seemingly nonexistent). The average mess has never seemed to bother him, while it can throw off my whole mood. Needless to say, there's a big gap between our two ideals. And although my current standards grew out of an unattainable model of perfectionism women are taught to chase, all the self-awareness in the world isn't helping the fact that a cluttered house stresses me out. We needed to find a shared standard, compromising in ways that resonated with both of us, in order for us to find an attainable balance.

There is a big camp of people (let's be real, men) who don't think shared standards should exist. *I have my standards, you have yours. If my standards bother you, you can go the extra mile to bring it up to your standard or else you can learn to live with it. It's not my fault that you can't handle the mess. It's not hurting anyone, it's just your personal preference. Why should I have to adopt your standard? Why should I have to change?* I've heard this argument over and over again. It's not a problem of *my* initiative. It's a problem with *your* standard.

As I noted earlier in this book, it's a pretty cruel argument. It argues that one person should either have to suffer or put in a disproportionate amount of work because the other person is too lazy to compromise. It implies that the work we have put into creating a life that keeps everyone comfortable and happy has no value—that we create our standards without purpose or meaning. It's an argument which states that our standards don't matter, that our feelings don't matter, that our work doesn't matter. When our identity is so wrapped up in emotional labor, it's an argument that says *you* don't matter.

This is why emotional labor is such a minefield of hurt and resentment. One person's arbitrary standard is another person's lifeline. There's a huge disconnect when our partners do not understand *why* we do what we do in regard to emotional labor. It's not only how we keep our lives running smoothly; it's how we strive to find happiness. What women seek through their high standards isn't merely perfectionism—it's the idea of freedom. When we are drawn into the comparison game, when we feel the pressure to "have it all," when we try every organizational hack in the book, it's because we've been led to believe that just around the bend we will find peace. We will find happiness. We will find the life hack that will finally ease our exhaustion, because we don't believe we can find that relief in our partnerships.

Yet after talking with hundreds of women and seeing the dynamic shift in my own relationship, I can see the lie that perfectionism is selling. There is no plateau of perfection I can reach that will help me care for everyone around me, keeping them comfortable and happy, without becoming utterly depleted. I can't do it all. No one can. Instead, we can evaluate what parts of our emotional labor are intrinsically important to us. We can soul-search for our real priorities—not the ones that have been predetermined for us but the ones that stem from us. Then we can do what we do best and rearrange our lives accordingly, with care and attention to detail, not for the benefit of others but for ourselves. We can find the relief we're searching for by setting boundaries, taking responsibility for ourselves, and surrounding ourselves with people, and especially partners, who do the same.

When I wrote my article for *Harper's Bazaar* and shared it with Rob, I was essentially drawing a line in the sand. I was saying, as clearly as I knew how, that we couldn't go on without him taking his share of responsibility in our life together. It was uncomfortable, difficult, and quite frankly, even harder than having a blow-up fight about emotional labor every few months. Implementing a shared standard that worked for both of us meant that both of us had to show up and struggle through our individual hang-ups together. I had to face my perfectionism, my desire for control, the social conditioning that tied my worth to my ability to perform emotional labor. He had to learn these skills for the first time. He had to face the ways he had unintentionally hurt me by ignoring emotional labor for so long. He had to confront the social conditioning telling him that emotional labor—anything that fosters connection to his whole life—is not for him. It was a whole lot of unpacking to do to figure out things like how to best handle laundry and toddler meltdowns as a team.

And to be honest, I'm still not sure we're ever going to be 100 percent on the same page. I can't give a foolproof four-step plan to find the perfect compromise. Although we've found a shared standard that works for us, it's been easier for me than it would be for most. Rob actively tried to pick up on what I do around the house and asked me to point out the things that bothered me (how had I never told him how much counter clutter bothers me?). He went all in for the sake of our relationship, which admittedly involved him attempting to adopt my standards as his own. And while he doesn't get it perfect, he gets it good enough, so I had to give up the perfectionist desire to tell him, "You're doing it wrong," or perhaps more accurately, "You could be doing it better." I have to constantly fight the urge to encourage perfectionism in him, to get him on board with the same level of impossible striving I am used to, because it is the only way I know how to be.

The more I let go of that perfectionism, the more we both benefit. I have the time and mental space to enjoy my family and my work, because I'm not so laser-focused on being in charge. Rob has the space to really lean into emotional labor without worrying about my hovering and judgment. Sharing emotional labor is sometimes more difficult than I like to admit. We get in each other's way. We don't see eye to eye all the time. But we do, without a doubt, find greater connection with each other as we figure out what balance should look like for us. We're working from different places of understanding but moving in the same direction for once.

When Rob took on more emotional labor, I became happier and more satisfied with our relationship, which made *him* more apt to keep doing it. When we were both happy and sharing the responsibility of our life together, emotional labor wasn't such a drag anymore. In fact, we both enjoyed it, because doing emotional labor together made us feel more in tune with each other. More understood. We were no longer shying away from conversations about what was and was not working, because we were past the point of keeping score or trying to win when it came to emotional labor. We were able to trust each other to do our fair share and learn from each other as we aimed to find what shared responsibility and standards would look like for us.

What truly brought us to a balance where we both felt comfortable was the fact that both of us were finally doing the necessary work to understand each other. We were actively working our empathy muscles as we looked at each other's life experiences. Rob was listening to and processing my lived experiences as I laid them out for him. He was no longer responding with defensiveness, but showing an understanding that led naturally to action. He was giving me what I genuinely wanted—not perfectly folded towels or clean countertops like I thought I wanted, but a partner who truly saw me.

Cathy Adams, cohost of the *Zen Parenting* podcast along with Todd Adams, says that this is really our desire, no matter what the subject. "At the end of the day, all we really want is for someone to say, 'I see you, I hear you, I recognize what it is that you are doing,'" she says.[4] Our desire for our partners to recognize our emotional labor stems from a desire for deeper connection. Partners who recognize and understand this work help us feel loved.

The true benefit of full partnership, however, doesn't come from men's understanding and action alone. We also have to see our partners, not only for what they currently do but for their potential in the realm of emotional labor. Men still don't have full equality on the home front, and they have been raised in a culture that deters them from pursuing it. Even men who do want to step up may not do so out of fear of doing or saying the wrong thing. Women have played a role in this by snatching back the reins to do it our way every time an imperfect effort is made. We need to create a space that not only welcomes mistakes but allows men to find their own way in emotional labor—approaches that may be brilliant and methods we would never think of on our own. They deserve that opportunity for human wholeness. They deserve to discover the value of emotional labor for themselves.

Emotional labor is, in many ways, women's bastion of control in a world that limits our power. But holding on to control for the sake of control is no way to live. We're not benefitting from our perfectionism as much as we think we are, and neither are men. Men need to feel confident in their roles at home, free from maternal gatekeeping, in order to fully participate in their lives and break the cycle that says they can't be caring, can't be vulnerable, can't be intuitive, can't be organized, can't be competent in emotional labor.

We have to destroy the narrative that bars men from enjoying the fullness of a work life, personal life, and home life that they have a hand in creating. Just as we still lack women's skills in the workplace, we lack men's skills and innovation in the home. We can't keep holding tightly to control and expecting everyone around to adapt to us. We need to work together, to find a new way to harness the power of emotional labor for men and women alike.

Working alongside my husband to balance the emotional labor in our home has been an eye-opening experience. He has brought new perspective to so many things I believed about myself: that I was naturally superior at emotional labor, that I could never let go of control, that I always knew the best and only way to keep our family comfortable and happy. On the flip side, he has learned the joy of moving into the deeper waters of his life. He is worth every bit as much in our home and our life as I am, and that is a powerful feeling he did not know before. He knows what it means to take responsibility for his own life, and that has helped him redefine how he views masculinity and how he determines his self-worth. He can draw value from all parts of his life, because for once, all parts of his life are his own. He is more fully present in our home, in our marriage, in our family, in his friendships. He is more wholly engaged in his life, and I am more free in mine. The balance is not perfect—I doubt it ever will be—but I've found that perfect isn't a goal worth striving for anymore. What we have instead is progress and a real sense of equality. Those two things give me hope, not only for our relationship but for the future.

What we have gained for ourselves, for each other, is wholly worth the effort and struggle. Full stop. Yet I know that this journey doesn't end with us. When I look at our sons and our daughter, I know that for the first time they are seeing us working from a place of true equality. They are not sensing and seeing resentment building day after day, year after year. They are not absorbing stale gender roles that will not serve them. They are not learning to keep a scoreboard tacked to the back of their minds. They see emotional labor, out in the open, being given and taken freely. They see us thanking each other for this work in equal measure. This is going to be their normal. This is going to shape the way they see themselves, the way they see the world.

One of the most shocking things I discovered when I began researching emotional labor was that there was no generational divide. My mother experienced this, just as my grandmother experienced it, just as I and my friends experienced it. The imbalance of emotional labor was insidious, crossing borders and boundaries unlike any sociological phenomenon I had ever known. Unlike the divide of domestic labor, which was easily visible and correctable, emotional labor has been sticky because of its invisibility. It has eluded us until now.

You cannot fight what you cannot see, but our eyes are finally open. We can see emotional labor and all its wide-spreading branches—all the ways it is intertwined in our lives. We see how it has held us back. We see how it can benefit us. Now I feel confident that we will do what we do best. We will take stock of the vast and complicated issues in emotional labor, connecting each piece with care. We will tailor solutions that suit each of us. We will move forward with confidence.

Our sons and daughters will not know the struggle with emotional labor that we have known. They will know better and do better. This work does not have to be shadow work, not anymore. It will become, in time, as second nature as the equality my generation has grown up with thanks to the feminists before us. We can fight to change the balance of emotional labor in our lives, and our children can change it in the world.

We will draw a line in history: the generational divide starts here.

ACKNOWLEDGMENTS

The journey to publishing this book has filled me with more gratitude than I ever knew possible. I am so thankful to everyone who helped make this book a reality, and there are many of you.

To my amazing agent, John Maas, who has been a constant source of support throughout the creation of this book. You have been my strongest advocate every step of the way, and you've fielded my anxious phone calls with the calm of a saint. Also, thanks to the whole Sterling Lord Literistic team, including Celeste Fine, Jaidree Braddix, Anna Petkovich, and Danielle Bukowski, all of whom have indulged my endless questions throughout the process.

To my editor, Libby Edelson, for believing in this book and making it better. To the whole HarperOne team—Judith Curr, Melinda Mullin, Jennifer Jensen, Laina Adler, Gideon Weil, Eva Avery, and Suzanne Quist—who have been so enthusiastic in their support from day one.

Of course this book would never have come into being without first writing my *Harper's Bazaar* article "Women Aren't Nags— We're Just Fed Up." Thank you to Binders, for giving me the inspiration, encouragement, and contacts necessary to get to this point in my writing career. Thank you to Olivia Fleming, for finally taking a chance on one of my cold pitches. An especially huge thank-you to everyone who read and shared the article. Your internet enthusiasm made this book possible.

To Heidi Oran, for being there through the ups and downs of writing life (and real life). To Michelle Horton, without whom I would have given up on my writing career long ago. To all my EM writers: Mary Sauer, Kelly Burch, Maggie Ethridge, Chaunie Brusie, DeAndrea Salvador, Gretchen Bossio, Lauren Hartmann, Briana Meade, Kristel Acevedo, Emily Lingenfelser, Jessica Lemmons, Katie Fazio, Krishann Briscoe, Erin Heger, Maria Toca, Katie Anne, Andie Murphy, and all the others who have offered their support, commiseration, and celebration, basically on demand, every step of the way.

To Melanie Perish, who did everything from beta read to bringing me diapers and home-cooked meals. My life as a writer would not be sustainable without your friendship. Thank you to the rest of our poetry and writers group, especially Mary Nork for always bringing us together. To Joe Crowley, I wish I hadn't waited to share news of this book with you. You are so deeply missed.

To Chris Coake, who has been mentoring me since I was going through a cut-my-own-bangs and wear-a-faux-fur-lined-bomber-hat stage of life. Thank you for making me a better writer and dealing with my ever-evolving awkwardness. Less thanks for sitting me down to discuss prospects of writerly doom I had not yet considered (namely impending depression over success and men trying to kill me for my feminist writing). To Seth Boyd, for nurturing my love of creative nonfiction and setting me firmly on this path.

To my mom and Nana, not only for being the kind of women who unwittingly raise a feminist writer, but also for watching my feral children so this book could actually get finished. To my dad for instilling within me a strong work ethic and endless confidence in my abilities. To my whole family, for supporting me through this process and through life. This book is a testament to your love.

To Mandy, for being my Gayle.

To Nicole, for being my Schynozzie.

To all my friends who talked emotional labor with me over dinner and wine and long car rides: Jade, Jamie, Kate, Karie, Alexis, Maria, Shana, and Mandy, again. To Reema, I am forever thankful for the multitude of ways our stories and lives are connected.

Last but not least, thank you to my partner, Rob, who has put forth full and enthusiastic support for this book from the very start. Thank you for letting me use our story without exception, for taking on emotional labor like a pro, and for always remaining open to growth and change. I love you.

NOTES

INTRODUCTION: AN INVISIBLE JOB IS NEVER DONE

1. Tiffany Dufu, *Drop the Ball* (New York: FlatIron Books, 2015), 44.
2. Kim Parker and Gretchen Livingston, "Seven Facts About American Dads," Pew Research Center, June 13, 2018, http://www.pewresearch.org/fact-tank/2017/06/15/fathers-day-facts/.
3. Sheryl Sandberg, *Lean In* (New York: Random House, 2013), 109.
4. Interview with the author, August 18, 2017.
5. Chaunie Brusie, "No, Dear Husband and Kids, You're Not Cleaning 'for' Me," Babble, https://www.babble.com/parenting/no-dear-husband-and-kids-youre-not-cleaning-for-me/.
6. Gemma Hartley, "Women Aren't Nags—We're Just Fed Up," *Harper's Bazaar*, September 27, 2017, http://www.harpersbazaar.com/culture/features/a12063822/emotional-labor-gender-equality/.
7. Arlie Russell Hochschild, *The Managed Heart: Commercialization of Human Feeling* (Berkeley: Univ. of California Press, 1983), 7.
8. Rebecca J. Erickson, "Why Emotion Work Matters: Sex, Gender, and the Division of Household Labor," *Journal of Marriage and Family*, April 15, 2005.
9. Jess Zimmerman, "Where's My Cut? On Unpaid Emotional Labor," The Toast, July 13, 2015, http://the-toast.net/2015/07/13/emotional-labor/.
10. "Emotional Labor: The MetaFilter Thread Condensed," https://drive.google.com/file/d/0B0UUYL6kaNeBTDBRbkJkeUtabEk/view?pref=2&pli=1.
11. Rose Hackman, "'Women Are Just Better at This Stuff': Is Emotional Labor Feminism's Next Frontier?," *The Guardian*, November 8, 2015, https://www.theguardian.com/world/2015/nov/08/women-gender-roles-sexism-emotional-labor-feminism.
12. Gemma Hartley, "The Amount of Emotional Labor We Put on Stay-At-Home Moms Is Horribly Unfair," Romper, August 29, 2017, https://www.romper.com/p/the-amount-of-emotional-labor-we-put-on-stay-at-home-moms-is-horribly-unfair-79612.
13. Erica Chenoweth and Jeremy Pressman, "This Is What We Learned by Counting the Women's Marches," *The Washington Post*, February 7, 2017, https://www

.washingtonpost.com/news/monkey-cage/wp/2017/02/07/this-is-what-we-learned
-by-counting-the-womens-marches/?utm_term=.ec335a3201fe.

14. Judith Shulevitz, "Mom: The Designated Worrier," *New York Times*, May 8, 2015, https://www.nytimes.com/2015/05/10/opinion/sunday/judith-shulevitz-mom-the -designated-worrier.html?_r=1.

15. Sandberg, *Lean In*, 78.

16. Hochschild, *The Managed Heart*, 85.

17. Interview with the author, August 18, 2017.

18. Yang Claire Yang, Courtney Boen, Karen Gerken, Ting Li, Kristen Schorpp, and Kathleen Mullan Harris, "Social Relationships and Physiological Determinants of Longevity Across the Human Life Span," *Proceedings of the National Academy of Sciences* 113, no. 3 (January 2016): 578–83, http://www.pnas.org/content/113/3/578.

19. Ayal A. Aizer et al., "Marital Status and Survival in Patients with Cancer," *Journal of Clinical Oncology* 31, no. 31 (2013): 3869–76, http://ascopubs.org/doi /abs/10.1200/JCO.2013.49.6489.

20. "Marriage and Men's Health," Harvard Health Publishing, July 2010, https:// www.health.harvard.edu/newsletter_article/marriage-and-mens-health; P. Martikainen and T. Valkonen, "Mortality After the Death of a Spouse: Rates and Causes of Death in a Large Finnish Cohort," *American Journal of Public Health* 86, no. 8 (August 1996): 1087–93, https://www.ncbi.nlm.nih.gov/pubmed/8712266.

21. Rep. Maxine Waters during a House Financial Services Committee hearing July 27, 2017.

CHAPTER 1: HOW DID WE GET HERE?

1. Maria Krysan, Kristin A. Moore, and Nicholas Zill, "Identifying Successful Families: An Overview of Constructs and Selected Measures," Office of Social Services Policy, May 10, 1990, https://aspe.hhs.gov/basic-report/identifying-successful -families-overview-constructs-and-selected-measures.

2. Sarah Bregel, "How to Say You Maybe Don't Want to Be Married Anymore," *Longreads*, November 2017, https://longreads.com/2017/11/20/how-to-say-you-maybe -dont-want-to-be-married-anymore/.

3. Interview with the author, December 13, 2017.

4. David R. Hibbard and Duane Buhrmester, "The Role of Peers in the Socialization of Gender-Related Social Interaction Styles," *Sex Roles* 39, no. 3–4 (August 1988), 185–202.

5. Interview with the author, June 11, 2018.

6. Interview with the author, June 10, 2018.

7. Micaela di Leonardo, "The Female World of Cards and Holidays: Women, Families, and the Work of Kinship," *Signs* 12, no. 3 (Spring 1987): 4410–53, https://www .anthropology.northwestern.edu/documents/people/TheFemaleWorldofCards.pdf.

8. Jeanne E. Arnold, Anthony P. Graesch, Enzo Ragazzini, and Elinor Ochs, *Life at Home in the Twenty-First Century: Thirty-Two Families Open Their Doors* (Los Angeles: Cotsen Institute of Archaeology Press, 2012).

CHAPTER 2: THE MOTHER LOAD

1. Stephanie Land, "The Mental Load of Being a Poor Mom," Refinery29, July 25, 2017, http://www.refinery29.com/2017/07/160057/the-mental-load-of-being-a-poor-mom.

2. "You Should've Asked," *Emma* (blog), May 20, 2017, https://english.emmaclit .com/2017/05/20/you-shouldve-asked/.

3. Rasheena Fountain, "Black Single Mothers Are More Than Scapegoats," *Huffington Post*, April 6, 2016, https://www.huffingtonpost.com/rasheena-fountain/black -single-mothers-are-_b_9619536.html.

4. Michelle Homer, "Community Rallies Around Houston Dad Struggling to Pay for Three Sons' Insulin," KHOU11, June 9, 2017, http://www.khou.com /features/community-rallies-around-houston-dad-struggling-to-pay-for-3-sons -insulin/447076681.
5. Dufu, *Drop the Ball*, 211.
6. Jami Ingledue, "The Mental Workload of a Mother," *Huffington Post*, July 24, 2017, https://www.huffingtonpost.com/entry/the-mental-workload-of-a-mother_us _59765076e4b0c6616f7ce447.
7. Brigid Schulte, *Overwhelmed: Work, Love, and Play When No One Has The Time* (New York: Farrar, Straus and Giroux, 2014), 185.
8. Lyn Craig, "Does Father Care Mean Fathers Share? A Comparison of How Mothers and Fathers in Intact Families Spend Time with Children," *Gender & Society* 20, no. 2 (April 2006): 259–81, DOI: 10.1177/0891243205285212.
9. Juliana Menasce Horowitz, "Who Does More at Home When Both Parents Work? Depends on Which One You Ask," Pew Research Center, November 5, 2015, http://www.pewresearch.org/fact-tank/2015/11/05/who-does-more-at-home -when-both-parents-work-depends-on-which-one-you-ask/.
10. Michael Kimmel, "Why Gender Equality Is Good for Everyone—Men Included," TEDWomen 2015, May 2015, https://www.ted.com/talks/michael_kimmel_why _gender_equality_is_good_for_everyone_men_included.

CHAPTER 3: WHO CARES?

1. "Men Deliberately Do Housework Badly to Avoid Doing It in the Future," *The Telegraph*, November 7, 2014, http://www.telegraph.co.uk/men/the-filter/11215506 /Men-deliberately-do-housework-badly-to-avoid-doing-it-in-future.html.
2. Deborah Arthurs, "Women Spend Three Hours Every Week Redoing Chores Their Men Have Done Badly," *Daily Mail*, March 19, 2012, http://www.dailymail .co.uk/femail/article-2117254/Women-spend-hours-week-redoing-chores-men -badly.html?ITO=1490.
3. Sarah M. Allen and Alan J. Hawkins, "Maternal Gatekeeping: Mothers' Beliefs and Behaviors That Inhibit Greater Father Involvement in Family Work," *Journal of Marriage and Family* 61, no. 1 (1999).
4. Interview with the author, November 28, 2017.
5. Madhura Ingalhalikar, Alex Smith, Drew Parker, Theodore D. Satterthwaite, Mark A. Elliott, Kosha Ruparel, Hakon Hakonarson, Raquel E. Gur, Ruben C. Gur, and Ragini Verma, "Sex Differences in the Structural Connectome of the Human Brain," *Proceedings of the National Academy of Sciences* 111, no. 2 (January 14, 2014): 823–28, https://doi.org/10.1073/pnas.1316909110.
6. Dufu, *Drop the Ball*, 4.
7. Interview with the author, December 18, 2017.
8. Interview with the author, December 1, 2017.
9. Schulte, *Overwhelmed*, 37.

CHAPTER 4: IT'S OKAY TO WANT MORE

1. Rufi Thorpe, "Mother, Writer, Monster, Maid," *Vela*, http://velamag.com/mother -writer-monster-maid/.
2. Lynne Twist, *The Soul of Money: Transforming Your Relationship with Money and Life* (New York: W.W. Norton, 2003), 44.
3. "Chore Wars: A New Working Mother Report Reveals Not Much Has Changed at Home," *Working Mother*, April 17, 2015, https://www.workingmother.com /content/chore-wars-new-working-mother-%20report-reveals-not-much-has -changed-home.

4. Hillary Rodham Clinton, *What Happened* (New York: Simon and Schuster, 2017), 133.

5. Interview with the author, December 20, 2017.

CHAPTER 5: WHAT WE DO AND WHY WE DO IT

1. Barry Schwartz, *The Paradox of Choice: Why More Is Less* (New York: Harper-Collins, 2004), 108.

2. Joel Hoomans, "35,000 Decisions: The Great Choices of Strategic Leaders," Roberts Wesleyan College, March 20, 2015, https://go.roberts.edu/leadingedge/the-great-choices-of-strategic-leaders.

3. Schwartz, *The Paradox of Choice*, 109.

4. Joanne Lipman, *That's What She Said: What Men Need to Know (and Women Need to Tell Them) About Working Together* (New York: HarperCollins, 2018), 1.

5. Wannabee Blunt, "Military Wives Are the Final Frontier of Feminism," Blunt Moms, http://www.bluntmoms.com/military-wives-final-frontier-feminism/.

6. Interview with the author, November 9, 2017.

7. Interview with the author, February 28, 2018.

8. Cheryl Strayed and Steve Almond, "Emotional Labor: The Invisible Work (Most) Women Do—with Gemma Hartley," *Dear Sugars*, May 5, 2018, http://www.wbur.org/dearsugar/2018/05/05/emotional-labor-invisible-work.

CHAPTER 6: WHOSE WORK IS IT ANYWAY?

1. Betty Friedan, *The Second Stage* (New York: Summit Books, 1981), 94.

2. Interview with the author, December 3, 2017.

3. Hochschild, *The Managed Heart*, 85.

4. Kimberly Seals Allers, "Rethinking Work-Life Balance for Women of Color," *Slate*, March 5, 2018, https://slate.com/human-interest/2018/03/for-women-of-color-work-life-balance-is-a-different-kind-of-problem.html.

5. Adrianne Frech and Sarah Damaske, "The Relationship Between Mothers' Work Pathways and Physical and Mental Health," *Journal of Health and Social Behavior* 53, no. 4 (2012): 396–412.

6. Gail G. Hunt and Susan Reinhard, "Caregiving in the U.S.," report for the National Alliance for Caregiving and AARP Public Policy Institute, 2015.

7. Interview with the author, December 7, 2017.

8. Judith Warner, "The Opt-Out Generation Wants Back In," *New York Times*, August 7, 2013, http://www.nytimes.com/2013/08/11/magazine/the-opt-out-generation-wants-back-in.html?pagewanted%3Dall.

9. Friedan, *The Second Stage*, 111.

10. John Adams, "The 'Mental Load' Is Real—but Feminists Are Wrong If They Think Only Women Feel It," *The Telegraph*, June 7, 2017, http://www.telegraph.co.uk/men/fatherhood/mental-load-real-feminists-wrong-think-women-feel/.

11. Interview with the author, December 22, 2017.

12. Anne-Marie Slaughter, *Unfinished Business: Women Men Work Family* (New York: Random House, 2015), 139.

13. Trish Bendix, "I Live with a Woman—We're Not Immune to Emotional Labor," *Harper's Bazaar*, October 9, 2017, http://www.harpersbazaar.com/culture/features/a12779502/emotional-labor-lgbtq-relationships/.

14. Sondra E. Solomon, Esther D. Rothblum, and Kimberly F. Balsam, "Money, Housework, Sex, and Conflict: Same Sex Couples in Civil Unions, Those Not in Civil Unions, and Heterosexual Married Siblings," *Sex Roles* 52 (2005).

15. Chimamanda Ngozi Adichie, *We Should All Be Feminists* (New York: Anchor Books, 2014), 34.

CHAPTER 7: A WARM SMILE AND A COLD REALITY

1. Interview with the author, January 26, 2018. Luckily, Mavrakis turned out to be fine after the needle stab.
2. Mona Chalabi, "Dear Mona, How Many Flight Attendants Are Men?," FiveThirty-Eight, October 3, 2014, https://fivethirtyeight.com/features/dear-mona-how-many-flight-attendants-are-men/.
3. Hochschild, *The Managed Heart*, 163.
4. Interview with the author, January 22, 2018.
5. Alison Vekshin, "Brothels in Nevada Suffer as Web Disrupts Oldest Trade," *Bloomberg*, August 28, 2013, https://www.bloomberg.com/news/articles/2013-08-28/brothels-in-nevada-shrivel-as-web-disrupts-oldest-trade.
6. Peter Holley, "'What Do Women Want?': A Company That Lets Women Hire Attractive Male Servants Says It Has the Answer," *The Washington Post*, October 11, 2017, https://www.washingtonpost.com/news/innovations/wp/2017/10/10/what-do-women-want-a-company-that-lets-women-hire-attractive-male-servants-says-it-has-the-answer/.
7. "Heartbreak ManServant," YouTube, December 7, 2015, https://www.youtube.com/watch?v=d-cFTVNqfLw.
8. Bureau of Labor Statistics, *Occupational Outlook Handbook* (Washington, DC: Department of Labor, 2016).
9. Andreas Schleicher, *Building a High-Quality Teaching Profession: Lessons from Around the World* (OECD Publishing, 2011), http://dx.doi.org/10.1787/9789264113046-en.
10. Interview with the author, June 30, 2018.
11. Robert B. Krogfoss, ed., *Manual for the Legal Secretarial Profession*, 2nd ed. (St. Paul, MN: West Publishing, 1974), 601.
12. Hochschild, *The Managed Heart*, 84.
13. Sandberg, *Lean In*, 41.

CHAPTER 8: TOO EMOTIONAL TO LEAD?

1. Michael Kruse, "The TV Interview That Haunts Hillary Clinton," *Politico Magazine*, September 23, 2016, https://www.politico.com/magazine/story/2016/09/hillary-clinton-2016-60-minutes-1992-214275.
2. Daniel White, "A Brief History of the Clinton Family's Chocolate-Chip Cookies," *Time*, August 19, 2016, http://time.com/4459173/hillary-bill-clinton-cookies-history/.
3. Clinton, *What Happened*, 136–37.
4. Joshua Green, "Take Two: Hillary's Choice," *The Atlantic*, November 2006, https://www.theatlantic.com/magazine/archive/2006/11/take-two-hillarys-choice/305292/.
5. Leslie Bennetts, "On Aggression in Politics: Are Women Judged by a Double Standard?," *New York Times*, February 12, 1979, https://www.nytimes.com/1979/02/12/archives/on-aggression-in-politics-are-women-judged-by-a-double-standard-one.html.
6. David Frum (@davidfrum), Twitter post, September 26, 2016, https://twitter.com/davidfrum/status/780580701422755840.
7. Clinton, *What Happened*, 122.
8. Clinton, *What Happened*, 134.
9. Clinton, *What Happened*, 133.
10. Clinton, *What Happened*, 134.
11. Marcus Noland, Tyler Moran, and Barbara Kotschwar, "Is Gender Diversity Profitable? Evidence from a Global Survey," Peterson Institute for Institutional

Economics Working Paper Series, February 2016, https://piie.com/publications /wp/wp16-3.pdf.

12. Jack Zenger and Joseph Folkman, "Are Women Better Leaders Than Men?," *Harvard Business Review*, March 15, 2012, https://hbr.org/2012/03/a-study-in -leadership-women-do.

13. Sonia Muir, "Heidi versus Howard—Perception Barrier to Be Hurdled," *Agriculture Today*, March 2012, https://www.dpi.nsw.gov.au/content/archive/agriculture -today-stories/ag-today-archive/march-2012/heidi-versus-howard-perception -barrier-to-be-hurdled-commissioner.

14. Madeline E. Heilman and Tyler G. Okimoto, "Why Are Women Penalized for Success at Male Tasks? The Implied Communality Deficit," *Journal of Applied Psychology* 92, no. 1 (January 2007): 81–92, https://nyuscholars.nyu.edu/en/publications /why-are-women-penalized-for-success-at-male-tasks-the-implied-com.

15. Drew DeSilver, "Despite Progress, U.S. Still Lags Many Nations in Women Leaders," Pew Research Center, January 26, 2015, http://www.pewresearch. org/fact-tank/2015/01/26/despite-progress-u-s-still-lags-many-nations-in-women -leadership/.

16. "Women and Leadership: Public Says Women Are Equally Qualified, but Barriers Persist," Pew Research Center, January 14, 2015, http://www.pewsocialtrends .org/2015/01/14/women-and-leadership/.

CHAPTER 9: WHAT QUIET COSTS

1. "More Than 12M 'Me Too' Facebook Posts, Comments, Reactions in 24 Hours," CBS, October 17, 2017, https://www.cbsnews.com/news/metoo-more-than-12 -million-facebook-posts-comments-reactions-24-hours/.

2. Interview with the author, December 4, 2017.

3. Irin Carmon and Amy Brittain, "Eight Women Say Charlie Rose Sexually Harassed Them—with Nudity, Groping and Lewd Calls," *The Washington Post*, November 20, 2017, https://www.washingtonpost.com/investigations/eight-women -say-charlie-rose-sexually-harassed-them--with-nudity-groping-and-lewd-calls /2017/11/20.

4. Julia Moskin and Kim Severson, "Ken Friedman, Power Restaurateur, Is Accused of Sexual Harassment," *New York Times*, December 12, 2017, https://www .nytimes.com/2017/12/12/dining/ken-friedman-sexual-harassment.html.

5. "The Criminal Justice System: Statistics," RAINN, https://www.rainn.org/statistics /criminal-justice-system.

6. Jane Mayer and Ronan Farrow, "Four Women Accuse New York's Attorney General of Physical Abuse," *The New Yorker*, May 7, 2018, https://www.newyorker.com /news/news-desk/four-women-accuse-new-yorks-attorney-general-of-physical-abuse.

7. Interview with the author, November 9, 2017.

8. Leslie Morgan Steiner, *Crazy Love* (New York: St. Martin's Press, 2009).

9. Leslie Morgan Steiner, "Why Domestic Violence Victims Don't Leave," TEDxRainier, November 2012, https://www.ted.com/talks/leslie_morgan_steiner_why_domestic _violence_victims_don_t_leave.

10. Steiner, *Crazy Love*, 93.

11. Interview with the author, February 4, 2018.

12. Margaret Atwood, *Second Words: Selected Critical Prose 1960–1982* (Toronto: House of Anansi, 2000), 413.

CHAPTER 10: FINISHING THE FIGHT

1. Betty Friedan, *The Feminine Mystique* (New York: Dell Publishing, 1963), 30.

2. Friedan, *The Feminine Mystique*, 19.

3. Friedan, *The Feminine Mystique*, 50.
4. Darla Halyk (New World Mom), Facebook post, February 8, 2018, https://www .facebook.com/NewWorldMom/posts/1827440660622445.
5. Miranda Larbi, "'I Can Do It All, but All of It Is Not Mine to Do' Should Be the Feminist Anthem of 2018," *Metro*, February 18, 2018, http://metro.co.uk/2018/02/18 /can-not-mine-feminist-anthem-2018-7321935/.
6. Interview with the author, February 28, 2018.
7. Interview with the author, March 16, 2018.
8. Interview with the author, March 12, 2018.
9. Interview with the author, March 13, 2018.
10. Betty Friedan, *The Second Stage* (New York: Summit Books, 1981), 157.

CHAPTER 11: NATURE VERSUS NURTURE

1. Interview with the author, March 7, 2018.
2. Barry Hewlett, *Intimate Fathers: The Nature and Context of Aka Pygmy Paternal Infant Care* (Ann Arbor: Univ. of Michigan Press, 1991).
3. Emma Seppala, "Are Women More Compassionate Than Men?," *Greater Good Magazine*, June 26, 2013, https://greatergood.berkeley.edu/article/item/are_women _more_compassionate_than_men.
4. Julie Blindel, "Iceland: The World's Most Feminist Country," *The Guardian*, March 25, 2010, https://www.theguardian.com/lifeandstyle/2010/mar/25/iceland -most-feminist-country.
5. Joanne Lipman, *That's What She Said: What Men Need To Know (and Women Need to Tell Them) About Working Together* (New York: HarperCollins, 2018), 224.
6. "Jóhanna Sigurðardóttir: 'Gender Equality Did Not Fall into Our Laps Without a Struggle,'" Women Political Leaders Global Forum, February 27, 2014, https:// www.womenpoliticalleaders.org/j%C3%B3hanna-sigur%C3%B0ard%C3%B3ttir -gender-equality-did-not-fall-into-our-laps-without-a-struggle-1989/.
7. Ivana Kottasová, "Iceland Makes It Illegal to Pay Women Less Than Men," CNN Money, January 3, 2018, http://money.cnn.com/2018/01/03/news/iceland-gender -pay-gap-illegal/index.html.

CHAPTER 12: TALKING ABOUT EMOTIONAL LABOR

1. Interview with the author, March 13, 2018.
2. Interview with the author, November 9, 2017.

CHAPTER 13: CREATING A CULTURE OF AWARENESS

1. Interview with the author, December 11, 2017.
2. Gretchen Rubin uses the phrase "Outer order, inner calm" often in her work.
3. Friedan, *The Second Stage*, 159.
4. Interview with the author, April 16, 2018.

CHAPTER 14: OWNING OUR WORTH

1. Interview with the author, November 17, 2017.
2. Interview with the author, March 15, 2018.
3. Gretchen Rubin, *Better Than Before: What I Learned About Making and Breaking Habits—to Sleep More, Quit Sugar, Procrastinate Less, and Generally Build a Happier Life* (New York: Random House, 2015), 223.
4. Brené Brown, "3 Ways to Set Boundaries," *O, The Oprah Magazine*, September 2013.

CHAPTER 15: FINDING BALANCE

1. Friedan, *The Second Stage*, 147.
2. Interview with the author, December 1, 2017.
3. Lisa Evans, "Why Are Women Entrepreneurs Paying Themselves Less Than They Deserve?," *Fast Company*, March 17, 2014, https://www.fastcompany.com/3027709/why-are-women-entrepreneurs-paying-themselves-less-than-they-deserve.
4. Interview with the author, April 16, 2018.